SO-BFS-875

PLANNING FOR WATER REUSE

LIST OF AUTHORS

DUANE D. BAUMANN
JAMES E. BERTRAM
NEIL M. CLINE
DANIEL M. DWORKIN
JOHN N. ENGLISH
O. O. HART
W. H. J. HATTINGH
RICHARD D. HEATON
DONALD E. MATSCHKE
JEROME W. MILLIMAN
JOHN H. SIMS
LUCAS R. J. VAN VUUREN
LEON WEINBERGER

PLANNING FOR WATER REUSE

EDITED BY

DUANE D. BAUMANN

AND

DANIEL M. DWORKIN

1978

MAAROUFA PRESS, INC.
CHICAGO

Eric Moore, Advisory Editor

© 1978 by Maaroufa Press, Inc.
All rights reserved
Library of Congress Catalog Card Number: 77-083289
ISBN: 0-88425-008-3
Manufactured in the United States of America

Designed by First Impression

CONTENTS

FOREWORD

GILBERT F. WHITE

In their efforts to meet growing demands upon their fixed water resources, the planning agencies of modern nations are able to draw upon a large battery of engineering and economic measures. The agencies are, however, often impeded by three problems: They have trouble accommodating their mode of analysis to assure thorough and balanced consideration of unconventional techniques for managing water. They find themselves trying to improve standards of quality in the face of scientific uncertainty as to the consequences of expanding chemical and biological threats to human health. Finally, they are obliged to adjust methods of professional thinking and forms of administrative organization in order to deal effectively with the new opportunities and uncertainties.

When one examines the question of how best to plan for water reuse as one component in the design of urban water supply and distribution systems, all three of these problems are illuminated. The papers assembled by Duane Baumann and Daniel Dworkin review the full range of these problems from the standpoints of economics, engineering, geography, medicine, psychology, and related disciplines. By bringing together into a single document and into a coherent framework these several points of view, *Planning for Water Reuse* helps advance techniques of water planning at the same time that it provides detailed information about reuse. Its relatively simple model for comparing alternatives of water supply and water demand management offers an analytical structure within which the new and unconventional can be evaluated along with the traditional. This approach is needed in order to appraise the social feasibility of water reuse and various demand management practices in comparison with engineering devices to increase supply.

Since the planned treatment and distribution of effluent in the Chanute, Kansas, system during the drought of 1956–57, an annoying question attaching to any proposals for direct water reuse is the possibility of creating new hazards to health through the accumulation of viruses or trace substances. It often is argued that a well-managed waste and water treatment program involves fewer health dangers than the poorly managed supplies that prevail in many cities. The hard fact is that at least one-third of the urban population in the United States is served by surface supplies in which at least one out of every thirty gallons has been used previously. On some streams the proportion is much higher. An explicit decision to establish reuse for potable supplies requires conscious, public review of issues that are swept under the rug in the continuation of existing supply. The troublesome situation is that we do not understand the carcinogenic and other effects of viruses or many trace substances that currently find their way into supplies.

Much opposition to candid examination of direct reuse opportunities comes from members of professional groups. It is important to understand the origins of this opposition and how it relates to the attitudes and behavior of users of water supply in cities where reuse is proposed. *Planning for Water Reuse* shows that it may be as important also (1) to examine prevailing consumer preferences and the way in which professional and nonprofessional persons interact in arriving at decisions about municipal improvements and (2) to look into health effects and the comparative technical and economic feasibility of alternative techniques.

We have a long distance to go in improving methods of analysis, in probing full environmental effects, and in organizing public planning so that scientific information is used in a balanced and discriminating fashion in arriving at public decisions about natural resources. The thinking and experience with water reuse that has been drawn together by Baumann and Dworkin and their contributing authors is a solid step in that direction.

The University of Colorado, Boulder
March 1978

PREFACE

During the early 1960s, there was a prolonged drought in the northeastern United States. Public response to the imminent crises was to initiate long-range plans for increases in water supply, while, in the short run, a few emergency measures were employed, such as restrictions on water use, emergency transfers, and experimentation with weather modification. Although recycling of renovated wastewater was a viable alternative, it was not seriously considered.

Research on the practicability of water reuse, however, has continually increased during the past decade. The United States Office of Water Resources and Technology has a special research program on water reuse, as well as a five-volume bibliography on the subject. The American Water Works Association (AWWA) is currently concerned with the practicability of water reuse for urban areas, such as the newly established water reuse project in their research foundation. The United States Environmental Protection Agency (EPA) has focused on the health effects related to water reuse and is evaluating the full range of possible applications, including nonpotable uses.

The U.S. Army Corps of Engineers sponsored a seminar on the issues involved in planning for water reuse. Professionals from the government, universities, research foundations, and consulting firms were invited to Holcomb Research Institute in Indianapolis for one week in July 1975. The seminar was organized around three salient issues:

1. economic evaluation of recycled, renovated wastewater, among other alternatives of water supply provision;
2. assessment of risk to public health; and
3. the question of public and professional acceptance.

Many of the papers that appear in this volume were presented at the seminar; the remainder have been solicited. The contributors represented several disciplines that relate to the decision to reuse water: economics, engineering, geography, planning, psychology, and public health. To encourage serious consideration of the practicability of water reuse in planning for future urban water supply needs, the papers in this volume contribute to a better understanding of the three major questions discussed at the seminar. In addition, the volume focuses upon the experiences of the reuse of renovated wastewater as specific urban places and closes by identifying future directions in both research and implementation.

Duane D. Baumann
Daniel M. Dworkin
Southern Illinois University, Carbondale

ABBREVIATIONS
USED IN THIS TEXT

a.	are
ac	acre
ac-ft	acre-foot
ARRP	ammonia removal and recovery process
AWT	advanced wastewater treatment
AWWA	American Water Works Association
bbl	barrel
bg/d	billions of gallons per day
BOD	biochemical oxygen demand
BOR	Bureau of Outdoor Research (U.S.)
Btu	British thermal unit
bu	bushel
cfs	cubic feet per second
cm	centimeter
COD	chemical oxygen demand
C-SELM	Chicago-South End Lake Michigan
EPA	Environmental Protection Agency (U.S.)
F	Fahrenheit
gal.	gallon
Gl	gigaliter (G = 10^9)
GNP	gross national product
ha.	hectare
HERL	Health Effects Research Laboratory (EPA)
HEW	Department of Health, Education, and Welfare (U.S.)
hp	horsepower
in.	inch
kg	kilogram
kl	kiloliter
km	kilometer
kwh	kilowatt-hour
l	liter
lb	pound
m	meter
M	mega- (M = 10^6)
mg/d	millions of gallons per day
mg/l	milligrams per liter
μg	microgram
M&I	municipal and industrial
mi	mile
ml	milliliter

mm	millimeter
mo	month
MW	megawatt
MWD	metropolitan water district (Los Angeles)
NDCP	no discharge of critical pollutants
ng	nanogram ($n = 10^{-9}$)
NIWR	National Institute of Water Research (South Africa)
OCWD	Orange County Water District (California)
O&M	operation and maintenance
OR&D	Office of Research and Development (EPA)
ppm	parts per million
SAPPI	South African Paper and Pulp Industries
SIC	standard industrial classification
SM	static mixer
SMSA	standard metropolitan statistics area
TAT	Murray's Thematic Apperception Test
TDS	total dissolved solids
WHO	World Health Organization (U.N.)
WPCF	Water Pollution Control Federation (U.S.)
yr	year

Water Reuse for Cities: An Appraisal

Duane D. Baumann
Daniel M. Dworkin

The concept of water reuse is seldom, if ever, seriously considered in the process of planning for future urban water demands. The exclusion of planned water reuse and virtual reliance upon traditional engineering works are remarkable in light of the potential savings and the substantial amount of reused water that millions of Americans inadvertently ingest each day. The goal of this appraisal is threefold:

1. to assess the potential of water reuse for our cities now and in the future;
2. to appraise the factors that may have accounted for the low rate of adoption of planned reuse; and,
3. to describe a simulation model designed to evaluate water reuse relative to other alternatives of municipal water supply provision.

DEMAND FOR WATER: PRESENT AND FUTURE

One prediction is certain: The future demand for water in the United States will continue to increase, while the supply will remain relatively fixed. In 1970, the United States withdrew 365 billion gallons per day (bg/d), of which 87 bg were for consumptive uses.[1] The estimated average annual stream flow in the conterminous United States is approximately 1,200 bg/d,[2] and it is doubtful that this amount will be greatly changed in the next ten, twenty, or fifty years.[3] Hence, the rate of change in demand will determine the nature of our water resource management problems.

The exact rate of increase and nature of demand for water in the future, however, is highly uncertain. As the National Water Commission aptly recognized, there are pitfalls and problems in basing planning decisions on a single projection:

Duane D. Baumann and Daniel M. Dworkin are on the faculty of the Department of Geography, Southern Illinois University, Carbondale, Illinois.

> How much water will be used, where, and for what purposes will depend on the policies that are adopted. A range of "alternative futures" is possible, depending upon population levels and distribution, per capita energy consumption, rate of national income growth, technological development, water pricing policies, consumer habits and lifestyles, various governmental policies, and other variables.[4]

For example, research has demonstrated that increases in the price of water would lower domestic use primarily because of a decline in lawn sprinking,[5] while increases in the generation of thermal-electric and nuclear power will raise substantially the demand for water.[6]

The commission analyzed a range of possible outcomes, alternative futures, to assess the consequences of different combinations of the factors affecting demand, such as the interaction of variable levels of population, constraints regarding waste-heat disposal, amounts of dissolved oxygen required in fresh waters, and types of sewage treatment. Depending upon the combination of these factors, the projected demand for withdrawal in the year 2020 may be as low as 570 bg/d or as high as 2,280 bg/d—nearly twice the average annual stream flow.[7] Consumptive use of water is expected to increase from 87 bg/d in 1970 to between 150 to 250 bg/d by 2020.[8]

In shifting our focus from a national stance, we find that several regions of the country are already faced with an imminent threat of shortage, especially in the Rio Grande, Lower Colorado, and Great Basin regions, where withdrawals exceed mean annual stream flow (see table *i*-1). In addition, the Lower Colorado has a consumptive use of 5 bg/d, twice the mean annual stream flow, the deficiency being made up by groundwater and water transfers. Increasing population moreover has accelerated demand for municipal water supply.

As the process of urbanization continues, a large demand for water within a relatively small area will both add to the pressure for greater efficiency in the present use and create intense competition for the presently available supply; e.g., water for our urban population versus the demands for irrigation. Based upon one set of projections,[9] the relative importance of consumptive, municipal use is expected to increase, while withdrawals will remain approximately the same. In 1965 our urban areas consumed 5.2 bg/d, representing 7 percent of the total consumptive use: by 2020 consumptive use in urban areas is expected to rise to 24.6 bg/d, accounting for 16 percent of all consumptive use (table *i*-2). Whereas withdrawals for cities is projected to rise from 27 bg/d in 1970 to 74.3 bg/d in 2020, the proportion it represents of all withdrawals is seen as remaining approximately the same (7 percent) or even possibly declining

Table i-1. Stream Flow Compared with Current Withdrawals and Consumption (bg/d), Annual Flow Available

Region	Mean Annual Runoff[a]	% of yrs 50	% of yrs 90	95	Fresh Water Consumptive Use (1970)	Withdrawals (1970)[b]
North Atlantic	163.00	163.00	123.00	112.00	1.80	55.0
South Atlantic-Gulf	197.00	188.00	131.00	116.00	3.30	35.0
Great Lakes	63.20	61.40	46.30	42.40	1.20	39.0
Ohio	125.00	125.00	80.00	67.50	0.90	36.0
Tennessee	41.50	41.50	28.20	24.40	0.24	7.9
Upper Mississippi	64.60	64.60	36.40	28.50	0.80	16.0
Lower Mississippi	48.40	48.40	29.70	24.60	3.60	13.0
Souris-Red Rainy	6.17	5.95	2.60	1.91	0.07	0.3
Missouri	54.10	53.70	29.90	23.90	12.00	24.0
Arkansas-White-Red	95.80	93.40	44.30	33.40	6.80	12.0
Texas-Gulf	39.10	37.50	15.80	11.40	6.20	21.0
Rio Grande	4.90	4.90	2.60	2.10	3.30	6.3
Upper Colorado	13.45	13.45	8.82	7.50	4.10	8.1
Lower Colorado	3.19	2.51	1.07	0.85	5.00	7.2
Great Basin	5.89	5.82	3.12	2.46	3.20	6.7
Columbia-North Pacific	210.00	210.00	154.00	138.00	11.00	30.0
California	65.10	64.10	38.80	25.60	22.00	48.0
Conterminous U.S.	1,200.40				86.51	365.5
Total U.S.	1,794.00				88.00	371.0

SOURCE: Modified from National Water Commission, *Water Policies for the Future*, p. 9.

[a] Water Resources Council, *The Nation's Water Resources*, pp. 2; 3; 6.

[b] C. Richard Murray and E. Bodette Reeves, "Estimated Use of Water in the United States in 1970," Geological Survey Circular No. 676 (Washington, D.C.: U.S. Geological Survey, 1972), p. 17.

(5 percent) primarily because of expected efficiency in water use and a threefold increase in the demand for water for cooling in electric power generation.

Table i-2.   U.S. Estimated Water Use and Projected Requirements, by Purpose (bg/d)

	Use Projected Requirements (withdrawals)				Use Projected Requirements (consumptive use)			
	1965	1980	2000	2020	1965	1980	2000	2020
Rural domestic	2.4	2.5	2.8	3.3	1.6	1.8	2.1	2.5
Municipal (public-								
supplied)	23.7	33.6	50.7	74.3	5.2	10.6	16.5	24.6
Industrial (self-								
supplied)	46.4	75.0	127.4	210.8	3.8	6.1	10.0	15.6
Steam-electric power								
Fresh	62.7	134.0	259.3	410.6	0.7	1.7	4.6	8.0
Saline	21.8	59.3	211.2	503.5	0.2	0.5	2.0	5.2
Agriculture								
Irrigation	110.9	135.9	148.8	161.0	64.7	81.6	90.0	96.9
Livestock	1.7	2.4	3.4	4.7	1.6	2.2	3.1	4.2
Total	269.6	442.7	803.6	1,368.2	77.8	104.5	128.3	157.0

SOURCE: Modified from Water Resources Council, The Nation's Water Resources, pp. 1–8.

As demand for water increases, shortages will be most acute in urban areas. Cities are faced with the prospect of having to import water from distant sites. As sites for new reservoir construction become increasingly scarce and resistance to interbasin transfers grows, new policies will necessarily be formulated and implemented. Again, we rely upon the final report of the National Water Commission:

> To increase efficiency in water and use and to protect and improve its quality, and to do these things at least cost and with equity to all parts of our country ... require major changes in present water policies and programs.[10]

In response to the increase in demand, however, cities have traditionally chosen to increase the available supply. Except under emergency conditions such as drought, alternatives that would lower demand have been ignored. The most common response of forty-eight Massachusetts communities during the drought of the early 1960s, aside from the unenforced pleas for restrictions on water use, for example, was to plan for increases in supply, new sources, improvements in present supply, emergency sources, and a cloud-seeding experiment.[11] Those adjustments directed toward a reduction of demand were rarely considered or adopted (figure *i*-1).

Figure i-1. Nature of Adjustments Made by 39 Massachusetts Communities During 1963–1966 Drought

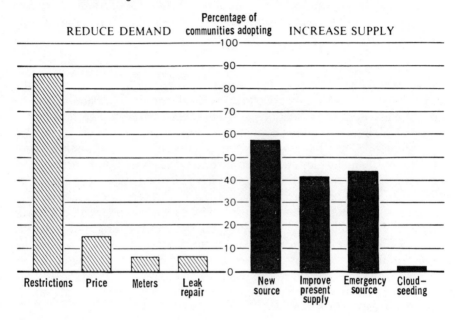

Adapted after Russell, Arey, Kates, *Drought and Urban Water Supply*, p. 71.

This traditional reliance upon technology designed to modify the environment, instead of policies directed toward changing schedule of demand, has been equally pronounced in another water resource problem. White has succinctly noted that "... For a long time it was out of the question for a planning officer to study any way of dealing with flood losses other than by constructing engineering works or by providing relief."[12]

THE CHOICE OF ALTERNATIVES

Among the range of alternatives available for coping with urban water resource problems, the reuse of renovated wastewater is a potentially attractive one. It is not, however, to be considered the panacea for all future urban water resource planning problems; instead, water reuse

should be considered as one alternative in combination with other adjustments in balancing the supply of, and demand for, water for our ever-
increasing urban areas. Although the implications and potential of reuse
is the substantive focus of this report, we reiterate the need in municipal
water resource planning for a thorough consideration of each available
alternative. Following a review of the alternatives for balancing supply of,
and demand for, municipal water supply, attention will focus on those
factors affecting the planning and adoption of recycling renovated water
(table *i*-3).

Modify Water Supply

The major source for municipal water supply in the United States, accounting for 75 percent of total capacity, is water from the diversion of rivers
and streams. Recent projections indicate that surface water flows will
represent a slightly higher proportion of the total water used to satisfy
future demands. As urban areas have grown, however, streams nearest the
cities have been developed, and future opportunities for diversion are
becoming scarcer. Among those regions in the United States that are more
susceptible to a shortage of water, interbasin transfers are required.[13]

Transfer of water can be expensive. The economic, political, environmental, and technological difficulties increase with the length of transfer
required. The area in which the water originates, the *donor region,* is
usually rural and often has a higher incidence of individual well users.
There is a tendency to regard the water as belonging to the region and to
view its transfer as necessary only because of unreasonable use of profli-
gate urban water users.[14]

Groundwater, which currently represents 25 percent of total municipal
supply, is expected to decrease slightly in proportion to the use of surface
water.[15] Sources capable of sustaining high withdrawal rates are limited in
distribution; and while groundwater is the predominant source of self-
supplied individual users, most major cities using groundwater do so as a
supplement rather than as a sole source of supply.

Desalinization and weather modification are other potential sources
that may, in selected circumstances, serve to augment conventional supplies. Although highly variable, weather modification in some instances
has considerable potential, such as increasing snow pack and, subsequently, spring runoff during years when winter reservoir storage is low. Desalinization, on the other hand, is comparatively expensive, requires large
amounts of energy, and it is most promising on a small scale and in unique
situations.[16]

Although efforts to reduce seepage and evaporation have had little
success, reduction of water loss by identifying undetected leaks can be
substantial: in some cases as much as 15 percent of the water withdrawn
may be unaccounted for because of leakage.[17]

Table i-3. Alternatives for Balancing Supply and Demand for Municipal Water Supply

Do Nothing	Modify Supply	Modify Demand

Accept shortage
Unplanned rationing
	1. Increase supply
	   Divert new streams
	   Provide increased storage
	   Use groundwater
	2. Increase efficiency
	   Reduce reservoir
	    evaporation
	   Eliminate leaks
	   Increase runoff
	   Reduce evaporation
	3. Weather modification
	4. Desalinization
	5. Renovated wastewater
	   Nonpotable uses
	   Potable uses
		1. Restrictions
		2. Price elasticity
		   Peak pricing; i.e.,
		    peak summer pricing
		   Marginal cost pricing
		3. Meters
		4. Educational campaign
		   emphasizing water use
		   conservation
		5. Technological innovations
		   and application; e.g.,
		   changes from water
		   cooling to air cooling

Modify Demand

Although other alternatives are available and practicable, planners traditionally have seen supply as the variable in the supply-demand equation.
Whereas price has been shown to be a significant variable, it is usually
disregarded as a method of controlling water use.[18] Marginal efficiency
theory in welfare economics suggests that marginal costs should equal
price; however, the decreasing block-rate pricing system, which is common to most cities, encourages high water use and prices the last gallon
of flow, which has most often been the most costly, at the lowest price.
Increasing block rates, peak summer pricing, and yearly rate changes
based on the supply in storage have all been proposed as methods of
reflecting marginal cost in the pricing of water.

Rationing and restricting uses have been used as a management tool
predominantly during crises: periods of drought. While the cost to consumers during periods of water restriction has been low, however, it is
usually not regarded as a method of planning for water supply.[19] In one
city, the prohibition of using once-through cooling water was an economic
benefit to industries that installed cooling towers and consequently saved
in water bills more than the costs of the investment in recirculating equipment, even when a discount rate of 20 percent was used.[20]

Little evidence is available to evaluate the effects of encouraging the
public to reduce the amount of water consumed. The available evidence
suggests, however, that such pleas were largely ineffective during the
drought of the early sixties in the Northeast.[21]

PLANNING FOR REUSE

Renovation and reuse of municipal water is neither a new concept, nor is
it an inherently efficient method that should be employed to supply water.
It can be as inadvertent and unplanned as the withdrawal and use of water
from a river with upstream users. On the average, for example, approximately one-third of the population in the United States relies upon municipal withdrawals from streams containing 1 gallon (gal.) of previously used
water for every 30 gal. withdrawn; and, in some instances, the ratio of
previously used water is as high as one-fifth.[22] Likewise, Koenig suggests
that of the water withdrawn for municipal supply, up to 18 percent was
effluent.[23] Or, water reuse can be direct and planned, as in a factory where
water from one process is directed with or without treatment to a second
in a series of cascading uses. In the municipal system, planned reuse
involves the collection and treatment of sewage and the use of the effluent
for irrigation, recreation, industry, or for return directly through an intervening body of water or aquifer for general municipal use.[24]

At the federal level, the potential for water reuse has long been recognized by groups such as the Senate Select Committee on National Water Resources (early 1960s).[25] In 1965 the Water Resource Planning Act required that reuse be considered one of the alternative methods of meeting future demand for water.[26] In the National Water Commission Act of 1968, the commission was required to:

> ... review present and anticipated national water resource problems, making such projections of water requirements as may be necessary and identifying alternative ways of meeting these requirements—giving consideration, among other things, to conservation and more efficient use of existing supplies, increased usability by reduction of pollution, innovations to encourage the highest economic use of water, interbasin transfers, and technological advances including but not limited to desalting, weather modification, and wastewater purification and reuse....[27]

Likewise, the Water Resources Council recognized the potential value of reuse:

> The large withdrawals estimated for 2020 in relation to run-off indicate that even with increased in-plant recycling a large increase in reuse would be required.[28]

In the final report, the National Water Commission recommended that the reuse of renovated wastewater "... should occupy a prominent spot in future planning for overall water resources utilization."[29] In addition, the commission made the following specific recommendations:

> The Commission believes that direct reuse of water for industrial purposes and that indirect reuse for purposes of human consumption will increase. Where feasible, such indirect reuse should be minimized by limiting wastewater reuse to processes that do not involve human consumption. This will have the effect of releasing for human consumption potable water now being used by industry. However, previously demonstrated successes in protection of public health in instances where municipal water supplies are derived from indirect reuse suggest that increases in such indirect reuse for human consumption should not be discouraged.
> In regions where a high-quality source of water is used for irrigation of cropped fields of recreation turf areas such as golf courses and a source of treated municipal waste-

water is available, arrangements for water exchange should
be considered. Nutrient-rich municipal waste-water could
be used for irrigation and exchanged for high-quality water
which could be used for domestic and industrial use.

Direct reuse of water for human consumption should be
deferred until it is demonstrated that virological and other
possible contamination does not present a significant
health hazard. Further knowledge on this subject is necessary, and the Commission endorses the research program
recommended by the American Water Works Association.[30] [For American Water Works Association (AWWA)
Policy Statement (1971), see appendix B of this volume.]

DEFINITION OF REUSE

The term *reuse* as applied to water is universally understood as "using
water again." Confusion, however, abounds concerning the exact nature
of the type of reuse implied; that is, whether it is planned or unplanned
and inadvertent; whether it is direct or indirect; or whether it is for
potable or nonpotable uses. The terms describing the treatment, if any, of
the water and the method in which water once used reaches the next user
are interchanged to the extent that any work on reuse of water will profit
from an operational definition.

We use the words *planned reuse* to refer to wastewater that is collected
and purposefully provided for additional use. *Inadvertent* or *unplanned
reuse* results when water is withdrawn and used from a stream with an
upstream discharger. This designation is different from that of the National Water Commission, which equates *planned* as *direct* reuse and
unplanned as *indirect* reuse, and so defines these:

> Direct reuse ... is made by the first user who recycles the
> water through the same system after suitable treatment.
> Indirect reuse occurs when effluent is discharged into a
> water body by the "first user, diluted by natural forces and
> then withdrawn, treated (if necessary), and used by
> others."[31]

The commission's terminology would fail to distinguish between the
planned reuse in Windhoek, South West Africa, where effluent is treated,
discharged into a reservoir, diluted, and withdrawn and used again; and
the unplanned reuse in a city such as New Orleans, where the reuse
component is part of the raw water source.

In the present appraisal, direct and indirect reuse are used to designate two types of planned reuse. *Direct reuse* is "the transmission of water collected as waste, either with or without treatment to an additional use." *Direct reuse* is provided in the United States for irrigation of agriculture and parklands, lawns, and for the grasslands associated with highways; for processing and cooling water in industry; and for forming man-made water bodies for fishing and boating and for scenic enhancement. *Indirect reuse* is "the use of wastewater to recharge aquifers or to build up groundwater supplies that will be later used as a source of supply." These definitions have also been used by Symons[32] and others.

Reuse of renovated effluent can serve as a source of potable and nonpotable water, and it can be furnished directly to the user or be used indirectly to recharge an aquifer that then serves as a source of supply. Both the end use, potable or nonpotable, and the method of distribution, direct or indirect, impose different requirements on the physical design of the system and the safeguards to protect human health and well-being.

Potable Reuse

Direct. While there are, at present, no municipal systems utilizing direct potable use of renovated water in the United States, it has been used in the past in Chanute, Kansas, and is now being used in Windhoek, South West Africa. In Chanute, the effluent was processed and returned directly to the distribution system. This direct return, with external sources used only to supply losses, is designated a *closed circuit* or a *pipe-to-pipe system*. Denver, Colorado, is presently planning a system of this type, investigating "potable reuse with the eventual goal of a nearly closed-loop system in the late 1990's."[33]

In Windhoek effluent is stored in reservoirs and later mixed with water from conventional sources to provide for municipal supply. The important distinction between the two systems is the delay between when effluent is collected and its later reuse, allowing in the interim an extended exposure of the effluent to the natural elements.

Indirect. In the United States the most extensive indirect reuse of water for potable supply is in Whittier Narrows in the Los Angeles, California, metropolitan area. Here 50 million gallons per day (mg/d) of treated effluent are collected and applied to gravel beds, charging the aquifer in the area. The effluent stored as groundwater is pumped up and used for both irrigation and general municipal use.

Nonpotable Reuse

Direct. Most planned reuse of water is for nonpotable purposes, supplied directly from the treatment plant to the user. This category includes most of the present uses for irrigation, industry, and recreation. Some of the proposed innovative uses include dual distribution systems for cities in which separate supply lines would furnish the highest quality potable water for drinking, cooking, bathing, and laundry, while lower quality reused water would be furnished for toilet flushing and for irrigation of lawns and gardens.

Indirect.   Nonpotable reuse of water does not usually require the extra treatment obtained from allowing the effluent to pass through layers of earth. There are, however, some places that reuse nonpotable water indirectly. One previously mentioned is Whittier Narrows, which uses the water for both potable and nonpotable uses. An innovative plan for nonpotable reuse has been prepared for Lubbock, Texas, where wastewater, previously applied directly to the land for irrigation, will be obtained by pumping the underlying watertable. It will then be used to fill a series of recreational lakes that will also serve as reservoirs for industrial use. The project, which is presently under construction, has been funded in part by the Bureau of Outdoor Recreation (BOR) and the U.S. Department of Health, Education, and Welfare (HEW).

In the future, if land treatment of sewage (a method that has been investigated by the Corps of Engineers as an alternative to more conventional methods of treatment) is adopted, extensive opportunities for indirect nonpotable reuse will be provided. In this method of treatment, settled sewage is applied to farmland area. The land then can be underdrained and the water would be available for reuse.

THE FUTURE OF REUSE

If reuse is not at present a least-cost method of supplementing the capacity of municipal systems, its economic attractiveness will increase in the future. The reasons for the increasing economic efficiency of reuse compared to conventional stream flow and storage fall into two major categories: (1) the growing cost of providing conventional flows; and (2) the decreasing cost of providing renovated water.

The Increasing Costs of Water Supply

Water as an Economic Good.   In most analyses of the cost of water supply, the water itself is considered a free good; the cost results from diversion, regulation, and transmission. By definition, a *free good* is one available to all users without scarcity, a situation that would result in zero price.[34] As water becomes less available, the concept of water as an economic good is emerging. Since the late nineteenth century, Western courts have regarded water as personal property once it has been lawfully diverted,[35] and a number of institutions have been formed to provide an orderly market in the sale and transfer of water rights.[36]

The increasing value of water can be shown in a number of instances.

The North Poudre Irrigation Company issued 10,000 shares of stock, each representing a right to receive water as an owner of the company. In five years (1960–65), the value of the shares increased from $200 to $600 a share. The owners were assessed $89 a share over the period for which they received 31.2 acre-feet (ac-ft) of water, an average cost of $2.85/ac-ft.[37] The price of the stock represents the value of anticipated benefits the stockholder assumes will be generated. As this changes, it indicates the change in the assessment of the future worth of receiving 5.2 ac-ft of water a year. In 1965, the investors valued the discounted benefits of receiving this water for less than $3/ac-ft at three times the 1960 rate. The 1975 price has risen to $2,900 a share, continuing at only a slightly slackening rate the continued price escalation.

Increasing Costs of Storage. The costs of providing storage are increasing because of: (1) increasing cost of sites; (2) decreasing storage potential of sites available; and (3) increased opportunity costs of flooding the land. Wollman and Bonen[38] found a probable rise in the cost of land and relocation costs, although the data collected over the past fifty years were somewhat contradictory. Since 1955 the cost of undeveloped land, farmland, and recreational land has been rising. There are no markets in dam sites, but land along rivers should share in the continued rise of the price of land.

The average potential of storage can be expected to fall, since those sites that have the greatest potential for storage and, therefore, lower costs per unit of storage are utilized first. Size is critical in cost calculations: dams impounding 10 million ac-ft or more cost on the average $26/ac-ft of storage, while those storing less than 20 thousand ac-ft cost an average of $186/ac-ft of storage.[39]

Major conflicts arise over competing uses of some areas; e.g., a scenic valley that is considered for a dam site. The first historical battle was over the Hetch Hetchy Valley, an area that was flooded to provide municipal water for San Francisco. In many other areas now flooded, little weight was given to the costs of the loss of unique landscapes.[40] Action by environmental groups has focused attention on this problem, thereby further affecting the supply and the cost of available dam sites.

Decreasing Returns from Storage. As the amount of storage increases for any stream, there is a decreasing yield available from any further increase in storage.[41] As a result of providing increasing levels of yield in critical water areas of the country, many streams are approaching maximum levels of storage (defined as "the point at which any increase in storage would reduce net flow due to evaporation"). The Colorado, the Rio Grande, and the Upper Missouri rivers have all exceeded the point of maximum useful development.[42] If the costs of providing storage are constant, the decreasing yield for each new unit of storage causes the resulting flows to be more costly.

Increasing Costs of Transmission.   The increase in distance between the source of supply and the point of use is raising the cost of water transmission. Those areas of the country that have captured the total available local supply are dependent upon interbasin transfers for more water. If transmountain diversions are planned, expensive tunnels and high-energy inputs may be required. While most transmountain developments are only partially for municipal use, some cities (for instance, Colorado Springs and Aurora, Colorado) have built and now operate such diversion projects solely for municipal use.

As part of the increasing costs of diversion, transmission losses can become a major factor in rising costs. The Fryingpan-Arkansas project calculates a 7-percent loss for every 100 miles of transmission.[43]

Decreasing Costs of Effluent

While the costs associated with water supply are rising, the costs for providing water for reuse are declining primarily because of the upgrading of effluent discharged by municipal systems. If the full cost of treating sewage to the level of completely renovated water is divided into primary, secondary, and advanced wastewater treatment (AWT) components, slightly more than half (in South Lake Tahoe, California, 56 percent) should be ascribed to AWT.[44]

Under Federal Water Pollution Control Act Amendments of 1972,[45] the federal government established standards that require secondary treatment of all municipal sewage and additional treatment in some areas of special need. Whatever the pollution control requirements, whether for secondary or advanced treatment, the substantially treated water produced will be available for distribution and reuse. Thus, the new federal legislation will provide water for reuse at decreasing costs for residual treatment. Though substantial research efforts have been completed,[46] however, water reuse still remains only a potential source of water available to municipalities.

THE PRACTICABILITY OF REUSE

Any consideration of the practicability of recycling renovated wastewater for municipal supply will necessarily require answers to three equally important questions: (1) What are the risks to health for each specific water reuse project, especially if human consumption of the renovated wastewater would occur? (2) To what extent would a proposed water reuse project be socially acceptable? Would the consumers accept reused water? and Would the politicians, public health officials, and engineers provide their endorsements? (3) Under what conditions is water reuse an economically efficient alternative for municipal water supply?

Public Health

Public health concerns are, for the most part, restricted to those uses in which drinking or bodily contact is planned. There are at present no U.S. cities processing effluent for direct potable reuse. Windhoek, South West Africa, has provided the only long-term example of direct introduction of effluent into the municipal supply. The sewage is treated to a tertiary level and includes a final filtration through activated carbon before being mixed with the conventional surface flow. Up to one-third of the effluent in Windhoek is recycled for potable supply during periods when chlorine demand of the wastewaters is not excessive.[47] The water produced meets all of the standards set by the World Health Organization (WHO).[48]

From October 1956 to March 1957, Chanute, Kansas, treated and reused water as a direct augmentation to the municipal supply. While the quality of the renovated water met the standards established by the U.S. Public Health Service,[49] the chemical composition deteriorated markedly, and the water had a pale yellow color and an unpleasant taste and odor; it foamed when agitated.[50] During the same period of drought another community, Ottumwa, Iowa, also recycled renovated wastewater. No health problems were observed.[51]

In Denver, plans are being implemented to recycle renovated wastewater for all uses, including water for drinking. Currently a small demonstration plant (1 mg/d) is under construction, and a substantial research effort concerning water quality and health has been launched. Within ten years Denver may be recycling renovated wastewater at the rate of 100 mg/d.

In another experiment Santee, California, developed recreational lakes from treated effluent with a particular focus upon the occurrence of viruses and bacteria. Lakes containing the treated effluent served as a scenic background for picnicking; boating, fishing, and swimming activities were added later in successive stages. The swimming experiment was closely investigated, and even though viruses were commonly isolated from raw sewage, none was ever measured in the input to a final contact chlorination process.[52]

Although promising, the conclusions reached from these experiments should not lead to confidence concerning the relationship of health and the quality of renovated wastewater. Bacteria and viruses appear to be controlled under proper filtration and chlorination, but little is known concerning the occurrence and distribution of heavy metals such as chromium, mercury, and lead; and organochlorine compounds such as carbon tetrachloride, dichloro diphenyl trichloroethane (DDT), aldrin, dieldrin, and chlordane. There is evidence, moreover, suggesting that at least some organochlorine compounds are carcinogenic. The recently published study on the New Orleans, Louisiana, water supply noted heavy concentrations of chloroform and carbon tetrachloride; both are possible carcinogens.[53]

The lack of definitive information on water quality and health should not preclude serious consideration of water reuse as a possible alternative in planning for municipal water supply. The same problems exist for nearly all other alternative sources of municipal water supply; and by not considering planned water reuse, we are not increasing the assurance of the production of safe, potable water, since most surface water sources contain substantial quantities of effluent and organic agricultural wastes. In nearly all communities in the United States, there are no routine tests for viruses; in fact, the U.S. Environmental Protection Agency's (EPA's) drinking water standards have not yet established virus standards. The point is simply stated: the questions about health and water quality are unknown for both water reuse techniques and the currently operating, conventional treatment technologies. Communities continue to focus upon bacteriological standards, tastes, and odors, while the effects of organics, heavy metals, and viruses are not measured and remain unknown.

Conventional wisdom, however, assumes that most water produced in the United States is safe to drink, and the implementation of water reuse would necessarily raise the risks to health. Harris and Brecher, when discussing conventional water supply systems, succinctly note:

> Almost everyone supposes that such systems are under continuous surveillance by competent state and local health officials, that water samples are scrupulously tested at frequent intervals, that any flaws in a water system will be soon discovered and corrected—and that the water we drink therefore must be safe. Unfortunately, almost everyone supposes wrong.[54]

In a U.S. Public Health Service survey of 969 communities, ". . . only 10 percent [of the communities] had bacteriological surveillance programs that met the 'criteria', while 90 percent either did not collect sufficient samples, or collected samples that showed poor bacterial quality, or both."[55] And 61 percent of the operators of the 969 communities ". . . had not received any water treatment training at a short-school level or higher."[56] Finally, in the same survey, only 59 percent of the communities produced drinking water that was acceptable under the then-existing recommended standards of the U.S. Public Health Service, standards that were considered by many to be lax when compared to those established by WHO. Similar results were observed in a more recent study of 446 U.S.

communities by the comptroller general of the United States: 18 percent of the communities did not meet the standards, as measured by coliform, in two or more months during the preceding twelve months.[57]

With the passage and implementation of the 1974 Safe Drinking Water Act,[58] progress should be made towards improving the quality of our drinking water. With respect to the potential of water reuse, we would argue for a relativist perspective rather than an unattainable absolutist stance. With the completion of the Denver water reuse project, the quality of the finished product will undoubtedly be significantly higher than that of the tap water presently available in most communities in the United States. This conclusion is not new. Dean, for example, noted as early as 1965:

> ... we can make a better quality of water by treating sewage than is available in many of our cities. Controlled treatment of a known hazardous raw material can produce a safer product than routine treatment of a deteriorating source. Viruses can be removed from heavily polluted water ... and the cost is not unreasonable.[59]

Finally, the entire question of health is circumvented in those situations where water can be reused for purposes other than ingestion; e.g., industrial cooling, irrigation, and recreation. Indeed, it is for these noningestive uses that reuse will most likely be adopted, but savings to the community might be foregone if water reuse is not also considered as a potential source for potable use.

Public Acceptance

Although renovated wastewater may be relatively safe to drink, a second and equally important question concerns public acceptance, not only by consumers but by politicians, management personnel, public health officials, and consulting engineers. In essence, no program utilizing renovated wastewater can be implemented without their acceptance.

Recalling the fluoridation debates and being aware of the present-day, heightened public participation, water resource managers are particularly concerned about public acceptance of recycled wastewater. From an unpublished survey by Baumann of 300 municipal water managers in the United States in 1969, the most common reason cited by the 50 percent who opposed wastewater reuse was an anticipated rejection by the public. Similarly Johnson found that "It would appear that water managers know very little of consumer responses concerning renovated wastewater, but generally consider the public would not accept it."[60]

On the other hand, in a recent review of the literature, Baumann and

Kasperson concluded ". . . there is little evidence to support the wide-spread conviction among those charged with proposing solutions to the nation's water supply problems that public opposition constitutes the most important obstacle to the adoption of waste water reuse systems."[61] There is evidence, moreover, that the public will accept renovated wastewater for potable use provided they are aware of the technological character-istics of water treatment. Based upon survey data in five communities, Sims and Baumann suggest that what the consumers know and feel about drinking renovated wastewater is related to the individual's general level of education and his knowledge about water treatment, and is not related to unconscious threats of specific concerns, such as fear of contamination or beliefs concerning nature, technology, esthetics, authority, progress, or destiny.[62]

The recent experience in Denver supports these findings. In a survey of 500 persons, the initial response to the concept of recycling renovated wastewater was primarily negative. As the respondents were provided additional information concerning the implications of water reuse plan-ning, however, the rate of public acceptance increased until 85 percent of the respondents expressed a willingness to drink renovated was-tewater.[63]

In Windhoek, South West Africa, ". . . public acceptance has been very good."[64] And although sales of bottled water increased in the Chanute Kansas, experience, the majority of the consumers drank the renovated wastewater.[65]

The central question, then, is, Why do the managers and engineers perceive the public as unwilling to accept recycled, renovated waste-water, when the available evidence suggests that the consumers would not be, in fact, an obstacle in community adoption of such a program? Could it be that as a result of the process of professional socialization, the engi-neers, water managers, and public health officials are reluctant to innovate or change the established procedures of municipal water supply provi-sion? Hence, does the public become a scapegoat for their reluctance to consider and/or recommend a program of reuse? If so, a key obstacle in the consideration and adoption of alternative strategies of recycling reno-vated wastewater in municipal water supply planning may lie not so much in the minds of the consumer as in the perceptions of consulting engineers and public health officials, two influential groups in community decision making in planning for municipal water supply. In another study by Sims and Baumann,[66] ninety-eight consulting engineers (thirty-three firms) and twenty-two state public health officials (from nine states) were inter-viewed concerning the practicability of a community program using reno-vated wastewater. It is public health officials who ". . hold the more negative position—they begin by not liking the idea, then raise many and major objections to it, and in the end, find their reflection has strengthened their antagonism. Consulting engineers . . . begin with a far more favorable attitude, raise fewer objections and conclude with a perfectly even-split between endorsement and rejection.[67]

Economic Efficiency

How Is Reuse Presently Considered and Utilized?   Reuse of water is an especially attractive concept for: cities that are in water-short areas and have no alternative sources of supply; cities that have provided water by expensive transmountain transfers, particularly those in which reuse is restricted by the law of prior appropriation of imported water; cities that have innovative, aggressive water programs; and, finally, cities that can experiment with water reuse through federal funding. These cities have reason to be interested in reuse as a supplementary source of municipal supply.

How is reuse judged in economic terms? Colorado Springs sees reuse as a low-cost source of supply, costing approximately one-third as much as deriving its potable water supply from extensive transmountain diversions of water from the western to the eastern slope of the Rockies.[68] As a result, it is actively pursuing a program of water reuse.

Whittier Narrows, California, buys potable water from the Los Angeles Metropolitan Water District (MWD). It has calculated the cost of providing secondary treated effluent as approximately equal to the cost of water from MWD. Because treating and reusing water at Whittier Narrows will provide needed capacity in the downstream sewer lines, it is using the treated sewage to recharge an aquifer.

In both Colorado Springs and Whittier Narrows, only three factors were utilized to determine the efficiency of reuse: (1) the cost of an alternative source of water; (2) the necessary treatment to provide an effluent of suitable quality; and (3) the cost of providing and operating a plant to produce the effluent. Once these costs were determined, the analysis consisted of a comparison of the costs of reuse and the costs of the alternative source.

To provide these comparisons, extensive data have been provided on the effectiveness and cost of all sewage treatment processes. The Taft Water Center of the EPA has developed data on the cost and effectiveness of processes for treating wastewater for flow rates from 1 to 100 mg/d. For most analysis only a comparison with the costs of providing water from conventional sources provides a measure of the efficiency of reuse.

Johnson provided the first challenge to this method of calculating the costs of reuse. His study points out that some of the necessary treatment costs would be required for pollution control, whether or not water was reused.[69] The National Water Commission, in its final report, used this modification in setting out the methods for calculating the true cost:

1. The cost of advanced treatment to make wastewater suitable for reuse;

2. minus the cost of pollution control treatment measures otherwise necessary to achieve water quality standards;
3. minus the cost of water treatment of the supply being considered as an alternative to reuse; and
4. plus or minus the difference in conveyance costs between the reusable supply and its alternative, including allowance for the cost of separate supply lines if reuse is contemplated for industrial water supply only.[70]

Other cities are reusing water for different reasons. Santee, California, has provided reused water to fill lakes that are used as a focus for park areas for family gatherings and for boating and fishing. The reuse project was started by an innovative water manager who attracted federal funding to investigate the potential of reused water for recreation. South Lake Tahoe, California, is treating sewage to produce a high-quality effluent, which is then pumped out of the Tahoe watershed because of an agreement by the states of California and Nevada to export all wastes from the Tahoe basin. The water is collected in a lake in the adjoining basin, which is used for recreation and irrigation.

Although there are other examples of reuse, these were selected because they illustrate problems with the present conception and practice of the reuse of wastewater. In Santee and Whittier Narrows, reuse is being provided when there is extensive, unused capacity to furnish water because of the California Water Plan. In Colorado Springs, water is being reused during years when non-reused water is spilling from oversupplied storage reservoirs. South Lake Tahoe is pumping effluent of potable quality across a mountain range because of an agreement limiting discharge within the basin.

How Should Reuse Be Utilized?   Any consideration of utilizing reuse more efficiently must start with the concept of an integrated system—integrated both in management and in the distribution of water—so that either treated effluent or potable water could be furnished to nonpotable users. With this control, the manager could make a decision based on his judgment of the state of the system: to produce and distribute treated effluent or to use only the potable supply for all users. This would eliminate the unnecessary costs in production and distribution of effluent during periods when unused capacity exists in the potable water supply.

In general, there is a relationship between reuse and storage of flows that provides a guide to using treated effluent: Reuse systems cost less to build but are more expensive to operate than systems designed to divert and store flows. On the other hand, reservoir systems are expensive but have low operating costs, suggesting that reuse systems should be used only when water from storage is unavailable to meet the demands. In this way, reuse would function as a source of peak supply, while storage—with its low operating costs—would provide the necessary continual capacity. There are, however, limitations: Treated effluent is not usually considered to be acceptable as a source for potable supply and would be restricted to those uses previously identified and furnished with a separate distribution system for nonpotable effluent. These limitations, however, serve only as constraints on the realization of the full potential of the system.

Reuse, no matter how it is inplemented, provides a source of water that can delay or obviate the need for conventional additions to supply. In addition to supplying water, the presence of reuse as a standby source, not affected by periods of low flow, can increase system yield and provide planning flexibility by serving: (1) as a substitute for the high levels of assurance required in municipal systems; (2) as a means of mobilizing any oversupply in the system; and (3) as a means of shortening the planning cycle, allowing pragmatic evaluation of change in demand to replace present long-term projections.

Reuse to Supply Assurance. The yield of a water supply system based on storage of flows is usually expressed as a quantity of water available or assured 95 percent (or more) of the time. To achieve this level of assurance, some storage must be provided that will be required less than 5 percent of the time. There is an inverse relationship between assurance and yield, yield increasing as assurance declines.[71] By allowing the levels of assurance in a system to be relaxed, the yields withdrawn from the system could be increased, and reuse could furnish the additional water necessary to maintain the desired levels of assurance.

Mobilizing Excess Supply. While the yield of municipal systems is always calculated to provide high assurance levels, there is indication from cities that have been forced to restrict water because of drought that rationing or restriction of water causes little damage. There is, however, an indication that even a shortage less than 5 percent of the time is not acceptable to engineers. Engineering and reference handbooks urge conservative calculations. Social scientists, on the other hand, claim that yields are often, if not always, understated. As an alternative to this sometime-academic debate, renovation and reuse can provide a standby source that will allow the use of the present facilities until pragmatic evaluations of the response of the physical system to the demands placed on it can replace the engineering estimates of yield.

Shortening the Planning Cycle. The long time required for the development of new water sources requires long-term estimations of the future demand for water. In the past, there was little concern if the future demand had been overstated and if subsequent projects based on this inflated demand had resulted in temporary oversupply. The rapid growth in the use of water utilized any excess capacity. There are indications that the rapid growth in demand has slowed. Some factors, such as the low birth rate and the replacement of the single-family house with apartments and cluster homes, indicate that the present slow down will continue. Excess capacity added now under lower rates of growth will be utilized more slowly, with a consequent investment in idle-capacity for a longer period.

SUMMARY AND CONCLUSIONS

Water reuse is a viable and attractive alternative for the provision of municipal water supply. While the demand for water continues to increase in the United States, particularly in our burgeoning urban areas, the traditional alternatives for municipal water supply planning may be less appropriate or no longer practicable.

From the perspective of public health, the growing evidence suggests that while new criteria may be necessarily formulated and applied to determining whether our water is safe to drink, and although new problems may emerge—for example, contamination by carcinogenic chemicals —these problems are not unique to the planned reuse of water.

If recycled, renovated wastewater can be safe to drink and if, under specific qualifications, the concept is a socially acceptable and economically efficient alternative for municipal water supply planning, then why has the rate of adoption been so low? The answer may be related to the existence of two problems: (1) the unavailability of a methodology to assess the relative value of reuse and (2) the professional biases of consulting engineers, public health officials, and municipal water managers. An effort has been made to correct the first deficiency: A simulation model has been developed to evaluate the relative merits of specific water reuse systems (see chapter 3 of this volume). The second problem has been only defined and awaits additional research.

Water reuse should be integrated in the planning for municipal water supply. The thrust is no longer to determine whether reuse is possible; instead, attention should focus on programs and research on the diversity of opportunities for efficient implementations.

NOTES

1. The distinction between the two uses are as follows. withdrawal water is available for further use, while water consumed is not available for reuse, since it is either lost through evapotranspiration or incorporated into the product. See National Water Commission, *Water Policies for the Future* (Washington, D.C.: Government Printing Office, 1973), p. 9.
2. Water Resources Council, *The Nation's Water Resources* (Washington, D.C.: Government Printing Office, 1968), pp. 1–22.
3. We are assuming no significant change in climate, although planned weather modification efforts may be effective in selected local areas under unique atmospheric conditions.

4. National Water Commission, *Water Policies*, p. 3.

5. F. Pierce Linaweaver, John C. Geyer, and Jerome B. Wolff, *A Study of Residential Water Uses* (Baltimore: Johns Hopkins University Press, 1966), p. 78.

6. George David and Leonard Wook, "Water Demands for Expanding Energy Developments," U.S. Geological Survey Circular 703 (Reston, Va., 1974).

7. National Water Commission, *Water Policies*, p. 13.

8. Ibid.

9. Water Resources Council, *The Nation's Water Resources*, p. 8.

10. National Water Commission, *Water Policies*, p. 1.

11. Clifford S. Russell, David G. Arey, and Robert W. Kates, *Drought and Urban Water Supply* (Baltimore: Johns Hopkins University Press, 1970).

12. Gilbert F. White, *Environmental Quality and Water Development*, ed. C. Goldmand, J. McEvoy III, and P. Richardson (San Francisco: W. H. Freeman & Co., 1973), p. 161.

13. Nathaniel Wollman and Gilbert W. Bonen, *The Outlook for Water* (Baltimore: Johns Hopkins University Press, 1971), p. 18.

14. This is an attitude expressed commonly by groups such as SOS (Save Our Streams) in western Massachusetts; SOS is fighting the diversion to the Quabbin system. Also, see Marion Clawson, *Suburban Land Conversion in the United States* (Baltimore: Johns Hopkins Press for Resources for the Future, 1973), p. 130.

15. U.S. Bureau of the Census, *Statistical Abstract of the United States*, 93d ed. (Washington, D.C., 1972), p. 173.

16. National Water Commission, *Water Policies*, p. 345.

17. John Simmons, "Economic Significance of Unaccounted for Water," *Journal of the American Water Works Association* 58 (1966): 639–41.

18. The literature is extensive. See Charles W. Howe, "Municipal Water Demand," *Forecasting the Demands for Water*, ed. W. R. Derrick Sewell, et al. (Ottawa: Department of Energy, Mines, and Resources, 1968), p. 48.

19. Russell et al., *Drought and Urban Water Supply*.

20. Ibid.

21. Ibid.

22. National Water Commission, *Water Policies*, p. 306.

23. Louis Koenig, *Studies Relating to Market Projections for Advanced Waste Treatment*, U.S. Department of Interior Publication WP-20-AWTR-17 (Washington, D.C. 1966).

24. Examples of reuse applications are: irrigation, Lubbock and San Angelo, Texas; recreation, Santee and South Lake Tahoe, California; aquifer recharge, Whittier Narrows, California; direct reuse, Windhoek, South West Africa.

25. U.S. Senate Select Committee on National Water Resources, *Water Resources Activities in the United States* (Washington, D.C.: Government Printing Office, 1960).

26. Water Resources Planning Act of 1965 (PL 85–90), sec. 102; also, Water Resources Council, "Principles and Standards for Planning Water and Related Land Resources," *Federal Register* 38, no. 175 (September 10, 1973): 24778–869.

27. National Water Commission Act of 1968.

28. Water Resources Council, *The Nation's Water Resources*, pp. 1–23.

29. National Water Commission, *Water Policies*, p. 314.

30. Ibid., pp. 314–15.

31. Ibid., p. 306.

32. George E. Symons, "Water Reuse—What Do We Mean?" *Water and Wastes Engineering* (June 1968).

33. R. D. Heaton, K. D. Linstedt, E. R. Lennett, and L. G. Suhr, "Progress Toward Successive Water Use in Denver," mimeographed (October 1974).

34. Paul Samuelson, *Economics* (New York: McGraw-Hill, 1970).

35. W. A. Hutchins, *Water Law in the Nineteen Western States* (Washington, D.C.: U.S. Department of Agriculture, 1971), p. 27.

36. L. M. Hartman and D. Seastone, *Water Transfers* (Baltimore: Johns Hopkins University Press, 1970), p. 4.

37. Ibid.

38. Wollman and Bonen, *The Outlook for Water*, p. 25.

39. Ibid.

40. J. V. Krutilla and C. J. Cicchette, "Evaluating Benefits of Environmental Resources with Special Application-to the Hells Canyon," *Natural Resources Journal* 12 (January 1972): 1–29.

41. G. O. G. Lof and C. H. Hardison, "Storage Requirements for Water in the United States," *Water Resources Research* 2 (Autumn 1966): 323–54.

42. Wollman and Bonen, *The Outlook for Water.*

43. Southern Water Conservancy District, Brochure 6, n.d.

44. R. L. Culp and G. L. Culp, *Advanced Wastewater Treatment* (New York: Van Nostrand Rheinhold Co., 1971).

45. Federal Water Pollution Control Act Amendments of 1972 (PL 92–500), sec. 2770.

46. The U.S. Office of Water Resources and Technology has published a two-volume annotated bibliography concerning research related to water reuse. See U.S. Office of Water Resources Technology (formerly the U.S. Office of Water Resources Research), *Water Reuse —A Bibliography,* 2 vols. (Washington, D.C.: Water Resources Scientific Information Center, 1973).

47. National Water Commission, *Water Policies,* p. 313.

48. G. C. Cillie et al., "The Reclamation of Sewage Effluents to Domestic Use," *Third International Conference on Water Pollution Research* (Washington, D.C.: WPFC, 1966); also see G. J. Stander, "Water Reclamation in Windhoek," *Scientiae* 10 (January 1969): 3–14.

49. U.S. Public Health Service, *Drinking Water Standards* (Washington, D.C.: Government Printing Office, 1962).

50. Dwight Metzler et al., "Emergency Use of Reclaimed Water for Potable Supply at Chanute, Kansas," *Journal of the American Water Works Association* 50 (1958): 1021–57.

51. U.S. Senate Select Committee on National Water Resources, *Water Resource Activities in the United States: Present and Prospective Means for Improved Reuse of Water,* 86th Cong., 2d sess., print no. 30 (Washington, D.C.: Government Printing Office, 1960), p. 3.

52. John C. Merrill et al., *The Santee Recreation Project* (Cincinnati, Ohio: Federal Water Pollution Control Agency, 1967), pp. 108–16.

53. Jean Marx, "Drinking Water: Another Source of Carcinogens," *Science* 186 (November 20, 1974): 809–11.

54. Robert H. Harris and Edward M. Brecher, "Is the Water Safe to Drink?" *Consumer Reports* 39 (June 1974): 437.

55. U.S. Public Health Service, *Community Water Supply Study* (Washington, D.C.: U.S. Public Health Service, 1970), p. vi.

56. Ibid., p. 8.

57. Comptroller General of the United States, *Improved Federal and State Programs Needed to Insure the Purity and Safety of Drinking Water in the United States* (Washington, D.C.: General Accounting Office, B-166506, 1973).

58. Safe Drinking Water Act, 93d Cong., S. 433 and H.R. 1059.

59. Robert Dean in Berg, ed., *Transmission of Viruses by the Water Route* (New York: John Wiley and Sons, 1965), p. 470.

60. James F. Johnson, *Renovated Wastewater: An Alternative Supply of Municipal Water Supply in the United States,* University of Chicago, Department of Geography Research Paper No. 135 (Chicago, 1961), p. 92.

61. Duane D. Baumann and Roger E. Kasperson, "Public Acceptance of Renovated Waste Water: Myth and Reality," *Water Resources Research* 10 (August 1974): 673–74.

62. John H. Sims and Duane D. Baumann, "Renovated Waste Water: The Questions of Public Acceptance," *Water Resources Research* 10 (August 1974): 659–65.

63. Heaton et al., "Successive Water Use in Denver."

64. National Water Commission, *Water Policies,* p. 313.

65. Metzler et al., "Chanute, Kansas," pp. 1021–57.

66. John H. Sims and Duane D. Baumann, "Professional Bias and Water Reuse," *Economic Geography* (1976).

67. Ibid.

68. City of Colorado Springs, Colorado, Department of Public Utilities, 1970 Annual Report, p. 11.

69. Johnson, *Renovated Wastewater.*

70. National Water Commission, *Water Policies.*

71. Lof and Hardison, "Storage Requirements for Water."

PART 1

CRITICAL QUESTIONS

CHAPTER 1

Selected
Health Aspects
of Reclaimed Water
in South Africa
W. H. J. Hattingh

South Africa, situated in the drought belt of the globe, is not richly endowed with water. Any deterioration in the quality of the available water resources is, therefore, a matter of grave concern. Calculations show that the demand for potable water will outstrip the supply by the turn of the century.

Fortunately, it is known that more than 60 percent of the water supplied to a city becomes wastewater [see reference 28], and it is to this readily available source of water that attention is being given.

Reclamation of water for reuse is not a new concept [32]; in fact, it was already practiced in Roman times [1]. The first attempt at reclaiming water for direct reuse at Chanute, Kansas, was described in 1956 [25]. In South West Africa, the Windhoek reclamation plant was commissioned in January 1969, and it marked the first deliberate step towards the reclamation of purified sewage effluents for unrestricted reuse [40]. In November 1970, the Stander Reclamation Plant was inaugurated at Daspoort, Pretoria, to supplement research in this field. The chemical and microbiological qualities of the water produced by both plants have been studied intensively since 1966 [4, 7, 8, 10, 17, 18, 19, 26, 27, 28, 29, 35, 37, 38, 39, 40, 41].

The health effects of present-day potable water and those of reclaimed water, in particular, are of vital importance and form the basis of a great deal of current research [5, 20, 21, 22, 23, 31, 32, 34, 36, 42, 43].

An extensive research program to determine the health aspects of reclaimed wastewaters—by the collection of information on the type and quantity of the constituents in wastewaters, reclaimed wastewaters, and other potable water—has been outlined earlier by the NIWR in the Republic of South Africa [28]. This program has been in operation for a few years, and it is the purpose of this paper briefly to summarize the results of the surveillance program.

W. H. J. Hattingh serves as the senior coordinator for Technical Administration at the National Institute for Water Research (NIWR), Pretoria, Republic of South Africa.
Note: This paper is based on the results of the Division of Water Quality of the NIWR.

RESULTS

The analytical procedures to measure the sanitary quality, trace elements, pathogenic bacteria, viruses, and parasites have been outlined elsewhere [10, 28]. Analytical methods to relate and identify trace quantities of organic chemical residues are continually being developed and published as they become available.

Microbiological Quality

The following bacterial species have been determined: total plate count, total coliform count, fecal coliform count, *Escherichia coli I*, fecal streptococci, *Clostridium perfringens*, *Staphylococcus aureus*, and *Pseudomonas aeruginosa*. In addition, a $TCID_{50}$ virus count per 10 liters (l), using primary monkey kidney cells and a parasite ova count, have also been carried out.

Total Plate Count. The NIWR has proposed a total plate count of 100/milliliter (ml) [10], and it has been found to be a useful parameter to judge the quality of a potable water. It was found that when the reclaimed water from the experimental plant in Pretoria did not conform to this standard, it occurred during experimental runs only. When the plant was operated continually, the quality conformed easily to this standard.

Total Coliform Count. The reclaimed water exceeded the proposed standard [10] of a coliforms per 100 ml in 13.1% of the samples analyzed (145 samples). This figure compared favorably with a figure of 17.1% for water from conventional water supplies.

Fecal Coliform Count. Reclaimed water exceeded a standard of 0 fecal coliforms per 100 ml in 6.3% of the total number of samples analyzed (144 samples). The value was 8.4% for drinking water from other sources. Once again the times that the reclaimed water did not conform to the proposed standard coincided with experimental runs under nonoptimal operation.

The other bacterial counts formed a pattern similar to those discussed above and will, therefore, not be discussed in length. A bacterial problem that has arisen in the last few years is that of antibiotic microbial resistance. The bacterium *Escherichia coli I* is generally regarded as an indicator of fecal pollution. This bacterium has the ability to transfer resistance to antibiotic compounds to other pathogenic bacteria. This acquired resistance makes them resistant to treatment of diseases by antibiotics, with resultant serious complications. The behavior of these bacteria, however, is similar to the "wild" type, and they are equally susceptible to chlorination. They can, therefore, be removed easily in water purification plants. Their occurrence and significance in the water environment is at present being studied [11, 12, 13, 14, 15, 16].

Virus Counts. Only 1 out of 464 samples of conventionally prepared drinking water contained virus/10 l, while all of 144 samples of reclaimed water were free of virus. Among 1,128 samples that conformed to the virus limit of 0/10 l, 487 samples (i.e., 43.2%) exceeded, for instance, the total plate count of less than 100/ml [10].

Parasite Ova. No parasite ova were isolated from drinking water. Ova are efficiently removed by lime treatment in the reclamation process.

Chemical Quality

The interest in the chemical quality of the waters under study centers on compounds such as the polynuclear aromatic hydrocarbons, a group that contains the carcinogenic compounds, the chlorinated hydrocarbons (pesticides), the volatile halogenated compounds, and the quality of organic matter present.

The following results indicate the occurrence and concentration of these compounds in the feed water to a reclamation plant and the final water produced by the plant (tables 1-1 and 1-4).

Table 1-1. Polynuclear Aromatic Hydrocarbons Detected in Feed and Final Water of Reclamation Plant (Pretoria, Republic of South Africa)

		Water	
	Toxicity	Feed	Final
Dibenz(a,c)anthracene		$-$a	$-$
Dibenz(a,h)anthracene	***	$+$b	$-$
Benz(a)anthracene	*	$+$	$-$
Perylene		$-$	$-$
Benzo(ghi)perylene		$+$	$-$
Pyrene		$+$	$+$
Indeno(1,2,3,cd)pyrene	*	$+$	$-$
3-Methylpyrene		$-$	$-$
Benzo(a)pyrene	***	$-$	$-$
Fluoranthene		$+$	$+$
Benzo(b)fluoranthene	**	$+$	$-$
Benzo(j)fluoranthene	**	$+$	$-$
Benzo(k)fluoranthene		$+$	$-$
Coronene		$-$	$-$
22-Methyl cholanthrene		$-$	$-$
9,10-Benzophenanthrene		$+$	$-$

aAbsent.
bPresent.

The feed to the reclamation plant contained a total of ten different polynuclear aromatic hydrocarbons in the ng l^{-1} range, while the final water contained only two compounds that do not have any toxicological importance (pyrene and fluoranthene; see table 1-1).

The chlorinated pesticides in the feed and final water of the reclamation plant were "identified" by retention time only and are still awaiting more positive identification. The values reported in table 1-2 were much lower than those specified by the EPA [6]. The low values of this group of halogenated organic compounds should present no real threat to man.

Table 1-2.   Average (N = 11) Concentration (μg l^{-1}), Chlorinated Pesticides in Feed and Final Water of Reclamation Plant (Pretoria, Republic of South Africa)

| | Water | |
	Feed	Final
Lindane	0.10	0.07
α-Endosulfan	.03	.04
β-Endosulfan	.33	.02
Dieldrin	.05	.03
DDT	0.05	0.04

Table 1-3.   Average (N = 12) Concentration (μg l^{-1}), Volatile Halogenated Hydrocarbons in Feed and Final Water of Reclamation Plant (Pretoria, Republic of South Africa)

| | Water | |
	Feed	Final
CCl_4	0.02	0.66
$CHCl_3$	0.68	17.66
C_2Cl_4	1.39	0.07
$CHBrCl_2$	0.13	11.92
$CHBr_2Cl$	0.09	10.55
$CHBr_3$	0.17	4.38

The results in table 1-3 show that the volatile halogenated hydrocarbons (carbon tetrachloride CCl_4, chloroform $CHCl_3$, tetrachloro ethylene C_2Cl_4, bromo-dichloromethane $CHBrCl_2$, dibromo-chloromethane $CHBr_2Cl$, bromoform $CHBr_3$) were formed in the final water from the reclamation plant. Chloroform ($CHCl_3$) increased from an average of 0.7 μg l^{-1} to an average of 17.7 μg l^{-1} in the final water. This low value compares favorably with those reported elsewhere [2, 33].

The percentage reduction of organic material by the reclamation plant was 84% (table 1-4). The total number of peaks in the final water was almost the same as in the feed water, but a marked change had taken place in the distribution of the peaks. The final water mainly contained peaks

Table 1-4.   Average (N = 7) Concentration (μg l^{-1}), Organic Material in Feed and Final Water of Reclamation Plant (Pretoria, Republic of South Africa)

	Total Organic Material	No. of Peaks	Distribution* A	B	C	D	E
Feed	37	65	0	6	42	15	2
Final	6	56	0	1	13	34	8

*A : 10,000 ng l^{-1}
B : 1,000–10,000 ng l^{-1}
C :   100– 1,000 ng l^{-1}
D :   10– 100 ng l^{-1}
E :   1–   10 ng l^{-1}

(more than 61%) in the concentration range 10 to 100 ng l^{-1}, whereas the peaks in the feed water were mostly (65%) in the range 100 to 1,000 ng l^{-1}.

The identification of the small amount of organic material present in the final reclaimed water (table 1-4) rests on the fact that this material must be isolated and concentrated from the aqueous phase without altering the molecular structure of the organic material. This latter constraint is an important one, since a change in molecular structure may change the toxicity of a molecule and vice versa. A large amount of research is going into this problem. None of the concentration techniques used by the NIWR proved satisfactory. It would seem that a combination of techniques must be used. The molecular size distribution of the organic matter in purified sewage effluent and reclaimed water is vastly different. The former water consists mainly of molecules of molecular weight larger than 100,000, whereas the reclaimed water consists mainly of molecules with molecular weights less than 500. These molecules have molecular weights similar to some inorganic chemicals, and separating them is, therefore, difficult.

The approach to date has been to extract certain known groups of compounds (such as pesticides) with solvents and then to analyze these groups. Progress has been made, and enough information has been obtained to form a baseline for 1974. The mass spectrometer is used for final identification of the compounds isolated and separated by other methods. A word of caution is needed here: Generating results is no problem, but identification and interpretation is not so easy.

Biological Testing
An expert committee from WHO concluded in 1975 that it was impossible to give a full evaluation of the toxic potential of a water from a study of its chemical constituents only and recommended that a complete and

proper toxicological evaluation should also be made, using the final water intended for human consumption. This may require long-term feeding experiments with more than one species of experimental animal, supplemented by toxicological evaluation based on mammalian cell and organ cultures [43].

Two bioassay experiments using rats to study the toxicity of spent active carbon, drinking water, and reclaimed water have been reported [18, 38]. The results indicate that the organic matter chemically recovered from spent active carbon had no ill effects on rats when this material was subcutaneously injected [18]. Van Rensburg et al. [38] concluded that (1) only secondary treated wastewaters had obvious, deleterious effects on the test animals and (2) that no indication of the presence of carcinogens in reclaimed water was observed. The lifelong ingestion of spent activated carbon also had no deleterious effects on the animals. In addition to the biological evaluation of water fed to rats, an additional system utilizing fish as a sensor has also been developed by the NIWR. The method is based on a measurement of the increase in the breathing rate of fish when toxic compounds are present in the water [26].

To date all results utilizing fish and reclaimed water are negative; that is, no toxic compounds were detected.

Bioevaluation techniques using unicellular organisms are presently being studied and will be introduced as soon as possible. The advantage of these sensors is that the life span is short and results can be obtained in a shorter period of time.

Epidemiological Studies
Epidemiological studies will be very difficult to carry out, since water is part of the total environment with which man is constantly in contact. Water can be considered a vehicle for essential elements and nutrients in the diet of man. It can also serve as a carrier of toxic, pathogenic, parasitic, carcinogenic, mutagenic, and teratogenic agents, which are also present in the atmosphere, the fauna and flora, the soil, or man-made structures or materials. In order to show any ill effects, man must—to overcome his own natural or acquired absorption capacity, resistance, or immunity [24]—consume directly or indirectly sufficient quantities of these agents from all possible sources. Water is often, therefore, not the only causative agent for a number of disease outbreaks. The single most important factor in the causation and spread of typhoid in some developing countries is one of personal hygiene [3]. Clean habits are relatable to cultural attitudes as well as to the availability of an adequate water supply [1].

In spite of the difficulties outlined above, however, the South African Institute for Medical Research is at present conducting an epidemiological study in Windhoek, South West Africa. This is a small town in an arid region, and the only hospital treats all patients of the town. The medical profession, therefore, has direct access to all cases admitted, and these may then be carefully studied to obtain the disease pattern of the town. At this stage, no change in the normal disease pattern has been observed [10, 17].

SETTING OF STANDARDS

The rationale for setting standards to insure that drinking water does not constitute a health hazard is at present under review by the NIWR. As better and better analytical techniques become available, there is a tendency to lower the limits for certain standards. The question then arises, is this really necessary?

There is also a tendency to include more and more compounds and not to omit others that are perhaps less important. Will there ultimately be a list of standards containing 400 compounds or a selection of only those proven harmful to man? Will the effort be to obtain a sterile environment? or, finally, will there be a reasonable allowance of chemicals at certain concentrations?

A safety factor is built into the setting of a standard, however; if the standard is exceeded, nobody drops dead. The safety factor is only a guide to the level of a toxic material that can be tolerated over an extended period of time. Opinions have been expressed that a reservoir of water should be fully analyzed before its use. This is impossible. It takes up to thirty days to obtain an answer from some analyses, such as virus evaluations. Are reservoirs to be built for a large city to retain a day's consumption for thirty days? The NIWR, therefore, believes that technology is available to produce water of good quality. Analytical results may then be used to confirm that this technology and the control of the water purification processes have been correctly applied.

The more standards proposed and the longer time required to analyze a sample, the more complicated becomes a routine analytical control laboratory and the higher becomes the standard of education required of the analysts. There is no point in setting a standard if the analytical method is not available and if the standard cannot be enforced. If the latter constraints cannot be overcome, then it is better to have no standard at all.

DISCUSSION

Much controversy exists on the present-day use of chlorine as a disinfectant for drinking water. It is now known that volatile halogenated hydrocarbons are formed, and a study has shown that one of these compounds may be carcinogenic. Proposals are made to stop the use of chlorine, therefore, and much attention is focused on the use of other oxidants, such as ozone. This matter is presently under study by the NIWR, but no clear-cut result is yet available. We believe, however, that the use of chlorine to upgrade the quality of a secondary treated sewage effluent is wrong. Chlorine should be applied only to the disinfection of a drinking water containing very little organic matter, thereby reducing the risk of producing organo-chlorine compounds.

Based on the results obtained so far, the NIWR proposed the following microbiological standard for a potable water [10]: A total bacterial plate count of less than $100/ml$, a total coliform count of $0/100$ ml, and a virus count of $0/10$ l. There is some controversy, however, as to the volume of water that should be analyzed. Volumes of as much as 3,785 l have been proposed [9]. The rationale behind this reasoning is not clear, since if the pressure to increase the volume of water to be analyzed is maintained, then eventually a whole reservoir would have to be analyzed for virus before the result would be acceptable.

In those few instances in other parts of the world where an outbreak of disease has been experienced, gross pollution has been shown to be the cause. Under controlled conditions where proper disinfection has been applied, however, there has never been an outbreak. It has been the experience in the Republic of South Africa that whenever pathogenic bacteria or viruses—or both—have been isolated from a potable water, proper disinfection had not been achieved. This could be traced back to bad operating practice or inadequate control of disinfection. To date, no virus or pathogenic bacteria have been isolated from reclaimed water.

The NIWR has been conducting studies on the production and quality of water reclaimed from secondary purified sewage effluents for more than a decade. An extensive study of the quality of the major potable water supplies in the Republic of South Africa has been followed since 1973 and will be carried out over a period of ten years.

To date all results obtained indicate that there is very little wrong with our present drinking water supplies and that the reclaimed water compares favorably with these waters and also with all known standards set to safeguard the health of man. It is believed that present-day technology should be able to produce any quality of water desired, even from the most polluted sources. Studies [37] indicated, for instance, that when a pilot reclamation plant was inoculated with large concentrations (up to 4 mg/l) of compounds such as polynuclear aromatic hydrocarbons, chlorinated pesticides, organo-phosphate pesticides, heavy metals such as Hg, Pb, As, and cyanides, the final water produced by the plant contained concentrations of these compounds so low as to present no health hazard to man. These observations were confirmed by bioassay experiments [26, 28, 38].

REFERENCES

[1] Barnard, J. J. and Hattingh, W. H. J. "Health Aspects of Reuse of Wastewater for Human Consumption." Paper presented at the Conference on Drinking Water Quality, High Wycombe, England, 4–6 November 1975.
[2] Bellar, T. A.; Lichtenberg, J. J.; and Kroner, R. C. *Journal of the American Water Works Association* 66 (1974): 703.
[3] Campbell, J. M. and Le Roux, N. J. *S.A. Medical Journal* 43 (1969): 1408–11.
[4] Cilié, G. G.; van Vuuren, L. R. J.; Stander, G. J.; and Kolbe, F. F. *Advances in Water Pollution Research.* Vol. 2. Pp. 1–19. Edited by S. H. Jenkins and L. Media. Washington, D.C.: Water Pollution Control Federation, 1966.
[5] Dunham, L. J.; O'Gara, R. W.; and Taylor, F. B. *American Journal of Public Health* 57 (1967): 2178–85.
[6] Environmental Protection Agency. "National Interim Primary Drinking Water Regulations." *Federal Register* 40, no. 248 (December 24, 1975).
[7] Funke, J. W. and Coombs, P. National Institute for Water Research, CSIR, Project Report No. 4, 6201/6434. Pretoria, 1972.
[8] ———. National Institute for Water Research, CSIR, Project Report No. 5, 6201/6434. Pretoria, 1972.
[9] Gerba, C. P.; Wallis, C.; and Melnick, J. L. *Journal of the American Water Works Association* 64 (1975): 220–25.
[10] Grabow, W. O. K. and Isaäcson, M. "Microbiological Quality and Epidemiological Aspects of Reclaimed Water." Paper presented at the International Conference on Advanced Treatment and Reclamation of Wastewater, Johannesburg, June 1977.
[11] Grabow, W. O. K. and Middendorf, I. G. *Wat. Res.* 7 (1973): 1589–97.
[12] Grabow, W. O. K. and Prozesky, O. W. *Antimicrobial Agents and Chemotherapy* 3 (1973): 175–80.
[13] Grabow, W. O. K. and Van Zyl, M. *Wat. Res.* 10 (1976): 717–23.
[14] Grabow, W. O. K.; Grabow, Nora A.; and Burger, J. S. *Wat. Res.* 3 (1969): 943–53.
[15] Grabow, W. O. K.; Prozesky, O. W.; and Burger, J. S. *Wat. Res.* 9 (1975): 777–82.
[16] Grabow, W. O. K.; Prozesky, O. W.; and Smith, L. S. *Wat. Res.* 8 (1974): 1–9.
[17] Grove, S. S. "The Epidemiology of Reclaimed Water." Paper presented at the Fifty-first Conference of the Institute of Municipal Engineers of South Africa, Windhoek, June 1974.
[18] Hattingh, W. H. J. and Nupen, E. M. *Water S. A.* 2 (1976): 33.
[19] Henzen, M. R.; Stander, G. J.; and van Vuuren, L. R. J. *Prog. Water Technol.* 3 (1973): 307.
[20] Hueper, W. C. and Payne, W. W. *Am. J. Clin. Path.* 39 (1963): 475–81.
[21] Hueper, W. C. and Ruchhoft, C. C. *Arch. Ind. Hyg.* 9 (1954): 488–95.
[22] Janecek, J. and Chalupa, J. *Arch. Hydrobiol.* 65 (1969): 515–22.
[23] Maloney, G. W. and Davis, T. J. *American Journal of Public Health* 57 (1967): 2194–97.
[24] Martin, A. E. "Medical Considerations in the Abstraction of Potable Waters from Polluted Sources." Paper presented at the Spring Conference of the Society of Water Treatment and Examination, London, 1972.
[25] Metzler, D. *Journal of the American Water Works Association* 50 (1958): 1021.
[26] Morgan, W. S. G. "The Use of Fish as Biological Sensor to Detect Toxic Compounds in Potable Water." Paper presented to International Conference on Advanced Treatment and Reclamation of Wastewater, Johannesburg, June 1977.
[27] Nupen, E. M. *Wat. Res.* 4 (1970): 661–72.
[28] Nupen, E. M. and Hattingh, W. H. J. "Health Aspects of Reusing Wastewater for Potable Purposes—South African Experience." Paper presented at the Workshop on Research Needs for the Potable Reuse of Municipal Wastewater, Boulder, Colo., 17–20 March 1975.
[29] Nupen, E. M. and Stander, G. J. "The Virus Problem in the Windhoek Wastewater Reclamation Project. Paper presented at the Sixth International Conference of the IAWPR, Jerusalem, June 1972.
[30] Nupen, E. M.; Bateman, B. W.; and McKenny, N. C. "The Reduction of Virus by the Various Unit Processes Used in the Reclamation of Sewage to Potable Waters." Paper

presented at the Conference on Viruses in Water and Wastewater Systems, Austin, Tex.,
April 1974.

[31] Ottoboni, A. and Greenberg, A. E. *Journal of the Water Pollution Control Federation*
42 (1970): 493–99.

[32] Phillips, W. J. *Journal of the American Water Works Association* 66 (1974): 231.

[33] Rook, J. *Journal of the American Water Works Association* 68 (1976): 168.

[34] Smith, J. W. and Grigoropoulos, S. G. *Journal of the American Water Works Association*
60 (1968): 969–79.

[35] Stander, G. J. and van Vuuren, L. R. J. *Journal of the Water Pollution Control Federation*
41 (1969): 355–67.

[36] Tardiff, R. G. and Deinzer, M. *Proceedings of the Fifteenth Water Quality Conference.*
University of Illinois, Urbana-Champaign, 1973. Pp. 23–37.

[37] Van Rensburg, J. F. J.; Van Rossum, P. G.; and Hattingh, W. H. J. "The Occurrence and
Fate of Organic Micro-pollutants in a Water Reclaimed for Potable Reuse." Paper presented to the International Conference on Advanced Treatment and Reclamation of Wastewater, Johannesburg, June 1977.

[38] Van Rensburg, S. J.; Hattingh, W. H. J.; Siebert, M. L.; and Kriek, N. P. J. "Biological
Testing of Water Reclaimed from Purified Sewage Effluents." Paper presented to the
International Conference on Advanced Treatment and Reclamation of Wastewater, Johan-
nesburg, June 1977.

[39] Van Vuuren, L. R. J. and Henzen, M. R. "Process Selection and Cost of Advanced
Wastewater Treatment in Relation to the Quality of Secondary Effluents and Quality
Requirements for Various Uses." Paper presented at the IAWPR Specialised Conference
on Application of New Concepts of Physical-Chemical Wastewater Treatment, Vanderbilt
University, Nashville, Tenn., 18–22 September 1972.

[40] Van Vuuren, L. R. J.; Henzen, M. R.; and Stander, G. J. "The Full-Scale Reclamation for
the Augmentation of the Domestic Supplies of the City of Windhoek." Paper presented
at the Fifth International Conference of the IAWPR, San Francisco, 1970.

[41] Van Vuuren, L. R. J.; Stander, G. J.; Henzen, M. R.; Meiring, P. G. J.; and Van Blerk,
S. H. V. *Wat. Res.* 1 (1967): 463–70.

[42] World Health Organization. *Technical Report Series* No. 517. Geneva, 1973.

[43] ———. *Technical Paper Series* No. 7. Leidschendam, 1975.

CHAPTER 2

Economic
Considerations
in the Reuse
of Urban Water
Jerome W. Milliman

There appears to be a growing realization that reuse of urban wastewater
can be a promising source of water supply. Several basic factors are responsible for this growing awareness:

1. Increasing urbanization and industrialization throughout the world
   are clearly exerting greater pressures on limited fresh water resources. As a result, fresh water sources are becoming scarce and
   costly.
2. More and more communities are turning to polluted sources to meet
   their needs for new supplies. It has been estimated that about one-
   third of the United States population now uses water that is in part
   made up of wastewaters discharged only hours earlier from municipal or industrial sewers.[1]
3. The costs of treatment of wastewater are rising as a result of higher
   standards imposed on the treatment of wastewater before discharge. In some cases, the quality of discharged wastewater may
   exceed the quality of intake water into the system. When high-
   quality water is produced by waste treatment plants, the economics
   of reuse of wastewater becomes a serious consideration. This matter
   will become important when cities attempt to meet the zero-dis-
   charge goal set forth in the 1972 Federal Water Pollution Control
   Act.[2]
4. Finally, important developments are taking place in the technology
   of AWT. Progress is being made in processes for dealing with virus
   removal, heavy metals, and toxic organic materials. Increased attention is also being given to problems of system reliability and to
   monitoring capabilities.[3] It is now realized that most of the reservations that have been expressed regarding reuse of wastewaters apply with almost equal force to many conventional water treatment
   plants.

Jerome W. Milliman is professor of economics in the College of Business Administration, Bureau of Economic and Business
Research, University of Florida, Gainesville, Florida.

Increasingly, it is being recognized that the science and technology of water supply and water pollution control are much the same. What remains is a need to develop common institutional arrangements for the joint planning and management of water supply and waste treatment of systems. It is also clear that the economics of water supply and the economics of wastewater treatment must be brought together in a common planning and operation framework.

The present indirect use of wastewaters for urban water supplies is largely unplanned. Concern has been expressed with regard to serious problems involving the safety and reliability of treatment of conventional water supplies. This concern now extends to the planned reuse of wastewater, which, it seems, inevitably must be given serious consideration. The questions are, What is the best technology to make reliable and safe the reuse possibilities? and, How can wastewater be reused in an economic and efficient manner?

GENERAL ECONOMIC FACTORS FOR REUSE OF WASTEWATER

The proper perspective for economic planning for the reuse of urban wastewater must be that of viewing reuse as part of the *overall problem* of efficient management of water resources. The activities of water supply, wastewater disposal, water quality management, and possible reuse of wastewater are clearly interdependent *within* given urban areas and also *across* common watersheds or water basins.

One can argue that the widespread and growing concerns about the safety of municipal supplies, the water shortages and rising costs, and environmental quality and need for higher standards for wastewater discharges are largely problems both of inadequate institutional arrangements for the management of water resource and of failure to use economic principles.[4]

There are four factors governing economic planning for the possible reuse of wastewater:

1. Establish systems of regional water management.
2. Within urban areas, establish unified management of investment, pricing, operating decisions for water supply and waste disposal.
3. Adopt user charges for water supplies and the treatment of wastewater based upon marginal costs.
4. With regard to management and planning policy, rely on evaluation of benefits and costs of programs and projects for water resource investments and environmental quality management.

Systems of Regional Water Management

The need to develop regional systems of water management is probably best argued by Kneese and Bower in their study of regional water quality problems.[5] They argue that regional authorities are necessary: (a) to internalize major offsite costs of water pollution by balancing gains and costs between upstream and downstream users; and (b) to take advantage of large-scale treatment measures that might not be economical or available to individual cities of firms.

Although their work is primarily directed toward *regional* water quality management, it is clear that water quality management should be directly related to the total supply management of the hydrologic unit, including use of water for hydropower, recreation, flood control, navigation, and water supply.

In addition to a regional approach, Kneese and Bower stress the need for effluent charges as a means of providing economic incentives to minimize the costs of attaining environmental quality. Present water pollution control efforts in the United States have failed to emphasize comprehensive river basin planning and have not employed the effluent charges as a means of reducing the output of industrial and municipal waterborne wastes.[6]

The proper framework within which to view the desirability of reuse of wastewater is clearly the regional one. First, all water resource management should be coordinated across uses within a basin. Second, it is clear that there may be economies of scale in the treatment and transmission of wastewater for reuse that require a large-scale regional works. Third, reuse of wastewater upstream may have downstream benefits and costs that may not be considered unless a regional management framework is provided.

Integration of Water Supply and Sewerage Systems

As figure 2-1 illustrates, urban water and sewerage systems are only part of a combined overall system. A full system consists of supply, purification, storage, and delivery of water to users, followed by collection, treatment, and disposal of wastewater.

All too often, water and sewerage systems within an urban area are administered independently, so that the advantages of a combined operation are lost. Pricing and investment decisions for urban water supply are usually made independently of their effects upon wastewater operations. Yet, water supply policies inevitably affect wastewater policies. Combined planning and management of water and sewerage systems *within* an urban area offers many advantages from technical, managerial, economic, and social points of view.[7] Clearly, if we are to consider reuse of wastewater, integrated water and sewerage management will be required if efficient policies are to be developed.

Figure 2-1. Typical Combined Water Sewerage System

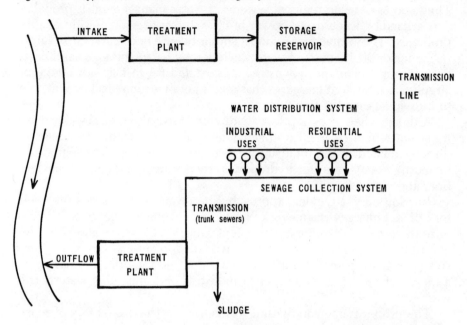

Yet Colorado Springs, Colorado, cited as a pioneer in the field of reuse of urban wastewaters, still has separate management of its water supply and sewerage departments.[8] The two even employ separate engineering consultants. Surely, one must recognize that the economic feasibility of the reuse of wastewater depends upon the rationalization of pricing and investment policies for water and sewerage. It is commonplace to observe that the market demand for reuse of wastewater depends upon price. The real question, of course, is how correct prices are to be determined for reclaimed wastewater, for sewage water, and for "fresh" water supplies in a coordinated framework.

Pricing for Water Supply, Sewage, and Reclaimed Wastewaters

It is generally recognized by economists that pricing policies for urban water supply and sewage leave a great deal to be desired. It is also understood that economic analysis of urban wastewater reuse depends upon its costs of production and its price, relative to alternative water sources available to prospective users. Unless "correct" prices are charged for "fresh" water supplies and unless the costs of wastewater treatment are correctly estimated and assessed, it will be impossible to determine the economic feasibility of wastewater reuse.

Economists agree that prices for water supplies should be based upon the marginal costs of production and delivery and the marginal costs of waste disposal. When marginal costs of service differ among users, then prices should differ in corresponding fashion. Yet, the conventional practice in the municipal water supply industry is to base prices or rates upon average costs.[9] In an age when costs of new supplies are rising, average cost pricing will seriously underprice water to final users. On the one hand, if water rates for conventional supplies are too low, water consumption will be excessive, thus increasing the "need" for reuse of wastewater. On the other hand, excessively low prices for conventional supplies may make "correct" prices charged for reclaimed water appear too high in relation to alternatives available to potential users.

In addition to the widespread use of average cost pricing, the water supply industry generally charges uniform rates that fail to reflect costs of service that vary over time and space.[10] Peak season pricing, for example, is seldom employed, even though water commodity costs and water system costs are much influenced by seasonal use. It is also clear that the costs of serving suburban customers may be much greater than those charged in high density areas. Uniform prices across time and space clearly produce inefficiencies in current water use. Again, inefficient prices for conventional supplies will make it virtually impossible to estimate "correct" prices for reclaimed water supplies.

Cost-Benefit Analysis for Water Supply, Sewerage, and Reclaimed Water
It is important that the economic feasibility of wastewater reuse be determined by careful cost-benefit analysis. Also, cost-benefit analysis of urban wastewater reuse on a *regional level* is a complex task.[11] There can be no quarrel with these statements. Yet, the irony is that the same kind of careful cost-benefit analysis has not been employed on conventional municipal water supply and sewerage projects, and it is not being employed now.

In conventional planning, the water industry traditionally forecasts water requirements (independent of prices, benefits, and costs) and then designs new capacity to meet requirements. After the engineering and physical planning have taken place, computations are made to determine accounting costs and the rate level (based upon average costs). On the one hand, it is evident that physical and financial planning are now basically separate activities that bring in the demand relations only by the back door. On the other hand, current practices concentrate upon financial feasibility (the self-liquidating character of the project) and virtually ignore an economic evaluation of general benefits and costs.[12]

In summary, the seriousness with which we approach economic planning for wastewater reuse will depend on four factors affecting economic efficiency: (1) use of a regional approach; (2) integrated planning across urban water supply and water disposal systems; (3) greater attention to rate structures based upon marginal costs; (4) greater use of cost-benefit analysis for water supply, waste disposal, wastewater reclamation.

SPECIAL ECONOMIC FACTORS IN REUSE OF WASTEWATER

In 1971 the reuse of municipal wastewater in the United States took place at approximately 358 areas generally located in the southwestern states of Texas, California, New Mexico, Nevada, Colorado, and Arizona.[13] Total reuse volume on an annual basis was estimated at 133 bg (exclusive of groundwater recharge). Treated urban wastewater was being used successfully for irrigation of a wide variety of crops and landscaping, for industrial cooling and process water, and for recreational lakes. At one site, Grand Canyon Village, Arizona, treated wastewater was used for toilet flushing. Irrigation use comprised 77 bg, or 58 percent. Industrial use was 53 bg, or 40 percent. The bulk of the industrial reuse, however, was due to one user in Baltimore, Maryland—the Bethlehem Steel Plant—which used 44 bg annually.

Reuse in other countries takes place at approximately fifty-five sites, with the bulk of the use being in Australia, Japan, Israel, South Africa, and Mexico. The most well-known reuse takes place in Windhoek, South West Africa, where reclaimed sewage is used for direct potable use, with monthly proportions going as high as 27 percent of total municipal water consumption there.

Is the reuse of wastewater economical? The obvious answer is "yes"— otherwise it would not take place. Clearly, the gains exceed the costs to the parties involved. Yet, an extensive study of the literature on wastewater reclamation indicates that the "obvious" answer of economic feasibility is not at all clear-cut. Better answers might be "probably," "perhaps," or, simply, "No one knows." It is a vain search to look in the extensive literature on reclamation of wastewater for careful studies of cost-benefit analysis, cost estimation (not just engineering estimates of average costs), and price policy and user charges. It is an interesting commentary on the rapid development of the science and technology of wastewater reclamation that apparently so little attention has been paid to the basic economic factors influencing the feasibility of reuse of urban wastewater. The remaining part of this paper therefore will contain some scattered comments on a few special economic factors that might influence the wastewater reuse question.

Integrated Management of Water Supply, Waste Treatment, and Water Reclamation System

Figure 2-2 illustrates a hypothetical system combining water supply, waste treatment, and wastewater reclamation for an urban area. The figure should show clearly that the administration and control of the community water supply and wastewater disposal (and reuse) systems should be combined, if possible.

Figure 2-2. Simplified Wastewater Reuse System

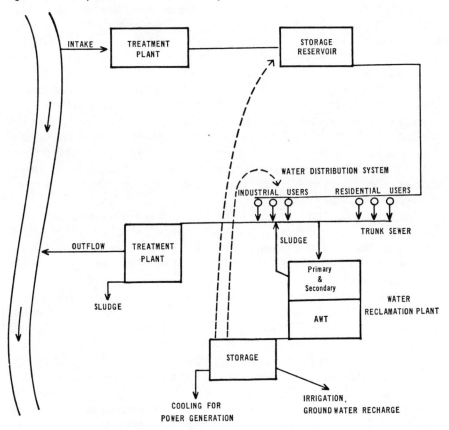

There are definite economies to be derived from combined management, including sharing of technical personnel and monitoring and testing facilities and integrating the physical layout of services to minimize costs of the total system. A water system is less costly, for example, when service can be made by gravity flow; the same logic applies to the operation of the sewerage system. If wastewater is not reclaimed, it may be economic to have the waste treatment plant located at the lowest elevation in the system. Yet, when a water reclamation plant is considered, its location must be carefully planned, not only to intercept and treat only high-quality wastewater (little or no industrial wastes), but also to minimize pumping and conveyance costs to potential users of the reclaimed waters. The costs of separate distribution lines for conveyance of reclaimed wastewater to potential users may greatly affect the market demand for reclamation.

The payment for the collection and treatment of wastewater should be considered an integral part of the water supply service, and water charges should include these costs.[14] At present, this is more the exception than the rule. When reclamation of wastewater is considered, it will be even more important to rationalize common water and sewage user charges. For example, the costs of reclamation will be very sensitive to the quantities and qualities of the wastewater. Municipal water uses that seriously degrade wastewater and make practicing reclamation more difficult should be charged higher prices. Also, uses that do not return water to the system (e.g., lawn watering, car washing) may reduce return flows and affect the quantities to be reclaimed, particularly on a seasonal basis. It is possible, for example, that these consumptive water uses may reduce return flows to reclamation plants at the very time that the seasonal demands for reclaimed water are the highest. Thus, consumptive uses may have to be given higher rates.

Figure 2-2 illustrates the possible kinds of reuse to be considered. Clearly, the extent and type of AWT will depend upon the kinds of potential reuse. Nitrogen and phosphorous may be valuable nutrients in reclaimed water destined for irrigation use, yet they are major problems in water destined for power station cooling.

Usually, it will be necessary to provide storage facilities for the reclaimed water in addition to careful monitoring and testing systems within the reclamation plant. This storage will allow for retention of reclaimed waters for a period of time (itself a purifying process) to allow for adequate observation and testing of the product water. Also, storage will be necessary to even out irregularities in the daily and seasonal inflows to the reclamation plant and to provide capacity to meet fluctuating user demand for the reclaimed water. For example, irrigation demands may be highly seasonal or vary from year to year, depending upon long-range climatic conditions. In such cases, it may be desirable to operate the reclamation plant on an intermittent basis, perhaps to supply peaks or special uses, and to use conventional supplies to meet base-load demands.

Regionalization of Water Management

Figure 2-3 illustrates a hypothetical system of regional water management. As indicated above, the case for regional water management is well established, even though the practice of regional management is not common. If the layout of a combined community water supply and community wastewater system can greatly affect total capital and operating costs, it should be the case that the regionalization of water resource management can lead to substantial cost savings. It is not clear, for example, that it would make good economic sense for each community to have its own wastewater treatment plant. Large-scale treatment plants usually have lower costs, even when extra conveyance costs are included. It follows also that it may be desirable to have regional water reclamation plants, rather than the local ones shown in figure 2-2.

The benefits and costs of wastewater reclamation, moreover, will clearly differ with regard to point of view: regional or local. If water is reclaimed and reused upstream, there will likely be important effects on the quantities, qualities, and timing of water flows to downstream users. Just as interbasin diversions of water resources may have important downstream effects, it is probable that upstream reclamation may have downstream effects not seen by upstream communities. Upstream reuse of water for irrigation at low-flow periods, for example, may cause hardship to downstream users. In addition, the return flows from irrigation waters may be of very poor quality.

Current federal grants for subsidy of municipal waste treatment plant construction induce planners to think in terms of "end-of-the-pipe" treatment instead of less costly alternatives.[15] Such subsidies moreover encourage each community to "go-it-alone," not considering large-scale regional treatment plants. Finally, the 1985 target of zero discharge (PL 92–500) will require cities to produce pollution-free treatment. It seems, therefore, apparent that the 1985 goal of zero discharge is grossly uneconomic and unrealistic.[16]

Higher standards of municipal water treatment, nevertheless, will cause cities to consider reusing high-quality wastewater rather than discharging it into rivers and making the water available to downstream users. On the one hand, the incremental costs of AWT attributable to reuse will decline as the "standard" treatment required for *all* wastewater is increased. On the other hand, the quality of treated water will begin more closely to approximate the quality of conventional water sources, so that recycling will be less objectionable. As a result, there may be uneconomic incentives for cities to reuse their own wastewater.

Even if zero discharge is not obtained, it is clear that effects of federal water quality policy may be highly uneconomic from a regional and national point of view. Surely decision makers must be obligated to examine the benefits and costs of the proposed increases in goals and in the methods for achieving improved environment management of water resources.

Dual Water Systems

If reclaimed wastewater is of the same quality as conventional water sources, then there will be no need to consider the cost of dual supply systems. By contrast, if the reclaimed water is of lower quality, then dual systems would be necessary.

Figure 2-3.   Regional Water Management

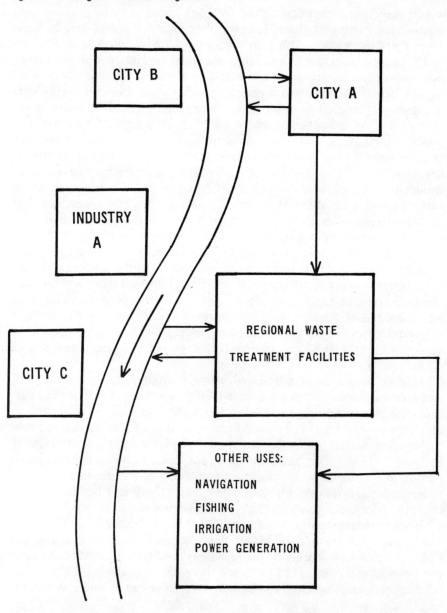

Two objections to dual systems are cited: cross-connections and cost.[17] If two systems—one for potable and one for nonpotable water—are present in the same area, extreme care must be taken in the layout of lines to avoid cross-connections. This danger is well recognized, already part of the planning for conventional water supply and wastewater systems.

The planning of dual systems does warrant a good deal of research. If the dual system is just a special line to some irrigation users, to a power plant, or to industrial users, the cost might well be reasonable. By contrast, if an *existing* municipal system is to be replaced more or less in its entirety by a dual system, the cost might be unrealistic. An intermediate case would be the cost of a dual supply system for a new community or a new area. Okun states that the costs of dual systems for new areas might be only 20 percent higher than conventional systems, particularly where the new construction would comprise highrise, multifamily dwellings.[18] The technology for dual systems now exists because the potable water system could use plastic pipe, and the pressures required for fire protection would be handled by the nonpotable water systems.

The case for dual systems seems more attractive when one realizes that only approximately 10 percent of the potable water supplied in large cities is really used for potable purposes; e.g., drinking and cooking. The remainder is used for industrial use, lawn watering, toilet flushing, fire protection, and the like. If commodity costs and costs of treatment are high relative to transmission and distribution costs, considering dual systems may make sense. In the past the reverse has been true, and there has been an effort to make *all* municipal water supply meet drinking water standards. Dual domestic systems are already in place in Grand Canyon Village, parts of Hong Kong, and in the Bahama Islands. In several cases, seawater has been used for toilet flushing.

One cost of a dual system apparently has not been recognized in the literature: Such systems may require dual metering devices, dual billing, and dual pricing policies. Perhaps it might not be necessary to have separate meters for each type of water for each user. It may turn out that only the potable supply should be metered or perhaps even that metering might not be needed at all. This last possibility might be feasible under a dual set of flat price structures based upon probable use indicators (e.g., number of toilets, size of lawn) that might serve as use proxies and avoid either dual or single meters. In any event, it is clear that a great deal more attention would be required to calculate marginal costs of dual supplies and to price structures and demand elasticities than is the case when only one product water is served to each user.

For the present, it is likely that reclaimed water may be of lower quality than conventional sources, so that dual systems of some kind will be needed. There is reason to believe that at some future date the advance of technology and the use of large-scale reclamation plants will make it economic in arid areas of the world to produce reclaimed water of impeccable quality. Under these circumstances there may be no need for dual systems.

There would remain, however, the need for integrated system planning and management that could consider the trade off between the extra costs of dual systems and the incremental of producing reclaimed water that is clearly potable.

NOTES

1. Daniel Okun, "Planning for Water Reuse," *Journal of the American Water Works Association* 65 (October 1973): 617–22.
2. Federal Water Pollution Control Act Amendments of 1972 (PL 92–500). See Edward Cleary, "Accommodating to New Imperatives in Water Pollution Control," *Journal of the American Water Works Association* 66 (July 1974): 437–40.
3. William Phillips, "Direct Reuse of Reclaimed Wastewater: Pros, Cons and Alternatives," *Journal of the American Water Works Association* 66 (April 1974): 231–37.
4. Jerome Milliman, "Policy Horizons for Future Urban Water Supply," *Land Economics* 39 (May 1963): 109–32.
5. Allen Kneese and Blair Bower, *Managing Water Quality Economics, Technology, and Policy* (Baltimore: Johns Hopkins University Press, 1968), ch. 10.
6. A. Myrick Freeman, Robert Haveman, and Allen Kneese, *The Economics of Environmental Policy* (New York: John Wiley and Sons, 1973), pp. 115–16.
7. Jerome Milliman, *General Economic Principles for Sewerage Planning and Operation,* Indiana University, Institute for Applied Urban Economics (Bloomington, 1968), p. 20.
8. Duane Baumann and Daniel Dworkin, "Planning for Water Reuse," Butler University, Holcomb Research Institute (Indianapolis, Ind., 1975), pp. 16–18.
9. Jack Hirshleifer, James DeHaven, and Jerome Milliman, *Water Supply: Economics, Technology, and Policy* (Chicago: University of Chicago Press, 1960), ch. 5.
10. Steve Hanke, "Water Rates: An Assessment of Current Issues," *Journal of the American Water Works Association* 67 (May 1975): 215–19.
11. Environmental Protection Agency, *Demonstrated Technology and Research Needs for Reuse of Municipal Wastewater,* EPA-670/2-75-038, Cincinnati, Ohio, p. 126.
12. Hirshleifer et al., *Water Supply,* pp. 123–24.
13. Environmental Protection Agency, *Reuse of Municipal Wastewater,* p. 136.
14. World Health Organization, *Disposal of Community Wastewater,* Technical Report Series No. 541, Geneva, Switzerland, 1974, p. 47.
15. Freeman et al., *Economics of Environmental Policy,* pp. 118–19.
16. Allen Kneese and Charles Schultze, *Pollution, Prices and Public Policy* (Washington, D.C.: Brookings Institution, 1975), p. 78.
17. Okun, "Planning for Water Reuse," p. 621.
18. Ibid.

CHAPTER 3

Evaluating Reuse: Daniel M. Dworkin
A Simulation Model
Applied to
Colorado Springs, Colorado

Colorado Springs, Colorado, has been reusing water as a supplement to the
water supply system for the past twenty years. The National Water Commission cited the city for reusing water as a means for delaying investment
in new source development [11]. While the prospect of providing reuse
rather than diverting water from across the continental divide seemed
attractive, there has been no attempt to evaluate the relative efficiency of
reuse when compared to new source development. A simulation model
was developed and used to evaluate reuse under a broad range of alternative places.

COLORADO SPRINGS

Colorado Springs is located on the eastern slopes of the southern Rocky
Mountains. It is the administrative seat and major city of El Paso County,
an area of sunshine and low precipitation. Lush green lawns and tree-
shaded streets are a feature of the older residential areas, which are in
striking contrast to the surrounding countryside, where summer grass
cover is mostly brown and sparse. The area was planned as a model city
in 1871 by W. J. Palmer, president of the Denver and Grande Railroad.
Much of the charm of the city can be credited to his planning, including
the present park system, to which he gave the initial impetus. It now
comprises more than, 3,000 acres [1].
    The area has been growing rapidly. The population of Colorado
Springs was nearly 37,000 in 1940. Seven years later it had risen to just
over 40,000, an annual growth rate of approximately 1 percent. By 1970,
the population had risen to over 135,000. This rate (6.5 percent) is more
than double that of the previous eleven years. Population estimates for
1977 (191,600) indicate a slower rate of growth, 4 percent annually for the
past seven years [7]. El Paso County, the Standard Metropolitan Statistics
Area (SMSA) encouraging Colorado Springs with a 1960 population of
143,742, had grown to 235,972 by the 1970 census, a 64-percent growth
rate, the sixth highest for SMSAs in the United States. Present estimates

indicate a population of 309,000. The city of Colorado Springs accounts for most of the rapid county growth. If the noncity residents of the county were considered, the growth was much slower: 73,548 in 1960; 100,912 in 1970; and 118,000 in 1977. The differential growth in the city and the county is causing the gradual domination of the area by the city of Colorado Springs (table 3-1).

Table 3-1. Change in Population, Colorado Springs and El Paso County, Colorado

	Colorado Springs	El Paso County	County Residents Only
1960	70,194	143,742	73,548
1970	135,060	235,972	100,912
1977 (est)	191,600	309,000	118,000
Increase (1960–70)	64,866	92,230	27,364
Increase (1970–77)	56,540	74,028	18,488

SOURCE: U.S. Census of Population, 1960, 1970, Chamber of Commerce, Colorado Springs, Colorado, 1977.

Employment in the area largely depends upon government agencies in both military and nonmilitary sectors, which account for nearly 25 percent of all nonagricultural jobs. The major installations are the North American Air Defense Command (NORAD), Peterson Field, the United States Army Air Defense Command (ARADCOM), Fort Carson, and the United States Air Force Academy.

The other two large categories, service industries and trade, are in part the result of the extensive tourist industry and the presence of a large number of military personnel. Eight hotels and 159 motels with 4,400 rooms serve the region, which also has 43 mobile home parks. These accommodate a booming tourist sector, drawn by attractions such as Pikes Peak and the Air Force Academy, as well as an average weekly population of 1680 convention-goers [6].

SUPPLY AND WASTE TREATMENT

The water supply system of Colorado Springs is a complex network of groundwater, surface water from local streams, a federal water project, interbasin transfers, and renovated water from returned sewage (figure 3-1). A combination of twenty potable and nonpotable reservoirs provides for the storage and release of flows. Prior appropriation doctrine governs

Figure 3-1. Colorado Springs Water Supply System

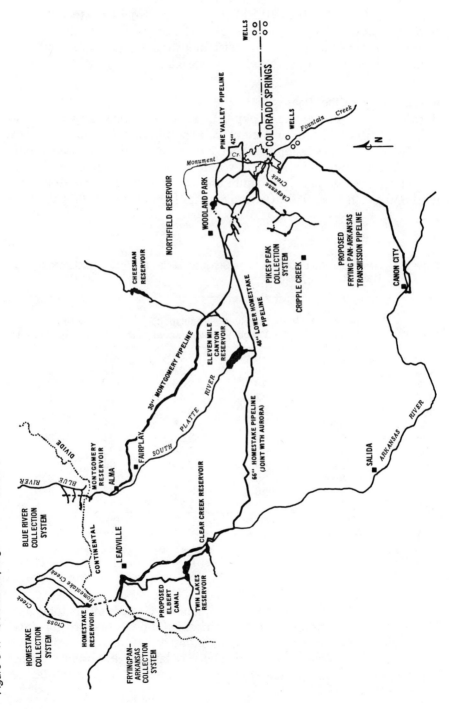

SOURCE: City of Colorado Springs, Department of Public Utilities, *Your Water,* p. 2.

the amount and timing of diversions, storage, and reuse. The use of potable water, which was less than 10,000 ac-ft annually from 1940 to 1947, rose to over 40,000 ac-ft in 1970. Five categories of use are identified by the water system: residential, commercial, industrial, military, and municipal (municipal use includes system losses as well as actual use).

Residential and Other Uses

Residential use is a product of population and per capita use. Changes in either will affect the total amount of water required. Population served by the Colorado Springs system has been increasing as a result of both annexation of other systems and growth within the present area served. In this period the average daily per capita use was 100 gal. Each dwelling unit used 350 gal./d at a 1960–70 average cost of 46.5 cents/1,000 gal. (table 3-2).

Table 3-2.   Residential Water Use, Average Summer Rainfall and Price of Colorado Springs Water Supply System

Year	Rainfall Apr. to Oct. (in.)	Price Received (¢/1,000 gal.)	Population (aver./acct.)	Daily Use gal./capita	Daily Use gal./acct.
1950	9.42	16	3.49	101	353
1960	5.36	40	3.32	112	373
1961	17.11	43	3.36	81	273
1962	8.08	42	3.40	107	364
1963	11.13	42	3.44	103	353
1964	5.60	41	3.48	121	421
1965	17.19	44	3.52	88	309
1966	11.78	42	3.56	106	375
1967	13.66	49	3.60	88	316
1968	8.85	55	3.65	100	365
1969	14.59	56	3.70	88	326
1970	11.21	58	3.75	98	367
Average	11.17	46.5*	3.52	99.4	349.6

SOURCE: Unpublished records, Colorado Springs, Colorado, Department of Public Utilities.
*Excluding 1950.

The other sectors represent the remaining 60 percent of total use. These all exhibit different trends. Commercial use has been rising since 1964. During the same period, use by industry has been declining, not only as a percentage of increased total use, but also in absolute terms. Military water use has accounted for approximately 18 percent of total use since 1960 (table 3-3).

Table 3-3.   Water Use by Category as a Percentage of Total Use, Colorado Springs Water Supply System

Year	Residential	Commercial	Industrial	Military	Municipal	Total (ac-ft)
1950	32.0	16.6	5.3	7.9	38.2	15529
1960	36.6	12.7	7.1	17.1	27.1	25754
1961	33.8	12.7	7.7	19.0	26.8	20927
1962	36.4	11.6	7.1	19.3	25.6	26937
1963	36.5	11.2	6.8	7.9	27.6	27156
1964	40.8	10.8	7.3	18.1	23.0	30623
1965	33.8	11.6	6.7	17.2	30.7	28528
1966	37.3	14.7	4.0	16.3	27.7	33947
1967	36.3	16.8	4.4	18.0	24.5	37492
1968	39.2	14.2	3.6	17.9	· 25.1	39240
1969	39.2	16.5	3.9	18.6	21.8	36550
1970	40.3	17.1	3.5	16.0	23.1	44206

SOURCE: Unpublished records, Colorado Springs, Colorado, Department of Public Utilities.

Water Supply; Investment in the Water System

As of 1970 the water supply system has an estimated capacity of 52,600 ac-ft/yr. With the present capability of providing renovated effluent, the total system capacity is estimated to be 56,200 ac-ft (table 3-4).

Table 3-4.   Present Estimated Capability of Colorado Springs Water Supply Sources

	Yield (ac-ft/yr)
Pikes Peak	13,000
Northfield	700
Cheyenne Creek	1,600
Wells (groundwater)	3,000
Blue River	10,000
Homestake (phase 1)	13,000
Monument Creek	1,300
Fryingpan-Arkansas (1st allotment)	10,000
Subtotal	52,600
Reuse	3,600
Total	56,200

SOURCE: Unpublished records, Chief of Operations, Colorado Springs, Colorado, Department of Public Utilities.

From 1930 to 1950, the total expenditure on water supply projects was less than $1 million. From 1951 to 1960, over $14 million were expended, and by the end of 1970 the total investment in water supply projects was nearly $63 million. If transmission and treatment are included, the total rises to $96 million (table 3-5).

Table 3-5. Value of Colorado Springs Water Supply System Facilities, December 31, 1970 (at cost, millions of dollars)

Source of supply	62.83
Pumping	1.75
Treatment	6.64
Transmission and distribution	23.72
General plant	1.14
Total	96.08

SOURCE: Unpublished records, Colorado Springs, Colorado, Department of Public Utilities.

The expenditures for the entire water supply and treatment plants for the 1961–70 period was over $60 million, an investment of over $1,000 for each additional resident served. Comparable figures for the United States during the period from 1955 to 1965 averaged $275 [9].

The investment has been used primarily to increase yield. The rated capacity of the system in 1961 was 24,000 ac-ft/yr, and in 1970 it had increased to 44,000 ac-ft (figure 3-2). On the average each acre-foot of added capacity cost $3,510, or, equivalently, $9.38/1,000 gal. of flow. The investment can be related to use rather than to capacity. The 1961 use adjusted for average rainfall condition was 21,200 ac-ft and rose to 38,000 ac-ft in 1970, a cost of $3,640, or $11.17/1,000 gal. for the additional water delivered.

The investment in capacity has a direct and substantial effect on the cost of water, interest and depreciation of which represented over half the expense incurred by the water division for 1970, resulting in a sharp rise in the cost and price of water delivered to the consumer.

Sewage Treatment and Reuse; Limitations

The sewer division charges users a fee based on water used by the customer in January. The treatment plant was upgraded in 1959 from primary to secondary treatment by the use of trickling filtration and clarification. Two types of AWT exist: one provides only sand filtration of the secondary effluent; and the other, a recently added pilot plant, uses a reactor clarifier and carbon filtration to produce a higher quality effluent.

Reuse renovation and reuse of effluent are controlled by the sewage division, which has been producing and distributing effluent since 1957. Originally, the motivation for reuse was a proposed sale to the highway department for irrigating the median strip. This never materialized, but preparations had been made and a nonpotable line, installed. Two users—

Figure 3-2. Estimated Yield and Annual Use: Colorado Springs

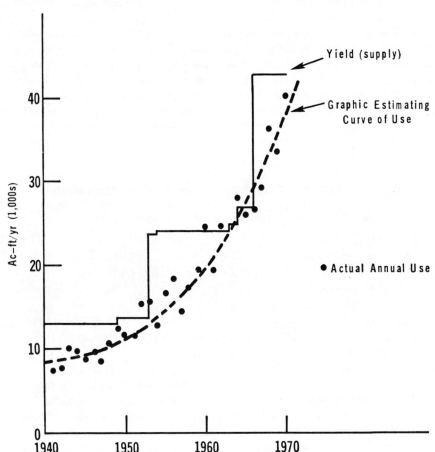

Kissing Camel Golf Course and Colorado College—started using the recycled water soon after it was available. Later, two years (1960 and 1962) of low rainfall and a restriction against irrigation encouraged others to use the lower cost, available effluent.

Present consumers of reused water, with the exception of a municipal electrical generating plant, are furnished secondary effluent, which has been further treated by filtration. This has produced a product that has been satisfactory for use in irrigation and that is sold at one-third the cost of potable water. Other users are being sought for the higher quality product produced as cooling water for the city-owned electrical generating plant, especially industry not normally able to locate in water-short areas. Both irrigation and industrial water will be delivered by separate, nonpotable supply lines. The present annual reuse capacity of both systems is 3,600 ac-ft.

As in most states with a doctrine of prior appropriation, the return flows originating in the Colorado Springs drainage basin have been appropriated and are not available for reuse. The only water that is available is imported flow, which is diverted from other basins. Some of the imported flows, as in the case of water from the Fryingpan-Arkansas project, are sometimes restricted. An accounting procedure is used to determine the amounts of water than can be reused. The records are monitored by the local irrigation district.

PLANNING FOR WATER SUPPLY: THE PLAN AND AN ALTERNATIVE

The city has extensive plans for the future water supply capacity. These include a second allotment of water from the Fryingpan-Arkansas project, a second phase of Homestake, and the Eagle-Arkansas diversion. Yield will be increased to nearly 100,000 ac-ft/yr (table 3-6 and figure 3-3), including reuse with an annual capacity of over 12,000 ac-ft.

A more flexible alternative is to consider reuse as a potential source of supply, placing control in the water department and providing a method of interchange so that either renovated effluent or water from the potable system could be supplied for nonpotable uses. If this were done, reuse could delay or obviate the need for conventional additions to supply by providing: (1) a substitute for high levels of assurance or reliability of supply; (2) a method of mobilizing oversupply resulting from the understatement of system yield; and (3) a method of shortning the planning horizon to allow the pragmatic evaluation of change in demand to replace present long-term projections.

Substitution for High Assurance Levels
A given stream and reservoir will produce a higher yield as the required level of assurance—the percentage of time when the stated yield may be expected—is relaxed. The resulting increase in yield is a function of the distribution of flows and the level of development of the stream (table 3-7).

To obtain the maximum level of assurance considered necessary for municipal supply, storage must be provided for at least the most severe drought on record; often extra storage is provided against the possibility of experiencing more severe droughts [2].

As an alternative, a standby reuse system could provide this assurance. Water could be supplied from storage until the levels were drawn down, so that the remaining capacity and minimum inflows could, with the renovation system, supply the expected demand. When storage levels rose, the renovation of water would be discontinued.

Table 3-6. Planned Additions to the Colorado Springs Water Supply System

Year	Plan	Yield (ac-ft)
1977	Eagle-Arkansas	5,000
1979	Homestake (2nd phase)	17,000
1985	Fryingpan-Arkansas (2nd allotment)	10,000
Subtotal		32,000
1979	Reuse	4,000
1983	Reuse	5,500
Subtotal		9,500
Total		41,500
Present capacity		56,200
Present and future total		97,700

SOURCE: Unpublished records, Colorado Springs, Colorado, Department of Public Utilities.

Figure 3-3. Colorado Springs Water Use and Supply Projection

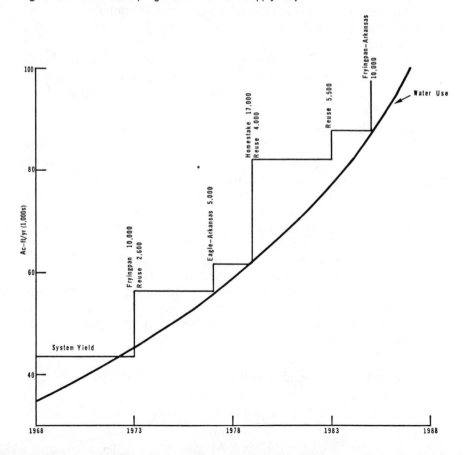

Table 3-7. Storage and Flow Relationships in the Colorado River Basin

% Mean Annual Flow	Resulting Yield	% Required Storage at Levels of Assurance		
		98	95	90
90	12.2	25.5	19.3	14.0
95	12.8	55.0	40.4	18.3
100	13.5			31.2

Adapted after Lof and Hardison, "Storage Requirements"; Wollman and Bonen, "Outlook for Water."
NOTE: Flow given in bg/d; storage given in millions of acre-feet. There is no deduction for reservoir losses.

Evaluation of Yield Estimates

In addition to allocating the provision of assurance to the reuse process, the water manager can employ the capacity of the reuse facility to provide a method of pragmatically appraising yield. There has been a long-standing academic debate over the engineering estimates of yield. Social scientists insist that such yields are understated [13], while engineers continue to provide more stringent methods of evaluation and to point out evidence of systems that have failed at the rated capacity [4, 8].

Reuse could provide a margin of reserve capacity that would allow additions to the system to be delayed until a pragmatic evaluation of yield replaces the engineering estimates. This could result in a substantial delay or could alleviate the need for conventional additions to supply.

Shortening the Planning Horizon

An additional benefit of the delay in increasing system capacity would be the shortened planning horizon in evaluating system demand. This would be possible because the decision to increase the capacity of reuse systems can be implemented much faster than those decisions that require diverting additional streams, providing new storage, or developing new groundwater sources. Often chemical treatment can be provided rapidly where interim reuse capacity is required [12]. Thus, estimates of future needs could be based on more current data and, because the economies of scale are not as great in reuse systems as in reservoirs and diversion tunnels, the capacity could be increased as required [3]. This consideration is increasingly important because of the present low birth rate; assessments of demand based on the extension of historic growth patterns may overestimate future demands for water.

The Economics of an Integrated System

In an integrated system, reuse would serve as a standby source while storage would provide water, when available, for the system. While providing a standby source may appear wasteful, such a plan would maximize the use of storage, with its low operating costs, and minimize the production of renovated effluent, with its high operating costs. As demand continued to rise, more conventional capacity would be indicated, either when the opportunities for the use of effluent were exhausted or when the costs of increasing the conventional capacity would be less than continuing to increase the use of effluent. As higher quality effluent was required to meet the demands for environmental quality, there would be increased incentive to reuse water. An integrated system could provide a more rational approach than one in which water from storage and water from reuse were produced and used independently.

TESTING THE ASSUMPTIONS: A SIMULATION MODEL

To test these hypotheses, a generalized computer model was designed to simulate the water supply and waste treatment of a municipal system (figure 3-4; see also appendix D). By using the model the water supply system of Colorado Springs was simulated. Stream flows and rainfall were generated by using the stream flow simulation program HEC-4 provided by the Hydrologic Engineering Center of the U.S. Army Corps of Engineers. Water demand models were based on multiple regressions of twelve years of monthly demand for the five sectors of use (residential, commercial, industrial, military, and municipal). The municipal use category included metered municipal use as well as all unaccounted-for variation between the metered amount released from the reservoirs and the amount billed to users. The regression models, the correlation coefficients, and the levels of significance are outlined in table 3-8.

In a preliminary set of regressions, rainfall for the month was used as one of the independent variables. The significance as measured by the test was low: 0.20. To include the effect of soil moisture carry-over, an index of rainfall was used. This is computed monthly as the accumulated departure from mean rainfall. The methodology is as follows:

$$RI_i = \sum_{j=1}^{i} (R_j - \bar{R}_j) \quad \text{for } i = 1, 2, \ldots, 12$$

where i is the current month, RI_i is the value of the rain index in the ith month, j is a summation subscript, R_j is the rainfall in the jth month, and $\bar{R}_j$ is the average rainfall for the jth month.

In the regression a dummy variable, season, is used. During the period from May to September the variable equals 1 when it would be included

Figure 3-4. Flow Diagram of the Model

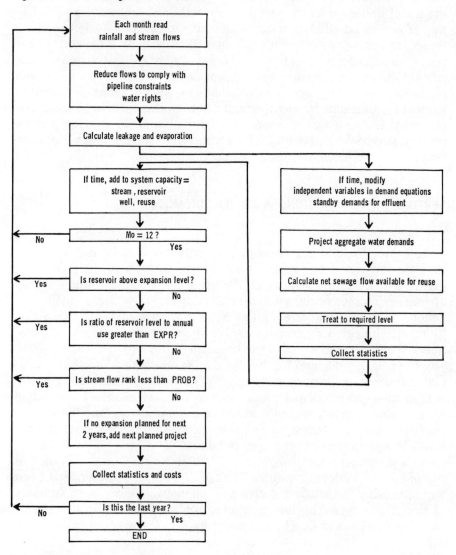

in the computations. All other times, season is set at 0 and is not part of the regression.

Equations of water demand are based on these models. The unexplained variation is included by adding the mean of the residuals and the product of the standard deviations multiplied by a random normal deviate.

The Simulations

Both the present plans for expansion of the water supply and reuse system and an alternative were simulated. The alternative provided no reuse

Table 3-8. Summary, Regressions of Daily Water Use (mg)

Sector	% Total Use (1970)	R²	Constant	Time	Season	Price	Population+	Index of Rainfall
Residential	40	0.76	-3.0500	0.0050	7.2800	-0.007	0.000079	-0.0600
Significance*			0.0500	.0500	0.0500	.100	.050000	0.0005
Commercial	17	0.29	-4.8600	.0410	1.0480	-.058	.000145	
Significance			0.0050	.0025	0.0025	.010	.000500	
Industrial	4	0.50	1.0900	.0070	0.5200	-.005	.000200	
Significance			0.0005	.0005	0.0005	.050		
Military	16	0.67	0.2840	.0200	2.2600	0.050	0.000500	
Significance			0.2000	.0005	0.0005			
Municipal	23	0.22	0.9150	.2400				
Significance			0.1000	0.0005				

NOTE: Here N = 144, time is accumulated in months, and seasons = from May to September and 0 at all other times.

*Significance as measured by t est.

+Industrial use population = employment.

capacity at the beginning of the simulation and made the addition of the Eagle-Arkansas and Homestake projects contingent on a decision process based on monitoring reservoir level, stream flow, and water use. In both the plan and the alternative, renovated water was restricted to nonpotable uses.

Decision for Reuse: The Alternative

Reuse capacity, if insufficient, is increased, and renovated effluent is produced when reservoir levels decline below a selected level; when the reservoir level rises above a higher level, reuse is discontinued. In the period before reuse capacity is added and when reuse is subsequently discontinued, potable water is furnished to all nonpotable users. When reservoir levels are low, the total monthly demand for each sector is partially met by renovated nonpotable effluent. Costs of increased capacity of the reuse system are invested in the first year of any decade and are based on the peak daily flow during the decade. Costs of construction and costs of operation are calculated separately (table 3-9).

Table 3-9.   Costs of AWT

	Costs	
	Construction (millions of dollars)	Treatment (thousands of dollars)
Coagulation and sedimentation	$.075Q^{.90040}$	$44/Q^{.01746}$
Granulated carbon adsorption	$.560Q^{.62487}$	$136/Q^{.19438}$

NOTE: $Q = mg/d$.

Decision Process for the Eagle-Arkansas and Homestake Projects

At the end of each year in the simulation a decision is made whether to add to the potable supply system. The three checks are: (1) Is the reservoir level higher than that required for expansion? (2) Is the amount of water in storage during the year greater than a set percentage of the annual use for the year? and (3) Is the total stream flow for the year less than a percentage of the combined record of historical and synthetic flows to that date? If any of the comparisons is positive (i.e., if reservoir levels are higher than the set expansion level, if the ratio of water level to total use indicates a higher percentage of annual use in storage, or if the rank of flows is less than might be expected a set percentage of the time), there will be no expansion. If all are negative, then a further check is made for the status of the second Fryingpan-Arkansas allotment. If it is scheduled for addition to the system within the next two years, neither of the other two plans will be used. If it is not, then the Eagle-Arkansas or, if it has already been added, the Homestake project will be scheduled for addition after two years. The two-year delay had been selected for Colorado Springs because much of the engineering and most of the diversion tunnels had been completed as part of other projects. To test the results, an additional series of simulations was run using a four-year delay.

Three population series were used (figure 3-5). The high population projection provided the population growth predicted by the consultants to the water division. Using the water demand models developed for the simulation and the high population projection, the resulting water demands were higher than the consultants' projections of a lowered per capita use not apparent in the historical data (figure 3-6). The medium population projection provides the estimated water use. A third projection assumes a lower growth for the system. The Pikes Peak Area Council of Governments has prepared high, medium, and low projections for El Paso County to the year 2000. These were compared with the populations simulated in the model. A comparison between the high and medium populations indicates the water system is projected to serve approximately 70 percent of the population of the county projected by the Pikes Peak Area Council of Governments. The low-growth series assumes that the water system will be serving nearly the entire projected population of the county by 2000 (table 3-10).

Both the plan and the alternative were simulated for a fifty-year period. Three population projections and three sets of stream flows were used. The first set of simulations is designed to simulate the daily potable water use predicted by the consultants: 52 mg/d in 1980 and 64 mg/d in 1990.

In the first simulation these rates are approximated in 1982, when the average withdrawal including nonpotable uses was 55.5 mg/d, and in 1991, when the total use was 69.3 mg/d.[1] (See also table 3-11).

Additions to Capacity: The Plan

To provide water to meet these demands, the plan used the scheduled series of additions; reuse capacity in 1974, 1979, and 1983; the Eagle-Arkansas River diversion in 1977; the Upper Homestake in 1979; and, finally, the second allotment from the Fryingpan-Arkansas project in 1985.

Using the decision process of mounting water use, reservoir levels, and stream flows, the alternative provided different timing of investments. The increments were the same, with the only difference being a .1 mg/d

---

[1] Although the alternative does not supply reused water on a continuing basis, these continual demands are incorporated into the industrial demand for water.

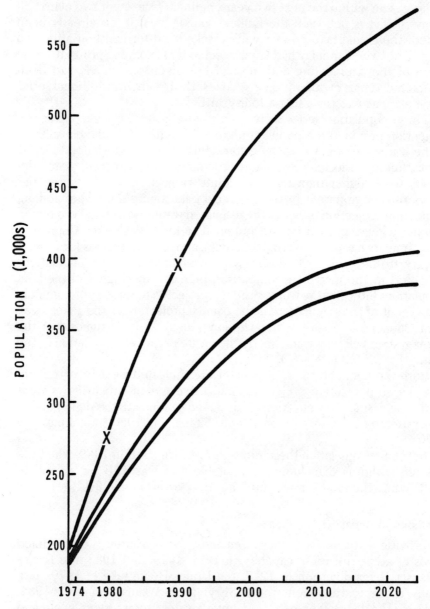

Figure 3-5. Population Growth Resulting from High, Medium, and Low Growth Rates

NOTE: X = consultants estimate of population.

higher in treatment capacity for the plan. The Fryingpan-Arkansas allotment, provided as the last addition in the plan in 1985, was the first

Figure 3-6. Population Growth and Daily Water Use

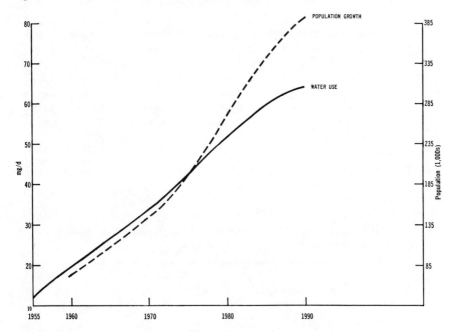

Adapted after Black and Veatch, *Report on Cheyenne Canyon Booster District and Templeton Service Area for Colorado Springs, Colorado* (Kansas City: Black and Veatch, 1972). Projections by Black and Veatch; graphic estimating curve by author.

Table 3-10. Comparison of Population: Pikes Peak Area Council of Governments for El Paso and Population Projected in Simulation Model (population in 1,000s at year's end)

Year	High Council	Model	%	Medium Council	Model	%	Low Council	Model	%
1975	312	211	68	310	206	66	293	206	70
1980	381	277	73	368	250	68	314	246	78
1985	467	333	71	417	286	69	328	277	84
1990	562	387	71	459	319	69	343	307	90
1995	673	450	67	504	343	68	354	334	94
2000	797	489	61	551	366	66	365	355	97

element at the same date for the alternative. The capacity to reuse effluent was first provided in 1996.[2] The Eagle-Arkansas diversion was delayed until 1998, and Homestake was finally brought into the system in 2000 (figure 3-7).

---

[2]The model combines all investment in water reuse into the first year of any ten-year period. Thus, while reuse capacity was provided and used in 1966, the investment is calculated from 1994. This is also true in the plan in which investments in 1974, 1978, and 1982 are all assumed for financial evaluations. to date from 1974.

Table 3-11. Simulated Water Use in Colorado Springs: Percentage of Use and Total Acre-feet (base year—1970 actual date)

	Residential (%)	Commercial (%)	Industrial (%)	Military (%)	Municipal (%)	Total (ac-ft)
1970	40.3	17.1	3.5	16.0	23.1	44206
1974	41.6	16.4	4.4	18.1	19.4	45554
1980	40.8	23.0	3.1	16.3	16.5	61129
1990	37.3	26.6	3.0	17.0	16.1	74481
2000	39.6	19.7	2.8	16.4	22.1	89495
2010	42.9	14.6	3.3	19.1	20.0	92477
2020	40.6	8.2	4.0	21.2	26.0	98790
2023	40.3	6.0	3.9	22.0	27.8	00673

SOURCE: Unpublished records, Colorado Springs, Colorado, Department of Public Utilities. Other data was projected using the simulation of the plan for Colorado Springs.

Figure 3-7. Investment Series in Water System for Colorado Springs, Medium Population Stream Flow Series 1

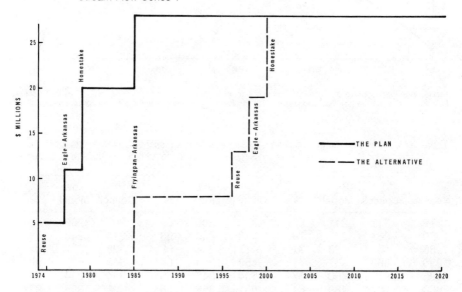

Reservoir Levels: The Plan and the Alternative

The operation of a water system can be evaluated by the reservoir levels, spillage, and the amount of water bypassed at the intakes. Constant high reservoir levels under conditions of varying stream flows are an indication of a system that is underutilized. The reservoir levels resulting from the implementation of the plan using the medium projection of population and the stream flow sequence exhibited little variation except during the final years of the simulation (figure 3-8). The alternative simulation uses storage more efficiently responding to low-flow years by a decline in the amount

Figure 3-8. Annual Minimum Reservoir Levels: The Plan (% capacity); Showing Eagle-Arkansas and Homestake Additions, Medium Population Stream Flow Series 1

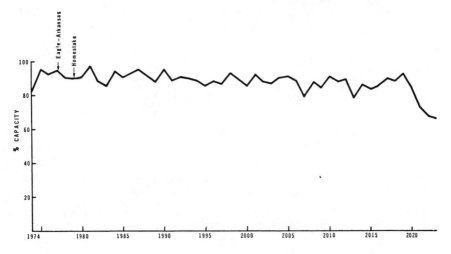

of water stored (figure 3-9). The spillage associated with both plans is markedly different. The plan spills water during 43 of the 50 years, projected against 12 in the alternative plan (figure 3-10).

The Costs: The Plan and the Alternative

As previously noted, the investments in water supply and water reuse facilities were substantially equal: only the timing was different. This is not true of the costs of operating and maintaining the reuse system. The plan reused 182 bg of water over the fifty years. Most of this, 165 bg, was treated to a tertiary level, using coagulation, sedimentation, and granulated carbon adsorption of the secondary treated effluent. The other 17 bg were treated only by sand filtration. The total costs of AWT were $23 million, or approximately 14 cents/1,000 gal. The alternative reused water only twice and accumulated less than $2 million in costs for the AWT process.

One could compare the plan and the alternative based on the difference on $21 million in cost of treatment, completely disregarding the timing of the expenditures. A more meaningful measure—weighing not only the expenditure, but also the timing—is obtained by discounting the expenditure to the present.

Using this method, the plan expenditures have a present value of $21.5 million; the alternative, $7.6 million. The equal costs for the water diversions and sewage treatment capacity have a discounted value of $9.5 million more in the plan than in the alternative, while the difference in

Figure 3-9. Annual Minimum Reservoir Levels: The Alternative (% capacity); Showing Eagle-Arkansas and Homestake Additions and Periods of Reuse, Medium Population Stream Flow Series 1

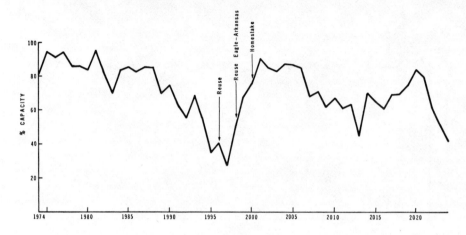

Figure 3-10. Average Monthly Spillage by Year: The Plan and the Alternative, Medium Population Stream Flow Series 1

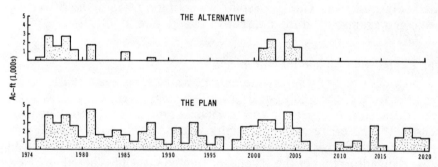

operations and maintenance (O&M) costs of reuse totaling $21 million more in the plan has been reduced to a difference in present value of $4.4 million (table 3-12).

It should be noted that the alternative plan has made an inefficient use of reuse capacity. For 1997, a large-sized plant has been provided that furnishes effluent for only two years. Even though this was an inefficient use of investment, it supports the point made previously: Reuse systems should be used for standby capacity. After this plan had been simulated once, parameters could have been adjusted ex post facto to provide either earlier implementation of the water supply projects or lower acceptable levels of the reservoir to avoid reuse. Two points are relevant: (1) Any

Table 3-12.   Colorado Springs Water Supply System, 1974–2023, Projected Operation: The Alternative Plan, Medium Population Stream Flow Series 1

	Plan	Alternative
Total water use 2023 (ac-ft)	106,000	106,000
Capacity of waste treatment plant		
Decade 1	12	0.0
2	12	0.0
3	12	11.9
4	12	11.9
5	12	11.9
Total reuse water processed (mg/d)		
Decade 1	19,000	0
2	40,000	0
3	40,000	1,400
4	40,000	0
5	40,000	0
Additions to capacity (date)		
Fryingpan-Arkansas	1985	1985
Eagle-Arkansas	1977	1998
Homestake	1979	2000
Present value (millions of dollars at 6.88%)		
Reuse capacity	2.2	0.7
Reuse O&M	4.8	0.4
Conventional capacity	14.5	6.5
Total	21.5	7.6

levels selected for the simulation ex post facto to minimize costs might not be optimum for other stream flow sequences; and (2) The provision for reuse, while not the most efficient in this application, has allowed for the delay in the water supply projects. Reuse is a low capital-intensive standby system and is functioning exactly as a reuse system should; that is, to provide the kind of assurance of yield that has been traditionally provided by understating the potential output of streams and reservoirs.

A second set of comparisons used the medium population projection and stream flow series 2. In this series the plan, insulated from changing stream flows because of the preselected sequence of additions, accumulated the same present value of investment as in the stream flow series. The present value of the investment required for the alternative declined by $100,000 (table 3-13). This was the result of delays in both reuse from 1996 to 1998 and water supply additions delayed from 1996 and 1998 to 2006 and 2008. In this second set of simulations, as in the first, the level of total water use reached 106,000 ac/ft. Although this was 6,000 ac/ft above the engineering estimate of yield, it has provided little stress for either the plan or the alternative.

Table 3-13. Colorado Springs Water Supply System, 1974–2023, Projected Operation: The Alternative Plan, Medium Population Stream Flow Series 1 and 2

| | Stream Flow Series | |
	1	2
Total water use 2023 (ac-ft)	106,000	106,000
Capacity of waste treatment plant (mg/d)		
Decade 1	0.0	0.0
2	0.0	0.0
3	11.9	12.5
4	11.9	14.2
5	11.9	14.2
Total reuse water processed (mg/decade)		
Decade 1	0	0
2	0	0
3	1400	2623
4	0	4026
5	0	0
Additions to capacity (date)		
Fryingpan-Arkansas	1985	1985
Eagle-Arkansas	1998	2006
Homestake	2000	2008
Present value (millions of dollars at 6.88%)		
Reuse capacity	0.70	1.02
Reuse O&M	0.40	1.11
Conventional capacity (water supply)	6.50	5.40
Total	7.60	7.53

The high population projection increasing to 511,000 by 2023 provides a test of the plan and the alternative at higher levels of water use. This projection closely resembles the population prediction of the consulting engineers for 1980 and 1990 of 278,000 and 394,000, respectively.

The water use sectors that will increase in this higher population series are residential, commercial, and municipal—all of which use population as one of the independant variables in the water use models. Industrial use that uses employment as an independant variable increased at a slower rate. Military use and nonpotable use were not affected.

The simulation of the plan ended after the thirty-sixth year. The reservoir went dry in January 2010. Water use had reached 135,000 ac-ft. Spillage was extensive in the early years of the simulation. When demands reached 133,000 ac-ft in 2002, the reservoir levels failed to recover sufficiently during high-flow years to meet the stress of low-flow periods.

The alternative continued to furnish water for the full fifty years. This required more investment in reuse plants and more reuse water produced during low-flow years. The Eagle-Arkansas project was provided in 1993 and the Homestake, in 1998. This was earlier than the previous simulation but still represented a delay from the scheduled additions of the plan (figure 3-11).

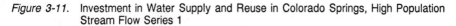

Figure 3-11. Investment in Water Supply and Reuse in Colorado Springs, High Population Stream Flow Series 1

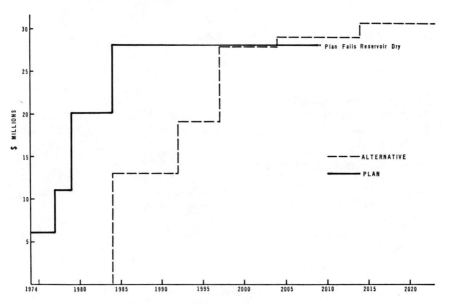

The present value of the plan is $21.1 million. The difference between this and the previous simulations is only in the exclusion of the last fourteen years of O&M costs. The present value of the alternative is $10.8 million for the thirty-six years. It increases to $11.9 million for the full fifty years (table 3-14).

Two other stream sequences, series 2 and 3, were used with the high population projection. In each of these the plan failed: in the former, during March 2006; and in the later, during March 2007. The alternative simulation in both sequences continued to furnish water for the full fifty years.

The present values of the investment required for the alternative runs were $11.2 for series 2 and $12.0 million for series 3 stream sequences. The present value of the required investment for the plan was approximately $21.0 million.

A final set of simulations was run using a low projection of population

Table 3-14.   Colorado Springs Water Supply System, 1974–2009, Projected Operation: The Alternative Plan, High Population Skip 48, Late Low Flow

	Plan	Alternative
Total water use 2009 (ac-ft)	135,000	135,000
Capacity of waste treatment plant (mg/d)		
Decade 1	12	0.0
2	12	26.4
3	12	27.4
4	12	32.0
Total reuse water processed (mg/decade)		
Decade 1	19,000	0
2	40,000	7,000
3	40,000	10,644
4	40,000	40,107
Additions to capacity (date)		
Fryingpan-Arkansas	1985	1984
Eagle-Arkansas	1977	1993
Homestake	1979	1998
Present value (millions of dollars at 6.88%)		
Reuse capacity	2.20	1.91
Reuse O&M	4.44	1.69
Conventional capacity	14.50	7.17
Total	21.14	10.77

that reaches 383,000 persons by 2023. In this, the alternative never required the second phase of Homestake. The present value of the investment was less than $6 million. The plan, again insensitive to external conditions, had a present value of $21 million.

For every assumed population and stream flow condition simulated, the alternative was a less costly method of supply than the plan. The costs of the alternative varied, depending on levels of supply and demand, while the costs of the plan were independent of these conditions.

Of the two methods of providing water for Colorado Springs, the plan is less desirable under conditions of low population growth. Under the assumption of high population growth, the plan failed in the fourth decade of operation. The alternative was able to supply demands for the full fifty years at a cost of $12 million or less (table 3-15).

The alternative is economically a more efficient method of providing a water supply for Colorado Springs. The additional expense of the plan arises from the cost of treating effluent for reuse when water from the potable supply system was available in quantities sufficient to meet the demands of all users and from the investment in conventional and reuse facilities that could have been delayed. The alternative plan provides

Table 3-15. Summary of the 6 Simulation Series: The Plan and the Alternative

Stream Flow Series	Population Projection	Years of Simulation	Present Value*	
			Plan	Alternative
1	high	35	21.1	10.8
2	high	32	20.9	10.0
3	high	33	21.0	12.0
1	medium	50	21.5	7.6
2	medium	50	21.5	7.5
3	medium	50	21.5	8.1
1	low	50	21.5	6.0
2	low	50	21.5	5.9
3	low	50	21.5	6.9

*In millions of dollars at 6.875%.

processing for water only when the supply in storage is low. Additions to conventional capacity are delayed until parameters measuring the supply and use of water indicate such a need. To provide further protection against premature investment, a decision for expansion is excluded during the extreme low-flow years.

REFERENCES

[1] Arnberg, Harvard J. *Department of Public Utilities: An Informal History (1872–1969)*. Colorado Springs, Colo.: Department of Public Utilities, 1969.

[2] Beard, Leo R. "Method for Determination of Safe Yield and Compensation Water from Storage Reservoirs." *Technical Paper 3*. U.S. Army Corps of Engineers Hydrologic Engineering Center, Sacramento, Calif., 1965.

[3] Berthovex, P. M. and Polkowski, L. "Cost Effectiveness Analysis of Wastewater Reuses." *J. Sanit. Eng. Div. Amer. Soc. Civil Eng.* 98 (SA6 1972): 869–81.

[4] Chow, V. T., ed. "Water-Resources Planning and Development Part II, System Design by Operations Research." In *Handbook of Applied Hydrology*. New York: McGraw-Hill, 1964.

[5] City of Colorado Springs, Department of Public Utilities. *Your Water Pure ... Precious ... Plentiful*. 1972. P. 2.

[6] Colorado Springs Chamber of Commerce. *Statistical Digest Revised Feb. 8, 1972*. P. k-7.

[7] Colorado Springs Chamber of Commerce, Economic Development Department. *Colorado Springs Community Audit*. Colorado Springs, Colo., April 1977.

[8] Fair, G. W.; Geyer, John C.; and Okum, Daniel A. *Water and Waste Water Engineering Water Supply and Waste Water Removal*. Vol. 1. New York: John Wiley, 1966.

[9] Howe, Charles W. and Linaweaver, L. P., Jr. "The Impact of Price on Residential Water Demand and Its Relation to System Design and Price Structure." *Water Resources Research* 3, no. 1 (1967): 18.

[10] Lof, G. O. and Hardison, C. "Storage Requirements for Water in the United States." *Water Resources Research* 2, no. 3 (1966): 340.

[11] National Water Commission. *Water Policies for the Future*. Washington, D.C.: Government Printing Office, 1973.

[12] Ockershausen, R. W. "In Plant Usage Works and Works Environment." *Science Technology* 8, no. 5 (1974): 420–23.

[13] Russell, Clifford S.; Arey, David G.; and Kates, Robert W. *Drought and Urban Wate Supply.* Baltimore: Johns Hopkins University Press, 1970.

[14] U.S. Bureau of the Census. *1970 Census Reports, P.C. (1) - A.* Washington, D.C.: Government Printing Office, 1970.

[15] Wollman, N. and Bonen, G. W. *The Outlook for Water.* Resources for the Future. Baltimore: Johns Hopkins University Press, 1971.

CHAPTER 4

Psychological Acceptance of Renovated Wastewater: Professional and Public

John H. Sims
Duane D. Baumann

This paper attempts first to provide information regarding the attitudes toward use of renovated wastewater of both the public at large and two specific professional groups involved in water reuse decisions: engineers and health officials. A second and more general goal is to demonstrate in a convincing manner how psychological factors influence a professional's "professional" judgment and behavior.

A review of three studies will serve these ends. The first study[1] makes two points: (1) it demonstrates how personality traits are differentially related to professional membership; and (2) it shows that the psychodynamics that distinguish the members of one profession from those of another can be either functional of dysfunctional. That is, they can either aid or hinder the performance of those tasks that define the professional's job.

The second study[2] shifts the focus from personality writ large to attitudes writ small. That is, it examines how two professional groups, public health officials and water engineers, view the use of renovated wastewater and relates those views to the groups' professional socialization.

Finally, the third study[3] under consideration treats the question of *public* response to the use of renovated wastewater—a question interesting in itself, but one taking on a special meaning in the context of comparison with what health officials and engineers *think* the public response to such use would be.

PSYCHODYNAMICS OF CIVIL SERVICE AND BUSINESS EXECUTIVES

In the 1960s, a group of social scientists from the University of Chicago, under the direction of W. Lloyd Warner, conducted a study of 7,000 federal civil service administrators.[4] As part of this research, several hundred randomly selected career civil service executives of grade levels 14 through 18 in Washington, D.C., were interviewed, usually for about four

---

John H. Sims is professor of psychology in the Graduate Department of Counseling Psychology, George Williams College, Downer's Grove, Illinois.

hours, and were given Murray's Thematic Apperception Test, commonly known as the TAT.[5] The interview was directed towards ascertaining how these men perceived the work role of the federal executive and the social structure of the Federal Civil Service; i.e., of the bureaucracy of which they were a part. The TAT was administered in an effort to identify what, if any, personality characteristics these men might have in common, characteristics that, perhaps, would distinguish them as a professional group. The remarks in the present paper are based upon the analysis of the TAT protocols of forty male career civil service executives, twenty with top-level GS 18 career civil service positions and twenty with GS 14 mid-management positions.

The TAT consists of a series of pictures that are somewhat ambiguous. For example, Card 1 shows a small boy and a violin. Now there is nothing ambiguous about the fact that the figure in the picture is a young boy and that the other clearly identifiable object in the picture is a violin. What the attitude of the boy is towards the violin, however, and what his feelings are about it, etc., are not explicit in the picture. These must be supplied by the viewer. And, indeed, these interpretations are exactly what the subject is asked to provide. For each picture shown, the subject is directed to tell a story that describes the situation portrayed in the picture, including what led up to the situation and how the situation will resolve itself. He is also asked to state what the person portrayed is thinking and feeling.

Now, since the stimuli of the pictures are in these respects ambiguous, the thoughts, feelings, and attitudes with which the storyteller endows the portrayed persons are indicative of the thoughts, feelings, and attitudes of the storyteller himself. What happens is that, in effect, when asked to interpret an ambiguous stimulus, one projects onto the stimulus one's personal view of himself in relation to the world.

Experience has shown that particular cards of the TAT tend to elicit stories that are relevant to particular areas of the personality. For example, Card 1 (the little boy and the violin) usually evokes a story that deals in some way with the issue of impulse versus control, with the relationship between personal needs and the demands of cultural agents, particularly with regard to achievement. Another card, number 6BM, which shows an elderly woman with a young man, not surprisingly tends to elicit stories that deal in some way with the issue of dependence versus autonomy, with the relation between the figure of the son and the maternal authority figure. Thus, through the selection of TAT cards, it is possible to obtain data pertinent to the particular areas of psychodynamics one wishes to investigate.

There are two areas of the personality of federal executives to be discussed here: The first is *achievement,* or the nature and strength of his desire to achieve; his perception of, and attitudes toward, external pressures to achieve; the difficulties he encounters in achieving; and his success and failure in achievement. The second area is the *relationship to maternal authority figures*, the nature and strength of the federal executive's emotional ties to such figures.

How the federal executive confronts the issue of achievement is illustrated by the following two contrasting stories told to Card 1:

> This is a picture of a talented little boy who's always wanted to play the violin. Now his parents have given him one of his own, and he is eager to begin lessons. He will practice diligently, many hours a day, but it will not be all sacrifice on his part, for he looks as if he'll enjoy the work. Finally, after many years, he'll become a fine professional musician, perhaps even a famous one, a Heifetz.

Now, the second story:

> This unhappy little boy is staring resentfully at his violin. His parents have insisted that he learn to play and he doesn't want to. It's practice time again, and while he'd like to avoid it, he knows he has to. And so, he'll pick it up and practice his lessons faithfully.
>
> It looks as if this will go on for years, and eventually he'll even learn to play the damn thing, but only fairly well, and he'll never really like it.

Following the logic that these stories are indicative of their storyteller's approach to achievement, it is clear that the two subjects show great differences in the nature and strength of their motivation to achieve and in their perceptions and attitudes toward external pressure to achieve. The first is not the story of a federal civil service executive at all. It was told by a business executive, in fact, an entrepreneur, the president and managing director of his own manufacturing company. It is typical of such men. The inner motivation to achieve: "[he's] always wanted to play the violin," "he is eager to begin"; the realization that work is necessary in order to achieve: "He will practice diligently, many hours a day"; the pleasure derived from work itself: "it will not be all sacrifice on his part, for he looks as if he'll enjoy the work"—all these are clearly shown in the story.

The second of these stories was told by a high-level career federal executive. It too is a typical story of the sample. Here the inner need to achieve is absent, and in its place is a conflict between an external pressure to achieve: "His parents have insisted that he learn to play"; and his desires, not for achievement in a different area, but for autonomy: "he doesn't want to." Note, however, that he does not resist; evidently the authority from which the press to achieve emanates is too powerful: "he'd like to avoid it, he knows he has to. And so, he'll pick it up and practice his lessons faithfully." This is expressed, in psychological jargon, as *defer-ence-compliance.* That is, he gives in to the demand that he achieve; or, rather, he gives in to the demand that he go through the motions to achieve. The emphasis, for the purposes of this study, is on what this leads to: namely, *work*—that is, he will "practice ... faithfully"; *a certain level of achievement*—that is, "eventually he'll even learn to play the damn thing, but only fairly well"; and *continuing emotional resentment*—that is, "[but] he'll never really like it."

When the stories to Card 1 of all forty federal executives are examined, the overall picture is, to a considerable extent, similar to that just present-ed. The majority see achievement as a conflicted issue. They are either pressed to achieve and do not want to, want to achieve but encounter obstacles, or need to achieve and yet want something else at the same time. In brief, achievement and strife seem inseparable.

When looking at the stories to see how the executives deal with these conflicts—what sources they mobilize to meet the difficulties that accrue to achievement—one finds them to be essentially *passive*. The heroes of these stories *want* to resist but rarely do; they *feel* resentment and hostility but rarely express it; they *fantasize* possible actions but rarely take them.

As a result, the issue of achievement is resolved somewhat equivocally. Most often the story ends not with clear-cut achievement, nor with clear-cut nonachievement, but simply with a giving in, with an acceptance that *one must do what one is told to do.*

Let us now examine a second area of the dynamics of federal execu-tives—that of the nature of their relation to maternal authority figures. The TAT stories relevant to this issue are those told to a picture that depicts an elderly, gray-haired woman standing with her back turned to a young, adult man looking downward with a perplexed expression and holding his hat in his hand.

Generally, the federal executives tell two types of stories to this card. The first and most frequent deals explicitly with the classic theme of conflict between parental control and autonomy, between emotional de-pendence and the "breaking of the silver cord." Typical is:

> This shows a mother and her son. The son has just an-
> nounced to his mother that he intends to leave home and
> marry a young woman whom the mother does not care for.
> The young man is wavering about the situation; he feels
> bad about it. He finally makes up his mind. He will go. But
> he will not feel good about it.

The majority of federal executives who tell stories of this type portray their heroes as accomplishing the developmental task of breaking the emotional bond with the mother. At the same time, however, their stories show that the breaking away was not easy; that it was, in fact, accompanied by feelings of guilt and self-doubt. Rarely is there any evidence that the future holds the promise of reestablishing their relationship with their mother on a new and mature level. Consequently, such stories suggest that, although the son has indeed left home *geographically*, an emotional residue of dependence remains.

The second common type of story told to Card 6BM runs so:

> This is a son who has come to tell his mother that her husband has been killed or has died suddenly of a heart attack. She is in a state of shock, trying to think of what she'll do now that she is without her husband. The young man is concerned about his mother's future, worried about whether he should take her into his own home, as he knows she'll be lonely.

Note, please, not a word about his own grief, for it is at least probable that his mother's husband was *his* father! Stories of this type present the mother figure as stricken by tragedy and in need of aid and comfort by the hero. Yet the hero does nothing to sustain her. Instead, he suggests that he perceives the in-need-of-nurturance mother as a threat to his autonomy. The widowed mother may reactivate a conflict thought to be resolved.

In summary, then, it seems that for the majority of federal executives in this sample, even when there is evidence that the struggle for independence from the mother has been obstensibly resolved by the hero leaving home, there remains the latent presence of an unbroken emotional relationship with the mother, a relationship that threatens to reappear should fate force mother and son together again.

This sample finishes a brief glimpse into but two aspects of the federal executive's psychodynamics. Now it would be worthwhile to discuss several elements of the structure of Federal Civil Service as they are perceived by the executives themselves.

For the career civil servant, by far the most important aspect of the organizational structure of the executive branch of the federal government is the dichotomy of personnel that exists regarding the functions of policy making (in the sense of making decisions and setting goals) and the functions of administration (in the sense of implementing policy).

This division of function between the elected or appointed *political* executive, who makes policy, and the *civil service* executive, who carries out policy, is by no means a rigid one. Civil service careerists are well aware of the fact that their professional knowledge constitutes an important part of the basis on which policy is made. As one civil servant says: "Government would be in a bad way if it weren't for people who stayed with it and really knew the inside and outside. You can't depend on people who are in and out in a few years."

However, the division between the functions of the political executive and the functions of the civil service executive, though elastic, remains. And civil servants emphasize it:

> It is not fair or right for him [i.e., for the civil service executive] to make policy decisions. The president selects men for this and the career man is the mechanic of the decision. That doesn't mean that you are a neuter or don't give advice. We help the boss make decisions. But a career man—it is not his prerogative. He is out-of-bounds if he begins to make policy. The man sitting across the chair has to face the public, the Congress, and the president, and there should be a clear line.

The executive quoted above voices what is the definitive essence of the role of the career civil service executive—he is the "mechanic of the decision." For, within the executive range, increases in level reflect increases in degree, not kind; in quantity of function, not quality. As one goes up the executive hierarchy, there is responsibility for a larger number of employees, for a larger geographic area, for a larger budget; however, in terms of both organizational and psychological dynamics, the task remains essentially the same—the carrying out of decisions made by others, the administration of policy.

There is another element of the structure of the Federal Civil Service of interest here. The original purpose of the Civil Service's legislated tenure of job occupancy (it is not easy to be fired) was to preclude political control, thereby protecting its personnel from arbitrary displacement following change of the party in power. Though perhaps never envisioned by its creators, the careerists see the principle and fact of tenure as serving not only to protect them from political change, but also to shield them from the vicissitudes of a free enterprise economy. According to two federal executives:

> Being in private industry was a very dangerous proposition. I knew many people who had been employed in private industry, and, because of economic circumstances, either of the company itself or of the country, their work had come to a halt and they had been put out of a job. Coming to work for the government, my employment was

> secure. Industry is a money-making thing. The decisions must be made from a purely economic standpoint. A person as a person gets more consideration in the government. If there was not work in my agency I feel sure that the government would find some kind of employment for me.

and

> The biggest difference between government and business is that you have the expectation in government that the organization will always need you and always have enough money to pay your salary. In private industry there's always a risk, in government you have your tenure.

It is clear, therefore, that the executives themselves choose as crucial two elements of the structure of the Federal Civil Service: first, the exclusion of policy making from its functions and the exclusive commitment to being the "mechanic of the decision"; second, its legislated personnel system and subsequent canopy of protection via tenure. From here, one can easily see the possible connections between the federal executive's perception of the Federal Civil Service's structure and those aspects of his personality already discussed.

To make two of those possible connections more explicit, consider the old saying, "Too many chiefs and not enough Indians." Perhaps its originator was concerned with making a bureaucracy work. For, does a bureaucracy need chiefs or Indians? Would an executive with a high level of need achievement, with an insistence upon his autonomy, with a drive to set up and accomplish his own goals, make a good "mechanic of the decision"? Or is the psychological base of the efficient administrator the willingness to follow orders or, at the very least, the begrudging deference-compliance to do what he is told? Is it not possible that the findings discussed above—how the federal executive feels about achievement and how he operates with regard to achievement—are positively functional in terms of serving the purposes of the Federal Civil Service?

Or, to switch the direction of the connection for the moment, is it not evident that the nurturant, protective personnel system of the Civil Service fulfills the dependence needs of the federal executive, who has never psychologically left home? Such functional connections between personality, occupational choice, and ability are crude. One would hope, however, that they are not so crude as to strain credibility. For, if they make sense at all, they lead to a most important further point:

Dwarfed by his political superiors, and outside the tradition of American free enterprise, it has been the lot of the career federal civil servant to be pinned against the wall in the glass case of a stereotype. The popular image of the civil servant is an unflattering one. It is that of a man who "doesn't have the stuff" for making it in the business world, who cannot "cut the mustard," and, hence, he is viewed as one who has retreated from the aggressive world of competition into the security of the "can't-be-fired" system of the Civil Service. Underlying this negative image is the belief that Civil Service organizations are second-rate business organizations, though they may be larger. The crucial structural and functional differences between them, with the exception of the protective personnel system, are ignored. Thus, the Civil Service executive is popularly seen as a second-rate business executive. His personality is defined negatively; he lacks qualities rather than possesses them. He lacks ambition, he is not aggressive, he does not have the ability to make decisions, he does not have the drive for achievement. In other words, he does not possess the personality characteristics of the successful business executive.

It should be clear, however, that executive ability is a function of personality dynamics and skills *within* a social setting. And the very personality characteristics associated with success in the business world may be dysfunctional in the social structure of the Civil Service organization. However, even if one insists that the particular personality characteristics of the federal executive just described *do* serve to aid him in the fulfillment of his duties, one can still ask if there might not be others that interfere with his work or, at least, direct or bias it.

Those psychological characteristics—values, attitudes, psychodynamics—that distinguish a given professional group do not appear by chance; there is a logic in them. Persons and professions seek each other out, first for training, then for practice. That is, professions attempt to select persons whose psychology is in harmony with their defining tasks, their social structure, and their ideology. Conversely, persons attempt to select professions the nature of whose work, social structure, and value system they perceive to be in harmony with their personality. Thus, persons become professional apprentices or trainees because both they and their trainers anticipate man and job will be well suited. And the training period is used by both parties to test that relationship and to increase the degree of "fit." As a result, a professional is far more than an expert by virtue of specialized knowledge; he is a man "cut from a certain cloth," identifiable not only in terms of information and skill, but in his ways of perceiving and thinking, in his feelings, his beliefs, in his loyalties and his prejudices.

PROFESSIONAL ATTITUDES TOWARD RENOVATED WASTEWATER

Little research has been done concerning the psychology of those professionals whose work involves them with environmental problems; rarer still is the study that explores how the psychological characteristics of such groups might influence their *work* with such problems. An example of how crucial this influence might be, the following study treats the question of how consulting engineers and public health officials perceive the persons and processes that would be involved in a community decision concerning a specific environmental issue—the use of renovated wastewater.

Because the study focused on identifying the unpremeditated feelings and attitudes of these two groups of professionals, as well as their thought-through professional opinions, a projective test was used as a device for initiating discussion of the problem. Respondents were shown a picture in which seven adult men in business dress are grouped in various attitudes around a conference table. Their instructions were:

> This is a picture of a meeting in a mayor's office which he has called to discuss the possibility of coping with an impending local water shortage through the use of reclaimed wastewater. I would like you to use your imagination and tell me a story about it. Who do you think are the various persons attending the meeting? What is going on at the moment? What are the men thinking and feeling and saying? How do you think this situation will turn out?

The first question asked of the executives was, Whom did they see as attending the meeting? That is, What interests are represented? What professions have members present? and, indeed, Who has been left out?

Of twelve ranked categories of persons identified as being present at the meeting, the first eight are either executive-administrators or professional experts: the mayor, a member of the city council, a consulting engineer, a public health official, a waterworks superintendent, a member of either the mayor's or the city engineer's staffs, and a legal counsel. Overwhelmingly, the respondents restrict membership in the decision-situation to government officials and their professional consultants. Rarely are nonelected representatives of the public (such as heads of community organizations) or representatives of business and industry (such as the chamber of commerce) mentioned. Apparently, there is the conviction that the question of a solution to an environmental problem should be left to them, as experts, and to public officials. The people themselves—both the general public and organized public groups—are left out. This de facto exclusion fits in with the disdain and fear of public opinion that Sewell[6] found to be characteristic of professionals.

With the question of who is involved in the meeting settled, the next step is to ask, What went on? That is, Who took what position on the question of using renovated wastewater, and why? Who was for and against? and What were their reasons?

Both professional groups are in complete agreement in their perceptions of themselves, each other, politicians, and the public. The consulting engineer is seen as the person most favorably disposed toward the reuse project (54 percent); the public health official, as most opposed (58 percent); and the mayor, as most neutral, undecided, or equivocal (76 percent). These assignments of a preponderant position contrast sharply with the perception of the "the public," which is seen as being more evenly distributed between positive (25 percent), negative (48 percent), and neutral (24 percent) attitudes. Clearly, both the engineers and health officials are far more certain of themselves and their professional brothers than of the unknown layman—at least insofar as the initial response to the idea of using renovated wastewater was concerned.

Even though the majority of both consulting engineers and health officials perceive themselves to be in opposition, these are general attitudes. What are the specifics, the causes (or rationalizations) of their positions? What are the distinguishing concerns of each professional group?

It is interesting that the professional sample most favorable to the idea of using reclaimed wastewater—the consulting engineers—is, at the same time, the group that finds it personally most repugnant: 46 percent admit to feelings of revulsion, and it is their first-ranked concern. The next three most frequently seen problems are: unfavorable public reaction (28 percent), health issues (22 percent), and technical feasibility (24 percent). This last figure is surprising; only one-fourth of the engineers raise questions concerning their own area of expertise—the technical problems involved in direct potable reuse.

The same logic suggests that public health officials also respond somewhat unexpectedly. Health issues involved in the use of renovated wastewater are *not* their first concern. That rank goes to their worried interest in what the public reaction will be (55 percent). And, indeed, their anticipation that the public may "cause trouble" is shown again in their concern about such a program's possible political consequences, an idea expressed with equal frequency (46 percent) to that of their concern for health issues (46 percent).

In sum, the two professional groups contrast greatly in the issues discussed at the meeting in the mayor's office. Engineers have but a single concern of first magnitude—that of expressing (and controlling) their feelings of revulsion to the use of renovated wastewater. While they acknowledge the problems of technical feasibility, public response, and health, they do not emphasize them. Public health officials, on the other hand, are primarily concerned with three questions, of which the health safeguards issue is but one. First and foremost is their anxiety over public response and political repercussions. Again, Sewell's research has anticipated these results:

> The problem of consulting public opinion poses a some-
> what different problem for the public health official than
> it does for the engineer. The effectiveness of the former in
> performing his tasks depends very much upon the extent
> to which his recommendations and regulations are under-
> stood and accepted by the public, and the extent to which
> he is able to overcome opposition (real or imaginary) from
> various groups.[7]

There is a third and final question to be asked concerning the stories: What is the meeting's final accounting? After the positions have been argued, who "votes" which way? The groups' concluding attitudes are much like the initial ones: twice as many consulting engineers (39 percent) as health officials (18 percent) favor the idea, and virtually twice as many health officials (68 percent) as engineers (38 percent) oppose it. What has happened in the course of the meeting is a shift toward a negative view; originally 54 percent of the engineers were favorably disposed toward the water reuse proposal and only 58 percent of the health officials were opposed. This movement is probably best viewed in the light of the professional conservatism—the well-known tendency of the invested professional to avoid the risk of change and to preserve the known and controlled status quo in his area of expertise.

The interprofessional differences that appear here are considerable. More than two-thirds of the health officials (68 percent) are against the use of renovated water, only 18 percent of them are for it, and even then for the "crisis time" only. This contrasts sharply with the final attitudes of the consulting engineers—as many are for it (39 percent) as against it (38 percent).

These differences are surely best understood from the differing perspectives of the two professions' areas of concern and their correlative differences in training. Consulting engineers are not directly involved with questions of public response or politics; their primary interest and responsibility is with the technical: its possibility and practicality. The public health official, on the other hand, is by definition responsible to the public. He must be concerned about its response. And, further, the potential consequences of his approval of a program to use renovated wastewater are far more threatening. The specter of possible widespread disaster must loom large in strengthening the health official's resistance to an unfamiliar system. His risks are far greater than those of the engineer.

It is apparent, then, that in telling stories about a hypothetical situation in which city authorities invite experts to consult with them on the possibility of a community program using renovated wastewater, consulting engineers and public health officials reveal their initial attitudes toward such a proposal; their perceptions of what problems might be encountered; their own personal concerns; and, finally, their considered professional stance. The data suggest strongly that, when asking for an expert's opinion, one gets far more than bargained for—far more, that is, than his purely expert judgment. One gets, in addition, his professional fears and prejudices.

With that general point firmly in mind along with the specific finding of these professionals' (particularly public health officials') anticipation of a negative public response to the idea of renovated water, the present paper can now focus directly on the question of public acceptance.[8]

PUBLIC ATTITUDES TOWARD RENOVATED WASTEWATER

A study of what the general public thinks and feels about water reuse encounters formidable difficulties from the beginning. These are principally of two kinds: First, except in rare instances, people have had no direct experience with recycled water; both the questions and the answers must be hypothetical. The "if . . . then" nature of such data suggests that their interpretations be approached with considerable caution. Second, psychological theory, previous research on water reuse, and the checkered history of public response to fluoridation[9]—all strongly indicate that the possible reasons for how the layman may react to the idea of using recycled water are both numerous and diverse and that they transcend the confines of sociology, psychology, and political science.

Working within these acknowledged limitations, the study now to be discussed had three aims: (1) to identify the nature and frequencies of public responses to the concept of recycled water according to its various uses; (2) to determine how such responses might be related to those standard sociological background characteristics of the sample (age, sex, race, education, social class, and religion) that previous research has indicated to be relevant; and (3) to attempt to break new ground by exploring a number of psychological variables seen as potentially determining acceptance or rejection of recycled water.

The relevant findings with respect to each of these aims are: First, 48 percent of the sample was willing to drink renovated water. It is important to emphasize that this finding reflects a minimal level of acceptance, since all other uses of reclaimed wastewater are more acceptable. That is, as was anticipated, acceptance of the idea of renovated water depends in large part upon the particular use intended. Responses to the various uses presented to the sample population display three levels of acceptance that correlate with three levels of closeness to the self. Thus, when use involves internalization of the water—drinking or cooking—acceptance is at its lowest level: 48 to 51 percent. Acceptance increases to between 78 and

81 percent as one moves to the somewhat less intimate uses involving body contact: swimming, fishing, washing, and irrigation of food products. Finally, acceptance reaches its highest level as use of renovated wastewater is perceived as being most distant from the self; 96 percent approve of its use for irrigation of golf courses and 94 percent approve of its use for industrial cooling. Contrast these figures with the public response anticipated by the professionals in the former study.

The second aim was to see if acceptance or rejection of renovated water for potable use could be related to social background factors. A most significant finding in several prior studies is the relationship of a person's attitude toward reuse and his formal education and knowledge of reuse.[10] Generally, the more formal education a person has, the higher the probability of his receptivity to using renovated wastewater. The present study supports this relationship: 26 percent of the respondents with a grade school education or less approved of renovated wastewater for drinking, whereas 63 percent of those with some college education approved of the idea.

Similarly, the study,[11] in line with the others, found a significant relationship between a respondent's knowledge concerning use of renovated wastewater and his level of acceptance. Even at a minimum, some knowledge concerning the concept of recycling renovated wastewater appears to have significant influence on a respondent's attitude. Of those respondents who could recall having heard about the notion of recycling renovated wastewater, 52 percent were in favor of drinking it, whereas only 24 percent of those who were unaware of the possibility would accept it as a source of drinking water.

The findings differed from conventional wisdom, however, regarding the connections between accepting renovated water and several other variables. Thus, changes in the price of water do not appear to affect significantly a respondent's willingness to adopt renovated wastewater. Increases in the price of water in order to maintain conventional sources of supply did not have any statistically significant effect on public acceptance of renovated wastewater. Regardless of the changes in price, the vast majority were unwilling to change their attitude. Public acceptance may change, but not under the penalty of price increases.

Another thesis suggests that a respondent's attitude is greatly influenced by his perception of the quantity and/or quality of alternative sources. But the present study suggests the absence of a relationship between consumers' perception of the existing source of supply and acceptance of renovated wastewater. Respondents were requested to rate their drinking water according to five criteria: overall quality to drink, cloudy material, taste, color, and odor. No relationship exists between his assessment of the five characteristics of water quality and his attitude toward renovated wastewater.

The third and final area of the study involves determining what psychological variables might be active in influencing response to possible use of renovated wastewater. How does one examine such an area? The methodological problems are, indeed, formidable. A search of the literature and of test compendiums failed to produce any standard instruments measuring variables of obvious relevance. Consequently, for the pilot study, conceived of as a hunting expedition, a sentence completion test consisting of twenty-nine items was designed to obtain data on the following six dimensions:

1. *Fear of, or disgust at, the incorporation of, or contact with, the impure.* Manifestations would range from exaggerated health concerns to body waste revulsion. A sample item is: If I were eating an apple and dropped it on the floor, I would ...
2. *Faith in science and accompanying trust in expertise versus suspicion of technology and mistrust of scientific authority.* An example is: When there is a problem concerning natural resources, the people to do something about it are ...
3. *Internal versus an external locus of control.* That is, the sense of being autonomous and efficacious in dealing both with the self and with the environment in contrast to a feeling that life is controlled by forces outside the self, such as God, luck, or fate. An example is: Getting ahead in the world results from ...
4. *Modern, innovative, progressive approach to problem solving versus a traditional, conservative "holding on" to established methods.* A sample item is: In making progress, man has ...
5. *View of the world in which technology is seen as interfering with nature's or God's ordained system.* Thus results a sense of the wrongfulness of manipulation of the environment. An example is: I believe that the practice of seeding clouds in order to make it rain ...
6. *Deep, essentially esthetic commitment to the "natural," as opposed to what is perceived as being artificial.* An example is: Given a choice between aerosol whipping cream and the kind that one has to whip oneself, I would buy _____ because ...

The results obtained from the sentence completion test were disappointing. Only two of the sentence stems produced responses that varied significantly according to whether the respondents accepted or rejected the idea of drinking renovated wastewater. First, regarding the practice of seeding clouds to induce rain, 52 percent of those who approved of drinking renovated wastewater viewed such technical manipulation of the environment positively; only 29 percent of those who disapproved of drinking renovated water did so. Second, on the sentence stem concerning fluoridation, 84 percent of potential drinkers of renovated water responded positively, as against only 70 percent of the nondrinkers. Both these differences are statistically significant, and both suggest that those respondents who accept the possibility of drinking renovated wastewater are also those who possess a greater confidence in the effectiveness of scientific technology in addressing environmental problems.

The difficulty with the generally negative findings, of course, is that they are ambiguous; one never really knows whether they reflect a true lack of difference or result from an insufficiently sensitive or erroneous instrument. If the researcher refuses to believe his results, he faces the accusation of displaying pigheaded tenacity toward his expectations; if he accepts them, he faces the accusation of using simpleminded and superficial measuring techniques.

What can one say, then, and with what level of confidence, about the question of public acceptance of renovated wastewater? The data reported here are consistent on two points: First, they reveal the presence of a relationship between public response to renovated wastewater and what may be termed *cognitive characteristics* of public knowledge and education. Second, the data show an absence of such a relationship with those variables labeled "psychological." In brief, what laymen think and feel about using recycled water appears to depend primarily upon what they know about it and their general educational level, rather than on unconscious fears of contamination or general belief and attitudinal systems concerning nature, technology, esthetics, authority, progress, or destiny.

These findings immediately raise two major questions: First, if variation in response to renovated water is related to variation in educational level, so that the higher the education, the more positive the response, it would be useful to know why. What is it about education that would lead to a greater acceptance of renovated wastewater? An answer is certainly not obvious, but perhaps it is reasonable to speculate that one relevant result of more education is increased confidence in science and technology as appropriate and effective means of coping with environmental problems. The two attitudinal items that were found to yield significant results support this argument.

The second major question arises from the nagging suspicion left by the negative psychological findings. Can it really be that the public takes so reasonable or, at least, so intellectual an approach to the intimate use of wastewater, to drinking what was once sewage? Might the preponderantly positive attitudes found reflect, in these days of environmental concerns, a desire in the respondents to be ecologically responsible? Might not the sublime rationality of the layman's response to the hypothetical use of renovated water collapse when he is confronted with the *actuality* of using it? Confidence will require research that puts the glass to his lips.

But this question and the suspicion that occasions it allow the issue to come full circle, ending where it began. The professional training, the socialization of a psychologist, dictates the conviction that surely there must be *something* unconscious at work in determining the layman's response to the use of renovated wastewater. Surely, it cannot be so simple or so open a matter as that of knowledge and education. But if one would accuse the engineer and the public health official of projecting their biases when they speculated on the resistance of the public, the present authors must have the grace to acknowledge their own bias in disbelieving what would appear to be the public's sweet reason.

NOTES

1. John H. Sims, "The Federal Civil Service Executive: The Psychodynamics of a Social Role," *American Psychological Convention Proceedings*, September 1969.
2. John H. Sims and Duane D. Baumann, "Professional Biases and Water Reuse," *Economic Geography* 52 (January 1976): 1–10.
3. Idem, "Renovated Waste Water: The Question of Public Acceptance," *Water Resources Research* 10 (August 1974).
4. W. Lloyd Warner et al., *The American Federal Executive* (New Haven: Yale University Press, 1964).
5. Henry A. Murray, *Thematic Apperception Test: Pictures and Manual* (Cambridge: Harvard University Press, 1943).
6. W. R. D. Sewell, "Environmental Perceptions and Attitudes of Engineers and Public Health Officials," *Environment and Behavior* 3 (March 1971).
7. Ibid.
8. Sims and Baumann, "Renovated Waste Water."
9. Robert L. Crain, Elihu Katz, and David B. Rosenthal, *The Politics of Community Conflict: The Fluoridation Decision* (Indianapolis: Bobbs-Merrill, 1969).
10. N. Ackerman, *Water Reuse in the United States* (M.A. thesis, Southern Illinois University, 1971); R. Athanasiou and S. Hanke, "Social Psychological Factors Related to Adoption of Reused Water as a Potable Water Supply," in *Urban Demands for Natural Resources*, Western Resource Conference (Fort Collins, Colo., 1970), pp. 113–24; D. D. Baumann and R. E. Kasperson, "Public Acceptance of Renovated Wastewater," in *Water Supply from Renovated Water—A Resource Manual for Massachusetts Planners, Public Officials and Citizen Groups*, Clark University (Worcester, Mass., 1972), pp. 95–119: W. H. Bruvold and P. C. Ward, "Public Attitudes Toward Uses of Reclaimed Wastewater," *Water Sewage Works* 67 (1970): 120–22; idem, "Using Reclaimed Waste Water—Public Opinion," *Journal of the Water Pollution Control Federation* 44 (1972): 1690–96; W. Bruvold, "Affective Response Toward Uses of Reclaimed Water," *Exp. Publ. Syst* 3 (1969): 1–12; J. F. Johnson, *Renovated Waste Water: An Alternative Supply of Municipal Water Supply in the United States*, University of Chicago, Department of Geography, Research Paper No. 135 (Chicago, 1971).
11. Sims and Baumann, "Renovated Waste Water," pp. 659–65.

CHAPTER 5

Industrial   Leon Weinberger
Water Reuse

Water resources, water needs, and water uses are too critical to the well being of society to allow misunderstanding or misapplication of data in planning. Hopefully, this presentation will provide some clarification and encourage the development of alternative projection methods by those having responsibility for determining the adequacy of water resources.

Published in 1968, the Water Resources Council's First National Assessment [4] estimated water use; projected requirements by purpose in the United States were developed. These are presented in table 5-1, an analysis of which indicates:

1. A distinction is made between withdrawals and consumptive use.
2. Considering withdrawals, agriculture and steam electric power are the greatest users.
3. Considering consumptive use, agriculture accounted for over 80 percent of the nation's total. Industry accounted for 5 percent.
4. Using 1965 as the base year, industrial requirements for both withdrawal and consumptive use were projected to increase fourfold by 2020.
5. Industry (less than 20 percent of the total) includes the activities of four standard industrial classification (SIC) groups: manufacturing, mining and mineral processing, ordnance, and construction.

The gross water demand, which would be the amount of water required if there were no recycling, is not shown in table 5-1.

Tables 5-2 and 5-3 are also developed from the First National Assessment [4]. For the manufacturing group, most of the water withdrawn was for process and power cooling, and the recirculation ratio (the ratio of gross water demand to water withdrawal) was projected to increase from 2.25 in 1965 to 6.3 in 2020.

The U.S. Bureau of the Census has a special report series on water use in manufacturing [3]. Table 5-4, derived from this report, reveals that

Dr. Leon Weinberger is affiliated with Environmental Quality Systems, Inc., Rockville, Maryland.

Table 5-1. U.S. Estimated Water Use and Projected Requirements, by Purpose (mg/d)

	Used 1965	Projected Requirements (withdrawals)			Used 1965	Projected Requirements (consumptive use)		
		1980	2000	2020		1980	2000	2020
Rural domestic	2,351	2,474	2,852	3,334	1,636	1,792	2,102	2,481
Municipal (public-supplied)	23,745	33,596	50,724	74,256	5,244	10,581	16,478	24,643
Industrial (self-supplied)	46,405	75,026	127,365	210,767	3,764	6,126	10,011	15,619
Steam-electric power								
Fresh	62,738	133,963	259,208	410,553	659	1,685	4,552	8,002
Saline	21,800	59,340	211,240	503,540	157	498	2,022	5,183
Agriculture								
Irrigation	110,852	135,852	149,824	160,978	64,696	81,559	89,964	96,919
Livestock	1,726	2,375	3,397	4,660	1,626	2,177	3,077	4,238
Total	269,617	442,626	804,610	1,368,088	77,782	104,418	128,206	157,085

SOURCE: Water Resources Council, The Nation's Water Resources, pp. 1–8.

Table 5-2.   U.S. Industrial Water Use, 1965 (public and self-supplied)

	Withdrawal	Gross Use	Recirculation Ratio	Consumption	Discharge
	(bg/d)	(bg/d)		(bg/d)	(bg/d)
Manufacturing					
Processing	10.6			2.0	8.6
Process cooling	18.5			0.2	18.3
Power cooling	8.0			0.1	7.9
Other	2.9			0.3	2.6
Total	40.0	90	2.25	2.6	37.4
Mineral industries					
Mining operations	0.19				
Processing	2.07				
Cooling	0.87				
Other	0.11				
Total	3.24	11.1	3.43	0.76	2.48

SOURCE: Water Resources Council, *The Nation's Water Resources,* pp. 4–2-2.

Table 5-3.   Projected Industrial Water Requirements (bg/d) in the Conterminous United States (public and self-supplied)

	1965	1980	2000	2020
Manufacturing				
Gross	90.00	164.3	349.0	763.0
Recirculation ratio	2.25	3.0	4.4	6.3
Withdrawal	40.00	54.8	80.0	121.0
Discharge	37.40	50.2	70.0	100.0
Consumption	2.60	4.6	10.0	21.0
Mineral industry				
Gross	11.10	20.0	33.0	88.0
Recirculation ratio	3.43	4.9	7.0	10.0
Withdrawal	3.24	4.1	4.7	8.8
Discharge	2.48	2.9	3.3	7.0
Consumption	0.76	1.2	1.4	1.8

SOURCE: Water Resources Council, *The Nation's Water Resources,* pp. 4–2-4.

1. Through 1973, for all manufacturing industries there is a continuing increase in gross water use. Between 1968 and 1973, however, a *reduction in total water intake* took place.
2. With the exception of paper and allied products, the major water use SIC categories showed decrease in total water intake.
3. Recycle ratios continue to increase.
4. With the exception of paper and allied products, the major use of

fresh water intake is for cooling and condensing for largest water users.

Table 5-4. Water Use and Recycle Trends in Manufacturing Industries, by Major Industry Group

	Year	Gross Water Intake (bg/d)	Total Water Intake (bg/d)	Recycle Ratio	Cooling and Condensing Fresh Water (bg/d) (% intake)	
All industries	1954	57.6	31.7	1.82		
	1959	71.9	33.2	2.16		
	1964	81.8	38.4	2.13		
	1968	97.8	42.4	2.31		
	1973	128.7	41.2	3.12	20.8	62.3
Paper and allied products (SIC 26)	1954	11.6	4.9	2.38		
	1959	16.6	5.3	3.12		
	1964	15.0	5.7	2.66		
	1968	17.9	6.2	2.90		
	1973	22.3	6.6	3.37	2.2	34.2
Chemicals and allied products (SIC 28)	1954	11.8	7.4	1.60		
	1959	14.3	8.9	1.61		
	1964	21.2	10.7	1.98		
	1968	25.8	12.3	2.10		
	1973	30.4	11.4	2.66	6.5	81.4
Petroleum and coal products (SIC 29)	1954	11.4	3.4	3.34		
	1959	15.8	3.6	4.38		
	1964	16.9	3.8	4.41		
	1968	20.0	3.9	5.08		
	1973	32.1	3.5	9.13	1.2	66.8
Primary metal industries (SIC 33)	1954	13.6	10.5	1.29		
	1959	15.5	10.1	1.53		
	1964	18.4	12.6	1.46		
	1968	21.3	13.7	1.55		
	1973	24.2	13.5	1.78	8.4	69.9

SOURCE: U.S. Bureau of the Census, "Water Use in Manufacturing."

It is important to note that the recycle (recirculation) ratio in 1973 for manufacturing was 3.12, whereas the projection in the First National Assessment indicated a 3.0 ratio by 1980. Clearly, industry is increasing water recycle faster than was expected in the early 1960s.

A recirculation ratio of 1.0 indicates a once-through system; i.e., no recirculation. A ratio of 2.0 indicates a total water intake equal to one-half of the gross water use; i.e., in the plant, water, on the average, is used twice between intake and discharge. To bring about a 50-percent reduction in water intake, the recirculation ratio must be doubled. It should also be apparent from the data that the greatest potential for reducing the intake water would be to recycle cooling waters.

Table 5-5 was developed by Kollar and Brewer [2]. The potential for industrial recycle as a means for reducing intake water requirements can be seen by comparing the highest recycling rate with the mean recycling rate.

Preliminary findings of the Second National Water Assessment (1975) are that, contrary to the first assessment, total water withdrawal is expected to *decline* between 1975 and 2000, due to increased recycling by industry, more efficient use in irrigation, and cessation of withdrawals of groundwater in areas where the groundwater reservoir is totally depleted. Water consumption is expected to increase as the uses of water expand. Of the 135.0 bg/d of water consumption projected for 2000, however, 93.9 bg/d (70 percent) will be for irrigation. Dr. M. Rupert Cutler, assistant secretary of agriculture for conservation, research, and education, has stated, "The blunt fact is, agriculture consumes more water through irrigation than all other uses. In fact, it accounts for about 80 percent of consumptive use in the nation."*

Kollar and Brewer [1] present the projections made in 1972 by the Water Resources Program of the Bureau of Domestic Commerce (BDC) for the Second National Assessment (table 5-6). Kollar and Brewer also report that the actual gross water demand in 1975 was 121 bg/d, and the total water intake was 42.2 bg/d in manufacturing. They further conclude that in 2000 the intake of water by manufacturers is projected to *decline* to 20 bg/d, due mainly to a reduction in intake water used for cooling.

It is most significant that in a period of ten years (between first and second assessments) the projections for intake water for manufacturing use in the United States for 2000 has been *reduced from 80 to 20 bg/d, a 75-percent reduction.*

Projecting water use on the basis of historic data and trends can result in estimates that depart significantly from actual requirements. Events over the past decade have alerted us to the need to reevaluate our projections:

1. passage of PL 92–500, the Federal Water Pollution Control Act Amendments of 1972;
2. recognized energy shortages;
3. increased costs of water and wastewater treatment;
4. national water shortages;
5. new approaches to water resources development.

---

*National Conference on Water, St. Louis, Mo., May 23, 1977.

Table 5-5. Water Recycling in the 20 Plants with the Highest Rates in 34 Major Water-using Industries, 1970

SIC	Industry	Gross Water Use (bg/yr)	Intake (bg/yr)	Mean Recycling Rate*	Highest Recycling Rate	10th Highest Recycling Rate	20th Highest Recycling Rate
2011	Meat packing plants	49.732	20.335	2.45	7.05	2.41	1.85
2015	Poultry dressing	3.473	1.990	1.75	4.28	1.30	1.14
2026	Fluid milk	8.118	0.859	9.45	71.71	7.92	3.96
2033	Canned fruit and vegetables	10.673	3.419	3.12	18.24	2.50	1.76
2037	Frozen fruit and vegetables	17.353	9.259	1.87	7.13	1.97	1.39
2046	Wet corn milling	53.986	32.109	1.68	11.91	2.31	1.11
2063	Beet sugar	58.949	16.829	3.50	22.24	2.97	1.84
2082	Malt liquors	64.350	12.675	5.08	10.00	2.85	1.11
2096	Shortening and cooking oils	48.106	5.425	8.87	113.53	8.23	1.30
2111	Cigarettes	60.765	2.292	26.51	33.39	15.31	1.11
2211	Weaving mills, cotton	74.289	1.186	62.64	285.31	64.25	27.99
2221	Weaving mills, synthetics	88.114	0.717	122.89	558.25	111.27	48.53
2231	Weaving and finishing, wool	19.163	2.637	7.27	93.44	24.19	1.18
2611	Pulp mills	713.440	208.179	3.43	7.57	3.84	1.41
2621	Papermills, except bldg paper	723.008	71.057	10.18	76.54	8.96	6.06

SIC	Industry					
2631	Paperboard mills	272.670	14.515	18.79	50.00	14.68	8.22
2812	Alkalines and chlorine	198.798	87.167	2.28	25.11	1.79	1.12
2813	Industrial gases	141.450	1.490	94.93	157.80	84.83	46.23
2815	Cyclic intermediate and crudes	327.354	55.446	5.90	160.00	13.45	2.24
2816	Inorganic pigments	120.387	50.222	2.40	15.22	1.53	1.11
2818	Industrial organic chemicals	962.830	35.142	27.40	48.18	23.20	15.80
2819	Industrial inorganic chemicals	505.919	16.670	30.35	70.95	30.10	23.81
2821	Plastic materials and resins	704.229	5.131	137.25	613.60	27.37	13.81
2823	Cellulosic man-made fibers	209.801	48.088	4.36	20.83	4.30	1.37
2824	Organic fibers, non-cellulosic	392.335	151.969	2.58	28.06	2.82	1.16
2834	Pharmaceutical preparations	70.621	15.385	4.59	104.73	7.36	1.11
2871	Fertilizers	282.251	23.373	12.08	90.60	9.72	2.45
2911	Petroleum refining	2,026.521	30.221	67.06	251.05	44.08	34.36
3241	Cement, hydraulic	20.868	4.320	4.83	97.35	2.58	1.77
3312	Blast furnaces and steel mills	394.549	29.050	13.58	95.13	18.66	6.76
3313	Electrometallurgical products	22.732	1.827	12.44	65.81	25.64	5.07
3321	Gray iron foundaries	35.396	10.254	3.45	15.23	2.86	1.82
3331	Primary copper	78.473	33.218	2.36	9.85	2.23	1.18
3334	Primary aluminum	65.519	15.723	4.17	10.10	3.50	1.66

Adapted after Kollar and Brewer, 1977.
*Recycling rates are obtained by dividing gross water by intake.

Table 5-6.   Projected Manufacturing Gross Water Demand

	Year	Volume (bg/d)
No recycling	1975	154
	2000	378[a]
Projected total water intake	1975	69
	2000	23[b]

Adapted after Kollar and Brewer, "Achieving Pollution Abatement."
[a]Increase over 1975, 145%.
[b]*Decrease* over 1975, 67%.

This paper has dealt with the quantity aspects of industrial use of water. The only *net use* of water by industry is the consumptive use; and if the quality of the water being discharged did not interfere with other uses, the total impact of industry on our water resources would be small: the goal, of course, of PL 92–500.

The following concluding comments can be made:

1. In discussing water requirements for industries, distinction must be made between water intake, consumption, total water demand.
2. Industrial use and manufacturers' use are not synonymous.
3. Within the past five years, projections for industrial water intake have been sharply reduced. A reduction in water intake is currently projected between now and 2000.
4. A more imaginative and creative approach should be taken to predict (and reduce) water requirements. Past practices, whether by industry, agriculture, or municipalities, need not be projected into the future.
5. The water requirements for a specific company can probably *not* be predicted based on national averages.
6. Withdrawal use of water by industry will decrease mainly because of cooling water recirculation. Process water requirements will also decrease, as will sanitary requirements.
7. Water withdrawal requirements will approach consumptive use, which is less than 5 percent of gross industrial water use.
8. In certain industries, dry processes can be substituted for wet ones. Consumptive uses can be reduced by nonevaporative cooling.
9. The consumptive use of water by agriculture accounts for 80 percent of the nation's total consumptive use.

REFERENCES

[1] Kollar, K. L. and Brewer, R. "Achieving Pollution Abatement." *Construction Review.* U.S. Department of Commerce, Office of Business Research and Analysis, Bureau of Competitive Assessment and Business Policy, July 1973.

[2] _____. *Journal of the American Waterworks Association* 69, no. 9 (September 1977): 468.

[3] U.S. Bureau of the Census. "Water Use in Manufacturing." 1972 Census of Manufactures. Special Report Series MC 72(SR).4. September 1975.

[4] Water Resources Council. *The Nation's Water Resources: The First National Assessment of the Water Resources Council.* Washington, D.C., 1968.

PART 2

PRACTICES

CHAPTER 6

Status
of Wastewater
Reuse
in South Africa

Lucas R. J. van Vuuren
O. O. Hart

Like most other countries, South Africa is confronted with problems of water pollution and diminishing water supplies. Direct reuse of wastewaters for irrigation and cooling and indirect reuse for domestic purposes have been practiced for several decades. More recently, the need for direct reuse has come to the foreground, and research has focused on wastewater treatment technology for implementation in various parts of the country. The reuse of effluent for agricultural, industrial, recreational, or direct municipal purposes already forms an integral part of the country's overall water management practice.

The country's average annual rainfall of 487 mm is theoretically equivalent to 1,630 Gl/d.[1] Ninety-one percent of the rainfall is lost by evaporation and transpiration, and only 9 percent reaches the rivers. The total runoff is comparatively small and, in fact, is less than the runoff of any one of the major rivers of Africa; e.g., the Zambezi River.[2] The assured runoff that can be made available by providing storage is 57.3 Gl/d. Underground supplies are estimated to be 3.1 Gl/d, giving a total supply of 60.4 Gl/d.

Irrigation demands by the end of the century can be expected to reach a total of 34.8 Gl/d. At an estimated 7-percent per year rate of increase, the demand for urban and industrial use will be 45.5 Gl/d by 2000, giving a total demand of 80.3 Gl/d, as against the assured supply of 60.4 Gl/d. This implies a deficit of 20 Gl/d; i.e., some 25 percent of the potential demand. The assured supply can, however, be increased to 75 Gl/d by increasing the net yield of impoundment reservoirs. In this case, the deficit would be reduced to 6.6 percent.

These figures indicate that South Africa is heading for a substantial water shortage.[3] On a regional basis the problem may become more accentuated and, in certain industrialized areas of the country, further progress is already prejudiced by water shortages.

The solution to the problem must be sought in better utilization of the available water; reuse must play a vital part. The challenges posed by this

Dr. Lucas R. J. van Vuuren is acting director for the National Institute for Water Research, Pretoria, Republic of South Africa.
O. O. Hart is the head of the Physiochemical Technology Division of the National Institute for Water Research, Pretoria, Republic of South Africa.

situation have forced the acceptance of the inevitable fact that water supply, wastewater reuse, and the control of pollution are inseparable components in a broad water conservation plan for every metropolitan area, as well as for the country as a whole.

AVAILABILITY OF WASTEWATER FOR REUSE

The average daily volumes of sewage effluent available and its usage in the twenty major cities and towns, as well as in some other minor towns and industries, are shown in table 6-1. These sources, representing a population of 5.8 million persons, produce an average 1,234 Ml/d of treated sewage effluent, or 210 l/d per capita. At present, 31.9 percent of this effluent is reused: 8.7 percent for power station cooling; 16.1 percent for irrigation of crops, parks, and sports fields; and 7.1 percent for industrial purposes. This last figure includes the utilization of an average 3 Ml/d for domestic consumption at Windhoek.[4]

In the case of the Vaal River Triangle, often called the industrial powerhouse of South Africa, the reuse pattern changes drastically, mainly because the water resources for this area are limited. Of the approximately 641 Ml sewage effluent available daily, 50 percent is being reused: 14.4 percent for power station cooling; 26.8 percent for irrigation; and 8.8 percent for industrial purposes.

AGRICULTURAL REUSE

The use of treated sewage effluents for irrigation has been practiced in South Africa for many years without any apparent deleterious effect on crops and soil. Before embarking on irrigation schemes using sewage effluent, several factors relating to quality requirements for plants, soil structure and drainage, pathogenic loading, and underground pollution have to be considered. Good drainage is of paramount importance when considering sewage effluent for irrigation because the effluent must be irrigated throughout the year, even during periods of excessive rainfall.

Irrigation with sewage effluents is an important adjunct of unrestricted reuse, since it provides bleed-off, which is essential for maintaining a total dissolved solids (TDS) equilibrium in a partially closed system. Henzen and Coombs[5] showed that an equilibrium level of .530 mg/l TDS can be maintained if 80 percent of the available sewage effluent in the Johannesburg metropolitan area is reclaimed and 20 percent is used consumptively for cooling and irrigation purposes.

Table 6-1. Daily Volumes of Sewage Effluents Available from Some Major South African Towns and Industries and Their Use (Ml/d)

	Population (1971)	Total Volume Effluent	Power Stations Cooling	Irrigation	Industrial
Johannesburg*/	1,181,321				
Roodepoort*	132,970	317.8	54.5	113.5	
Durban	716,585	229.3			10.2
Cape Town	651,090	143.0	9.1	0.5	
Pretoria*	518,314	86.0	37.6	16.5	
Port Elizabeth	390,982	88.0		6.8	
Germiston*	253,500	52.6		8.0	
East London	205,789	3.3			
Bloemfontein	160,000	25.0	6.5	0.3	
Benoni*	142,630	20.4		2.0	2.0
Springs*	141,690	29.5			29.5
Welkom	135,700	40.4			13.2
Pietermaritzburg	123,031	27.3		6.8	
Kimberley	115,200	8.0		1.6	1.1
Carletonville*	103,500	4.5		4.5	
Boksburg*	95,950	27.3			
Vereeniging*	93,090	10.2			
Krugersdorp*	91,100	17.0		13.6	
Brakpan*	85,702	7.0			
Windhoek	79,000	6.2			3.0+
Kempton Park*	71,160	25.5			
Klerksdorp*	65,050	5.8		5.8	
Randfontein*	50,398	4.5		1.4	
Bellville	46,700	9.1			1.1
Grahamstown	41,375	2.3		2.3	
Worcester	40,590	5.9		5.9	
Westonaria*	40,027	6.8		6.8	
Parys*	17.357	1.4			
Sasol*	30,230	23.0			23.0
Slurry	1,000	2.1			2.1
Ulco	2,550	0.1			0.1
King William's Town	16,600	2.3		2.3	
Modderfontein	6,400	1.9			1.9
Total	5,846,581	1,233.5	107.7	198.6	87.2
Percentage			8.7	16.1	7.1
Vaal River Triangle Total	3,113,989	641.2	92.1	172.1	56.4
Percentage			14.4	26.8	8.8

*Situated in the Vaal River Triangle.
+Average volume reclaimed for domestic use.

The presence of pathogenic organisms in sewage effluents precludes their use for the irrigation of certain crops, especially those that may be consumed raw. The major portion of sewage effluent reused for irrigation purposes is being applied for pasturage irrigation. Of these schemes, the most important is that of the City Council of Johannesburg, where a total volume of 113.5 Ml/d sewage effluent is being applied at a rate of 230 cm/a.[6] This is a rather high application rate with the result that between 40 and 50 percent of the effluent applied finds its way back to the river either as seepage or as runoff, particularly during wet weather. At this application rate, the potential fertilizing value of the effluent (34 mg/l as N and 23 mg/l as PO_4) is equivalent to applications of 730 kg nitrogen (as N) and 540 kg phosphorus (as PO_4)/a./ha.

The irrigated land is divided into uses for winter and summer grazing and summer crop production. The total summer crop production for 1970 was 9,000 tons of hay and 7,000 tons of silage, and the overall carrying capacity of the farms averaged at 4.2 animals/ha.

INDUSTRIAL REUSE

The population and industrial activity of the country is highly centralized. About 20 percent of the total water consumption is by cities, towns, industry, mining, and power generation.[7] It should be noted that industry and mining alone produce 40 percent of the country's gross national product (GNP), of which 81 percent is contributed by the four main metropolitan centers.[8] The most important of these centers is the Pretoria/Johannesburg/Vereeniging complex (Vaal River Triangle), which is responsible for about 45 percent of the country's industrial production. Natural water resources in this area are limited, however, with the result that interbasin transfers and effluent reuse will be inevitable to insure sufficient water by the end of the century. At present some 23 percent of the purified effluent available in the Vaal River Triangle is reused directly in industry and for power generation.

Another important center of economic activity is the Western Cape, where 11 percent of the purified sewage effluent available is presently being reused, mainly for power generation. With the exploitation of all the available sources in this area, including purified sewage effluent, there would be sufficient water in the foreseeable future.

The other important metropolitan centers, such as Durban and Port Elizabeth, have a reasonably assured supply of raw water for the future, although economics might swing the balance in favor of wastewater reuse.

Reuse for Cooling Purposes

There are two basic methods by which industry can reduce its potable water intake; namely, internal reuse of process water and wastewater reuse.

About 67 percent of the total demand for industrial water, the mining industry excluded, is required for cooling purposes, while 4 percent is used for steam generation.[9] The extent to which purified sewage effluent is currently being used as cooling water for power generation plants is reflected in statistics as shown in table 6-2.

Table 6-2. Reuse for Cooling in Power Stations

Power Stations ·	Power Station Capacity (MW)	Consumption of Reclaimed Sewage Effluent (Ml/d)
Cape Town (Athlone)	150	9.1
Bloemfontein	50	6.5
Johannesburg (Orlando)	300	22.7
Johannesburg (Kelvin)	360	31.8
Pretoria West	250	19.8
Pretoria, Rooiwal	120	17.8

For power station cooling, the major problem is control of the pH, alkalinity, and nitrogen-phosphorus relationships. A further problem is biological fouling as a result of excessible growth of bacteria, fungi, and algae. This is controlled by chlorination or addition of slimicides to the water circuit. Where chlorination is used, a shock dosage of the order of 5 to 7 mg/l or even less is applied.[10]

Pulp and Paper Industry

South African Pulp and Paper Industries (SAPPI) near the city of Springs was the first large manufacturing industry in this country to utilize purified sewage effluent as the major part of its water supply. The present water use is made up of 16 Ml/d from the Rand Water Board and a further 27 Ml/d of purified sewage from the Springs municipality.

Initially, the purified sewage used for process water received only limited tertiary treatment, consisting of sand filtration and low-level chlorination. The demand for paper of a higher brightness, however, called for further refinement of the purified effluent, which contains heavy metals, particularly iron, manganese, and copper; and organics, which are known to affect paper brightness. Research was conducted using various adsorbents, oxidants, and flocculants, such as lime and aluminum sulphate, to improve the water quality. These studies culminated in the design and construction of a full-scale, advanced treatment plant, which was commissioned in July 1970.

The full-scale plant comprises a flotation tank of 750 kl capacity; feed line (0.6 m) with booster pump; aeration vessel with high-speed disperser and air compressor operating at 10 psig; storage tanks and dosing equipment for aluminum sulphate, sodium hydroxide, and chlorine; and auxiliary equipment, such as pH and flow recorder controllers (figure 6-1).

Figure 6-1.   SAPPI Sewage Water Purification Simplified Flow Scheme

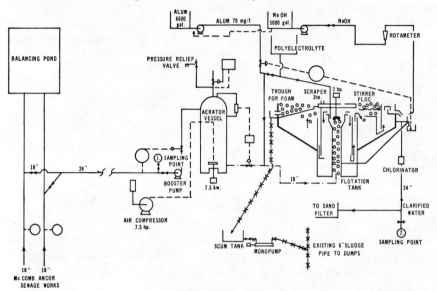

Aluminum sulphate is dosed at 75 mg/l into the feed line at a point succeeding the aeration stage. Approximately 1.4 mg/l of polyelectrolyte is added for improved flocculation and flotation, and sodium hydroxide (10 mg/l) is dosed in the effluent launder to adjust pH value. Prior to filtration approximately 3 mg/l of chlorine is added as a measure against algal growth. Operational results are shown in table 6-3.

The reclaimed water is of a quality such that it can be used in all sections of the mill without deleterious effect on the quality of the product paper. Very low turbidities (0 to 1 mg/l) in the form of suspended solids are carried over from the flotation unit, which has a hydraulic retention of less than thirty minutes.

Average costs for the first two years of continual operation (1970–71) are compared with costs for water as supplied by the Rand Water Board (see table 6-4). The annual savings by using reclaimed water instead of Rand Water Board water amounted to $220,000, which is of the same order as the initial capital expenditure. A cost saving of more than 50 percent in relation to conventional supply sources is currently achieved.

Table 6-3. Quality of Purified and Reclaimed Sewage Effluent from Full-Scale Plant at SAPPI (mg/*l*, where applicable)

Quality Parameters	Springs Purified Sewage	Reclaimed Water
pH	7.20	6.70
Conductivity	1,100.00	1,200.00
Color (Hazen units)	40.00	10.00
COD	75.00	40.00
Total phosphate (as P)	2.60–6.70	0.60–1.20
Methylene blue active substances	1.00–1.50	0.70–0.90
Iron (as Fe)	0.26	0.06
Manganese (as Mn)	0.55	0.50
Copper (as Cu)	0.45	0.02
Relative paper brightness in Elrepho units	76.90	82.40
Distilled water in Elrepho units	85.60	
Rand Water Board water in Elrepho units	82.40	

Table 6-4. Treatment Costs at SAPPI Water Reclamation Plant, 1971

	S.A. ¢/k*l*
Rand Water Board water	3.52
Springs purified sewage	0.22
Operation costs (chemicals, maintenance, and supervision)	1.21
Capital expenditure	
R159,000 at R14,000/yr, 25 M*l*/d for 325 d/yr	0.17
Total costs, reclaimed water	1.60

The Mondi Paper Company near Durban is another paper mill that uses secondary sewage effluent for process water. The total water intake to the mill presently amounts to about 1.6 M*l*/d of potable water and 10.6 M*l*/d of treated sewage effluent from the Durban Corporation's southern sewage works.

The factory's AWT plant has a capacity of 11.5 M*l*/d and incorporates chemical flocculation, foam fractionation, sand filtration, and activated carbon treatment, for which the carbon is regenerated on site. Cost estimates during 1974 indicated a total cost figure of about 9 cents/k*l* for the reclaimed water produced.[11]

The Chemical Industry

One of South Africa's largest industrial consumers and also the largest dynamite factory in the world, African Explosives and Chemical Industries, attacked its problem of water use, reuse, and effluent control in an admirable manner.[12] Their Modderfontein factory near Johannesburg had a potable water consumption in 1968 of between 450 and 500 Ml/mo. Intensive recycling and reuse of process waters reduced the factory's total fresh water requirements to 430 Ml/mo in 1973. Additional utilization of various classes of wastewaters, particularly for cooling purposes, reduced this volume still further. During the period 1962–68, the flow of strong effluent from the factory was reduced by more than 80 percent.

The stronger effluent, containing an appreciable amount of ammonium sulphate and ammonium nitrate, is used as a diluted liquid fertilizer for growing grass on an extensive area of land owned by the company. In this way, waste nitrogen salts are removed from the water environment.

Other Industries
The slurry process for the manufacture of Portland Cement can utilize treated sewage effluent effectively. The effluent quality need not be of a high standard, since all the water and organic matter is volatilized in the rotary kilns. Together, the Portland Cement factories at Slurry and Ulco use 2.2 Ml/d of treated sewage effluent in their slurry processes.

Other industrial applications of treated sewage effluents include:

1. 1.1 Ml/d for washing purposes at the De Beers Diamond Mines, Kimberley;
2. 1.1 Ml/d by South African Board Mills at Bellville;
3. 23 Ml/d by Sasol (the oil-from-coal industry) for the conveyance of ash from the power station, followed by maturation pond treatment and subsequent discharge into the Vaal River;
4. 13.2 Ml/d by gold mines in the Welkom area, particularly for slurry conveyance;
5. 2 Ml/d for cooling of plate metal and rollers in a steel mill at Benoni.

In general, it can be said that the major industries in the Republic are already water conscious and that these industries are endeavoring to modernize their factories and to keep abreast of new developments in order to cut down effluent pollution and fresh water requirements.

Unfortunately, water consciousness is largely lacking among industries that discharge their effluents into municipal sewers. This is no doubt inevitable so long as water remains relatively cheap (7.4 to 11.5 cents/kl to industry). Regulations for the discharge of effluents into municipal sewers are currently still based on limiting the concentration of pollutants, which does not encourage water conservation. The use of reclaimed effluents by industry, therefore, probably constitutes the most effective means for the conservation of water.

DIRECT AND INDIRECT REUSE OF WASTEWATER

With regard to the domestic use of reclaimed water, an objective appraisal of the question of direct and indirect reuse of wastewaters is necessary. This is a vexing and controversial issue, which in some countries has precipitated a stalemate in pollution control, in wastewater reuse, and in the upgrading of conventional water purification facilities.

It is necessary to state emphatically that the intake water for potable reclamation should consist of predominantly domestic wastewater that has undergone effective oxidative biological stabilization by any of the recognized systems.

The reservations that have been expressed regarding wastewater reclamation for domestic reuse—namely, the risk of infections, chronic toxicity, carcinogenic effects, sex hormone effects, and radiological effects—may apply with equal force to many conventional water purification plants treating natural waters that may be polluted. A critical evaluation of existing conventional water treatment plants, is, therefore, necessary.

Direct Reuse

The first plant for the reclamation of sewage for the direct potable reuse was commissioned in Windhoek, South West Africa, in October 1968, and, up to the end of 1970, had produced 1.8 Gl of reclaimed water.[13] The public's favorable acceptance of the reclaimed water is ascribed to the progressive disclosure of information via the press and to invitations to visit the plant.

The raw water is derived from a sewage treatment plant utilizing biofilters and then undergoes further biological purification in nine maturation ponds. The reclamation plant has a nominal capacity of 4.5 Ml/d, and the original plant that was constructed in 1969 essentially comprised facilities for algae flotation, foam fractionation, breakpoint chlorination, and active carbon polishing (figure 6-2). This plant has subsequently been modified to include high lime treatment and ammonia stripping (figure 6-3) because of the inefficient performance of the ponds with respect to ammonia removal.

A surface water supply undergoes purification in a conventional plant situated side by side with the reclamation plant.[14] The reclaimed water, after carbon adsorption, is blended with purified surface water and the admixed streams are then post-chlorinated to a free residual of 0.2 mg/l chlorine.

During a strict monitoring program that was followed over the course of several months, an average of 20 TCID$_{50}$/ml virus was found in the settled sewage entering the sewage purification works, and reovirus was

Figure 6-2. Schematic Flow Diagram of Original Windhoek Water Reclamation Plant

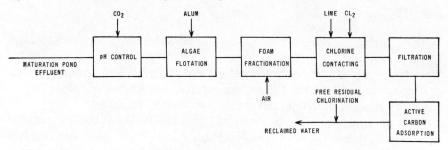

Figure 6-3. Schematic Flow Diagram of Modified Windhoek Water Reclamation Plant

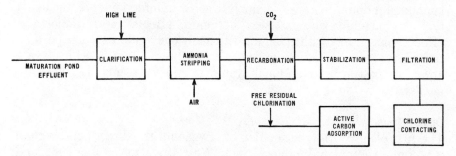

also isolated from the maturation pond effluent. As from the foam fractionation stage, no virus was ever detected in any of the hundreds of samples tested.

Escherichia coli I, or coliform bacteria, were never recorded after breakpoint chlorination, whereas the total plate count was drastically reduced within acceptable low levels. On several occasions, however, a significant increase in the total plate count was recorded after carbon adsorption, but post-chlorination effectively reduced these counts to below 100/m*l.*

The TDS of the reclaimed water increased from about 740 to 810 mg/*l*, mainly as a result of chemical dosing. Depending on the ratio of admixture of reclaimed water with purified raw water, the TDS of the blended water could be controlled well below 600 mg/*l*. After further dilution with borehole water, the TDS in the distribution system increased from 375 to 475 mg/*l* after integration.

After optimum operational conditions were established, a final quality reclaimed water could be produced prior to blending with a chemical oxygen demand (COD) of less than 10 mg/*l*, ABS of less than 0.2 mg/*l*, and nitrate of approximately 3 mg/*l*.

During the first two years of operation, the reclamation plant has contributed an average of 13.4 percent, with the monthly proportion ranging from 0 to 27.7 percent of the total water consumption at Windhoek. Cost estimates during 1970 confirmed that reclaimed water could be produced competitively with other supply sources.

Towards the beginning of 1971, the Swakop River water supply scheme was completed; and, following good rains in this area, the water situation was less critical. The water reclamation plant, therefore, was operated for short periods only and, later, was stopped due to a progressive further deterioration in the raw water intake quality while extensions to the sewage works were made.

Modifications to the reclamation plant comprising high lime treatment and ammonia stripping have been implemented with the view to achieve a higher ultimate utilization factor. Recommissioning of the modified plant was undertaken during 1977, and plant performance is highly satisfactory.

Although the critical water supply situation at Windhoek did not allow for a long and detailed epidemiological study before the introduction of reclaimed water, data were available from hospital and laboratory records on typhoid, other salmonella, shigella, and infectious hepatitis cases as far back as 1964. This valuable record served as a good basis against which the epidemiological studies, carried out during the operation of the reclamation plant, could be judged.

The success of the Windhoek reclamation scheme activated a concerted research effort by the NIWR at the experimental wastewater reclamation plant, Pretoria, on reduction of purification costs, improvement of unit processes, and the development of a multiple safety barrier reclamation system. By modifying the present Windhoek reclamation plant in accordance with the findings of this work, the full exploitation of purified sewage effluent, as a permanent component of Windhoek's water economy in both the short and long terms, has become a practical reality. Realizing these implications for Windhoek's future development when the Swakop River water supply is exploited to its full capacity within the next few years, the municipality of Windhoek has agreed to continue with water reclamation as a research and development project with financial support from the Water Research Commission. Future planning also provides for improved sewage treatment facilities.

Indirect Reuse

In South Africa several examples can be quoted where indirect reuse of domestic effluents is practiced. In the Johannesburg/Pretoria area, a substantial flow (321 Ml/d) of purified sewage, which is not utilized for industrial or agricultural reuse, finds its way in natural streams and water courses and thus, indirectly, into domestic water supplies. The increasing signs of eutrophication and deterioration in chemical and biochemical quality in these catchments are a matter of grave concern, and in some instances the conventional water purification plants have reached the stage where advanced techniques, such as activated carbon treatment, have become a dire need. The major problems encountered are the presence of algae and aquatic plants, and the occurrence of dissolved organics, nitrogen, and phosphorus. The following case histories demonstrate typical examples of the extent to which treated sewage effluents are used indirectly:

The Hartbeespoort impoundment reservoir essentially serves as an irrigation supply source for an area of about 13,400 hectares. It also serves as a recreational area for aquatic sport, such as angling, boating, and skiing. The township of Brits, population 20,000, and several smaller communities obtain water for domestic and industrial needs from this impoundment.

The average flow of the Crocodile River feeding this dam is 402 Ml/d. The Johannesburg metropolis within the catchment of the Crocodile is expanding rapidly, and approximately 47 Ml/d of purified sewage is disposed of into this catchment. An average 10 percent of treated sewage enters the Hartbeespoort Dam, and during the dry season it can be as high as 50 percent. The nutrient load is reduced by storage in the dam, but approximately 1.7 mg P/l and 1.4 mg N/l on the average still occur in the water extracted for irrigation and domestic purposes. These nutrients obviously do not pose a problem with regard to the quality for irrigation purposes. As a source for domestic water supply, however, these nutrients cause operational problems, and on several occasions public complaints of taste and odor in the domestic water supply have been received.

The existing water treatment works at Brits, completed in 1958 with a capacity of 3.5 Ml/d, has become inadequate to meet the growing demands in this rapidly developing area. The works is based on a conventional design comprising clarification, filtration, and disinfection. A new treatment works has recently been constructed where breakpoint chlorination and activated carbon units were included in order to treat adequately the increasingly polluted intake water.

The Rietvlei impoundment receives approximately 25 Ml/d of purified sewage from the township of Kempton Park, together with an average 25 Ml/d runoff. Treated sewage effluent therefore constitutes an appreciable proportion of the inflow into a dam that contributes to the potable supply for the city of Pretoria. The proportion of treated sewage in this dam is therefore higher than that of the Hartbeespoort Dam, but indications are that the self-purification capacity of this river is superior to that of the Crocodile River. Nevertheless, over the past years the problem of increased eutrophication also has had a significant effect on the control and operation of the water treatment plant, which has a capacity of 25 Ml/d.

Investigations are currently under way to improve separation of algae by the addition of ferric salts and polyelectrolytes. Studies on phosphorus removal from the purified sewage at source using chemical addition are also to be carried out. Future expansions to the sewage works will be based on current technological developments in the field of biological denitrification and phosphorus removal.

The Bon Accord Dam receives a relatively small stream of natural runoff that, along its course, is heavily polluted with purified sewage, agricultural seepage water, and industrial effluent. During the dry season, the upper reaches are essentially fed by purified sewage from the Daspoort sewage works (19 Ml/d) and effluent from a power station and steel foundry (about 10 Ml/d). This water enters the Bon Accord Dam at a rate of about 45 Ml/d. The average retention in the dam is four to five months, allowing for some degree of self-purification; however, this dam also shows marked signs of eutrophication.

During the dry season a minimum of 3.5 Ml/d of compensation water is released, and during the wet season the dam spills over. About 10 km downstream from the dam, 15 to 25 Ml/d purified sewage from the Rooiwal sewage works is allowed into the river. This river is the source for a purification works supplying a township of 18,000 inhabitants at a point 20 km further downstream.

In planning this water purification works during 1964, account was taken of the inferior quality of the raw water, particularly with regard to organic constituents. Surveys indicated the presence of 1 to 3 mg MBAS/l and COD of about 30 to 40 mg/l. The presence of 5 mg P/l and 6 mg NO$_3$(N)/l confirmed the presence of a substantial proportion of purified sewage.

The water purification works has a capacity of 4.5 Ml/d and consists of facilities for lime and alum flocculation, sedimentation, breakpoint chlorination, rapid gravity filtration, and active carbon adsorption treatment. The purified water is of acceptable potable quality, but chemical treatment costs are relatively high due to activated carbon treatment. Phosphorus is reduced below the 1 mg/l level and COD, below 15 mg/l. Presumptive *Escherichia coli I* has never been detected in the product water.

The above case histories of indirect reuse of domestic effluents are typical of several other catchments in South Africa. In terms of quantity these examples represent relatively small volumes of indirect reuse as compared with the Vaal Barrage, which receives the major part of the sewage effluent from the Johannesburg metropolis and Vaal Triangle. Because of the high dilution factor in the latter, the eutrophication effect is, however, less pronounced, although it is beginning to cause concern. The quality of the water in the Vaal Barrage reservoir has, however, deteriorated significantly over the past decade. Trends in future development have drawn attention to the need for more sophisticated sewage treatment plants and higher quality standards for domestic effluents in order to reduce pollution loads in this highly industrialized area. The implementation of activated sludge systems based on the principle of nitrification and denitrification and biological and chemical precipitation of phosphorus are envisaged for future and existing treatment plants.

Direct reuse of sewage effluent for recreational purposes is not practiced in South Africa. The presence of sewage effluents in impoundment reservoirs and rivers, as described above, could perhaps be regarded as a mode of indirect recreational reuse. The reason for this approach in South Africa should be seen in the light of the pressing demand for more water for unrestricted reuse, rather than for a limited application, such as for recreation. Research in South Africa is, therefore, primarily focused on direct wastewater reclamation for industrial and domestic purposes and, as a secondary objective, prevention of pollution of water environment.

FUTURE PLANNING

The water resources of the Republic have hitherto been utilized primarily for irrigation. Up to 83.5 percent of the total supply is currently consumed by agriculture. According to present evidence, there is no urgent need for additional, large-scale allocation of water for this use, and the emphasis is on increased yields of the land already under cultivation. It is therefore anticipated that by 2000 the proportion of water used for irrigation will be reduced to about 45 percent.

The position is different with regard to urban and industrial use of water. About 50 percent of the available effluents are already being reused in the Southern Transvaal, compared with only about 11 percent in the Western Cape. The potential of reclaimed water is thus relatively unexploited in the Western Cape. Statistics indicate that existing raw water supplies are already fully utilized, and interbasin transfer is possible only at high costs. Current research is, therefore, intensively directed towards future wastewater reclamation systems for the area.

An interesting new approach that is being pursued is the utilization of the vast underground storage capacity of sand beds in the Cape Flats area as an evaporation-free underground reservoir.[15] This area, in view of its suitable geohydrological characteristics, ideally lends itself as a storage reservoir for reclaimed wastewater. Research has reached the stage where a 4.5 Ml/d reclamation and recovery plant is under construction to serve as a research and demonstration plant from which full-scale design criteria could be derived. Unit processes under construction are essentially similar to those of the Stander Water Reclamation Plant at Daspoort, Pretoria, with the addition of infiltration and extraction facilities (figure 6-4) and the omission of ammonia stripping.

Figure 6-4. Diagrammatic Representation of Reclamation Scheme for Storage of Purified Sewage in the Sand Beds of the Cape Flats

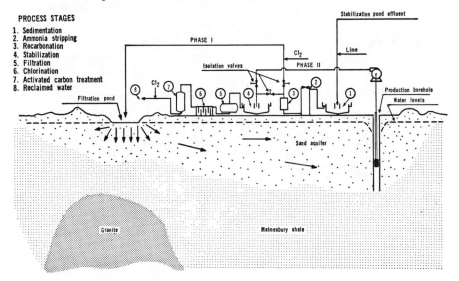

RESEARCH AND DEVELOPMENT

Research on wastewater treatment technology is centered at Pretoria under the auspices of the NIWR. Experimental facilities at the Daspoort sewage works comprise the Stander plant (4.5 Ml/d) and several pilot plants (100 kl/d), which are operated in parallel using various types of wastewater and employing various process combinations. These include biological denitrification, phosphorus removal, and integrated physical-chemical biological systems.

The Stander plant was completed towards the end of 1970 and serves as a research/demonstration facility for the determination of design and operational criteria.[16] Up to 1974 the plant was operated only on an intermittent basis, as this prototype unit necessitated extensive refinements and process modification with a view to optimization of performance and control.[17] These included automatic chemical dosing control, standby equipment, balancing facilities, active carbon regeneration, ozonation, and sludge dewatering. Since the beginning of 1975, operation of the plant has been in a semi-continuous basis, and the reclaimed secondary effluent is currently bled into an existing supply for cooling purposes (figure 6-5).

Figure 6-5.   Flow Diagram of the 4.5 Ml/d Stander Water Reclamation Plant (June 1975)

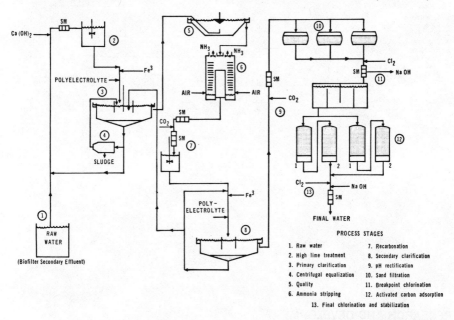

PROCESS STAGES

1. Raw water	7. Recarbonation
2. High lime treatment	8. Secondary clarification
3. Primary clarification	9. pH rectification
4. Centrifugal equalization	10. Sand filtration
5. Quality	11. Breakpoint chlorination
6. Ammonia stripping	12. Activated carbon adsorption
	13. Final chlorination and stabilization

The project is financially sponsored by the Water Research Commission, which also supports several other projects, including the Windhoek and Cape Flats water reclamation schemes. Satellite investigations involved bioassaying, epidemiology, process kinetics, and identification of residual organics. Close collaboration with the health authorities is maintained, and a ten-year water quality surveillance program has been launched.

CONCLUSIONS

Wastewater reuse forms an integral part of the overall management of the limited water supply sources in South Africa. The water balance of the country shows a serious deficit by the turn of the century, a deficit that can be made up only by exploitation of wastewater.

For direct domestic reuse, it is considered most essential that biological treatment be included as part of the process sequence and that toxic industrial effluents be separated. Balancing facilities should be provided, and ammoniacal nitrogen in particular should be maintained at a low level to insure breakpoint chlorination and disinfection control.

The current experience with the unrestricted reuse of domestic wastewaters is most encouraging, and it is with confidence that scientists and engineers are implementing several schemes in this country. It is realized that vigilant surveillance is required, not only of reclaimed wastewaters, but also of polluted surface water supplies. Public acceptance has been favorable, and collaboration with health and other state departments is maintained at all times.

NOTES

1. Gigaliter per day $= 10^9 l/d$.
2. S. P. Du Toit Viljoen, "Oorsig van die toekomstige waterbehoeftes van die Republiek van Suid-Afrika" (Paper presented at the convention, Water for the Future, Republic of South Africa, Water Year, 1970, Pretoria).
3. G. J. Stander, and A. J. Clayton, "Planning and Construction of Wastewater Reclamation Schemes as an Integral Part of Water Supply," *Journal of the Institute of Water Pollution Control* 70, no. 2 (1971): 228–34.
4. L. R. J. van Vuuren, and M. R. Henzen, "Process Selection and Cost of Advanced Wastewater Treatment in Relation to the Quality of Secondary Effluents and Quality Requirements for Various Uses" (Paper presented at the conference, Applications of New Consepts of Physical-Chemical Wastewater Treatment, Vanderbilt University, Nashville, Tennessee, September 18–22, 1972).
5. M. R. Henzen and Philip Coombs, "Reclamation of Water: The Key to Water Pollution Control" (Paper presented at a combined plenary session of the Second Rhodesian Scientific Congress, Umtali, September 5–11, 1971).
6. Val Bolitho, *Irrigation Farming—City of Johannesburg* (Report to City Engineer's Department, City of Johannesburg, 1970).
7. Stander and Clayton, "Planning and Construction."
8. Du Toit Viljoen, "Oorsig van die toekomstige waterbehoeftes."
9. M. R. Henzen and J. W. Funke, "An Appraisal of Some Significant Problems in the Reuse of Wastewater," *Journal of the Institute of Water Pollution Control* 70, no. 2 (1971): 177–86.
10. G. J. Stander and J. W. Funke, "Conservation of Water Reuse in South Africa" (Paper presented at the Symposium on Conservation of Water Reuse, part 4, Fifty-ninth Annual Meeting, American Institute of Chemical Engineers, Detroit, Mich., December 4–8, 1966; reprinted from *Chemical Engineering Progress*, Symposium Series 63, no. 78 (1967): 1–12).
11. John Voysey, personal communication.
12. A. T. Alexander, "Control of Liquid Effluent from African Explosives and Chemical Industries Ltd., Modderfontein Factory" (Paper presented at Symposium on Chemical Control of the Human Environment, Johannesburg, 1969).
13. A. J. Clayton and P. J. Pybus, "Windhoek Reclaiming Sewage for Drinking Water," *Civil Engineer, ASCE* 42, no. 9 (September 1972): 103–6.
14. L. R. J. van Vuuren, M. R. Henzen, G. J. Stander, and A. J. Clayton, "The Full-Scale Reclamation of Purified Sewage Effluent for the Augmentation of the Domestic Supplies of the City of Windhoek" (Paper presented at the Fifth International Conference on Water Pollution Research, San Francisco, July 26 to August 5, 1970, 1–32/1; 1–32/9).

15. M. R. Henzen, "Die Herwinning, Opberging en Onttrekking van Gesuiwerde Rioolwater in die Kaapse Skiereiland" (D.Sc. thesis).

16. Van Vuuren and Henzen, "Process Selection."

17. O. O. Hart, "Process Refinement in the Development of a Water Reclamation System" (Paper presented at the workshop, International Association on Water Pollution Research, Vienna, Austria, September 8–12, 1975).

CHAPTER 7

Water Reuse
in Agriculture,
Industry
and Recreation

James E. Bertram

The multiple reuse of water in Lubbock, Texas, is evolving as one solution to a growing demand for a depleting resource. Many cities in arid or semi-arid regions of the United States have considered, or will probably consider, similar courses of action in the near future.

The city of Lubbock is situated on the southern portion of the high plains of West Texas. The only noticeable variations in topography are numerous playa lakes, which are shallow depressions, varying in size from 10 to 1 square mile, and small canyons eroded by occasional surface runoff. Average annual rainfall is approximately 18 inches. Most rainfall runoff is trapped in playa lakes, where considerable surface water is lost through evaporation, averaging 73 in./yr.[1]

The high plains area of Texas has a rich agricultural economy. It has an underlying, large aquifer referred to as the Ogallala formation. Many cities, using water from the aquifer for domestic water supplies and numerous irrigated farms, are lowering the watertable from 1 to 3 ft/yr, while recharge averages only 1 in./yr or less.[2] The city of Lubbock, until 1968, took its entire water supply from the Ogallala. Recent engineering studies indicate that, based on Lubbock's estimated growth rate, peak daily domestic water demands will reach 141.3 mg/d by 1995, while maximum development of existing water sources will produce only 137.3 mg/d by 1995.[3]

RECLAIMED WATER AS A PROBLEM AND RESOURCE

Like most cities, the early history of sewage effluent disposal in Lubbock reflected a growing "problem" of what to do with the "wastewater." Early solutions in Lubbock involved large, man-made tanks near the reclamation plant.[4] By 1974, Lubbock's average daily use of potable water was 31.3 mg/d, of which an average of 16.3 mg/d, or 52 percent of the water used, flowed into the sewage treatment plants. It is estimated that the amount

---

James E. Bertram is the director of planning for the city of Lubbock, Texas.

of effluent could increase to 22 mg/d by 1990. Currently, most of the effluent is received by the southeast treatment plant (activated sludge process), which has a design capacity of 25 mg/d.

HISTORICAL REUSE APPLICATIONS

Crop Irrigation

The first change in attitude in Lubbock from effluent being "wastewater" to being a "resource" came with the decision in 1937 to irrigate cropland near the southeast reclamation plant. Frank Gray, a farmer, through a series of long-term contracts with the city, began spreading 1 to 1.5 mg/d on 200 ac.[5] By 1974, he had applied 14 to 15 mg/d to 5,000 ac (figure 7-1). Occasionally, Gray supplies water to an additional 200 ac adjacent to his farm.[6] During many times of the year, effluent ponds are formed in lower areas of the farm, where grazing cattle drink from them. In addition, Mr. Gray's domestic water supply comes from wells in the groundwater table beneath the farm. No adverse effects are known to have occurred from such ranching and domestic use.

In addition to the profits derived by Mr. Gray from his farming operation, several benefits have accrued to the city of Lubbock: (1) Nearby crop irrigation is a convenient method of disposing of the effluent while avoiding releasing water into the adjacent Yellowhouse Canyon streambed; (2) Crops remove much of the nitrogen that cannot be totally removed by percolation through the soil; and (3) The constant percolation of water through the soil has created an "artificially" recharged watertable, which has been raised to within a few feet of the surface under the Gray farm.

It is estimated that annual withdrawals of as much as 6 mg/d could be sustained for twenty years from this watertable.[7] This groundwater is reduced in biochemical oxygen demand (BOD), organic carbon, phosphorus, ammonia, virus, and bacteria and is available for reclamation as either industrial or recreational water after having undergone the equivalent of tertiary treatment.

Gray's farm consistently produces high yields of cotton, wheat, and grain sorghum and requires no additional fertilization. Production comparisons of typical crops on the Gray farm are shown in table 7-1.[8] In a long-term contract between Gray and the city of Lubbock, this water can be reclaimed and purchased for 1.5 cents/1,000 gal.

In terms of the priority of use or recommended sequence of multiple reuse, a recent research report by the Water Resource Center at Texas Technological University (Texas Tech) has recommended that "in most cases, irrigation be employed as mandatory first use."[9]

Figure 7-1. Applications of Water Reuse in Lubbock County, Texas

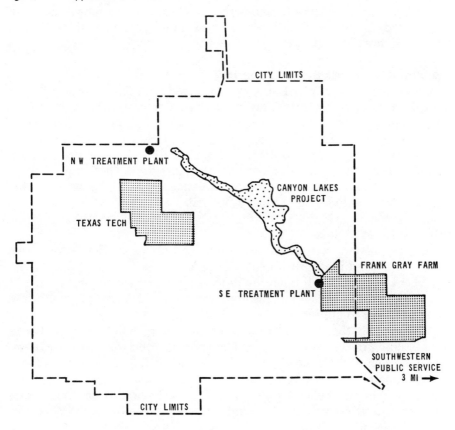

Table 7-1. Production Comparisons of Typical Crops

	Dry Land	Irrigation with Water from Ogallala	Irrigation with Effluent Without Fertilizing
Grain sorghum*	800–1,000	4,000–5,000	6,500
Wheat+	10–12	30–40	80
Lint cotton*	150–225	600–800	1,250

*lb.
+bu.

Texas Tech

In terms of historical sequence, Texas Tech was the second user and began receiving all of the effluent from Lubbock's northwest treatment plant in 1965. Currently, this water (1 mg/d) is used exclusively to irrigate farmland on the Tech campus. Long-range planning is under way to consider recharge of the watertable under the Tech campus for future domestic reuse and also to water turf areas of the campus entirely with reclaimed water (figure 7-1).

Southwestern Public Service Company

In May 1968, the city of Lubbock contracted with Southwestern Public Service Company (an electric utility) to provide treated effluent to be used as cooling water at the generating plant, southeast of the city. Southwestern Public Service could initially take 3.5 mg/d with two options to increase to 7.7 mg/d in June 1977, and ultimately to 12.35 mg/d by June 1986.[10] The water is piped directly to the electric production plant after secondary treatment at the southeast treatment plant. The water is purchased from Mr. Gray at 1 cent/1,000 gal.

Canyon Lakes Project

The most distinctive topographic feature in Lubbock is the Yellowhouse Canyon, extending approximately eight miles from northwest to southeast Lubbock (figure 7-1). It ranges in depth from 40 feet at the northern end to approximately 75 feet at the southern end; and in width from a few hundred feet to approximately one-half mile.[11]

Historically the canyon had become an eyesore, being used for dumping building debris, junk yards, caliche mining, wrecking yards, and even a sanitary landfill for the city of Lubbock. In 1967, during the City Planning Department's update of the Lubbock Land Use Plan, it was recommended that the Yellowhouse Canyon be reclaimed as an open space greenbelt and used to store reclaimed water in a series of recreational lakes. The Santee, California, project was used as an example of recreational applications of reclaimed water. Through a series of reports and a color slide presentation, numerous civic clubs and interested citizens were exposed to the proposal. Widespread acceptance of the proposal resulted in the project becoming the primary recreational goal in "Lubbock's Goals for the Seventies." Numerous citizens and civic clubs requested that the city council pursue an investigation of the project.

In 1968, the engineering firm of Freese, Nichols, and Endress was commissioned to complete a feasibility study on the project. In November 1969, the feasibility report concluded that "there is enough water available to support the proposed lakes and that, with proper monitoring and control, they can be kept safe and attractive for public use."[12] Conclusions of the report, relating to the first six lakes, include the following: (1) make-up water should be obtained from wells beneath the Frank Gray farm; (2) lakes 1 through 6 would be suitable for secondary contact activities; (3) concentrations of plant nutrients in the lakes would be substantial, and while algae and aquatic weeds could be expected, they could be adequately controlled; (4) all surface drainage from cattle feed lots would have to be abated; (5) induced aeration of the water should be employed: and (6) a continual water quality monitoring program should be established. The estimated capital cost of the first six lakes was set at $6,063,100.

Following a massive tornado on May 11, 1970, that damaged over seven square miles in the central and northeastern sectors of the city, a tornado-recovery bond election was held. It included $2.8 million for the Canyon Lakes project, which was approved by an approximate margin of 2 to 1. Subsequently, in 1971, $3.4 million from the State Parks and Wildlife Department and the BOR and $832,828 from the Department of Housing and Urban Development were tentatively committed to the project. BOR funding was conditional upon the water meeting state water quality standards. This requirement initiated a second report on make-up water by the firm of Freese and Nichols.[13] After investigating three alternatives—well water from beneath the Gray farm, effluent from the activated sludge plant, and in-plant, tertiary treatment of effluent—the report concluded that groundwater from the Gray farm should be used. By cost comparison, it was estimated that annual operations costs for 5 mg/d would be $229,000 (12.55 cents/1,000 gal.) for groundwater, $425,900 (23.33 cents/1,000 gal.) for activated sludge effluent, and $854,400 (46.81 cents/1,000 gal.) for in-plant tertiary treatment. The report concluded that groundwater is superior to other alternatives and that it is relatively free of virus and bacteria. A subsequent report by the Water Resource Center at Texas Tech supported the conclusions about virus and bacteria control; however, it raised concern over urban storm runoff that would be "considerably poorer in quality than treated domestic sewage."[14] The Water Resource Center is currently under contract to the city as the project's "water quality monitoring agent." Water quality monitoring equipment is being constructed with the Canyon Lakes dams, and an active program is under way to clean up the urban watershed. In the initial phase of the project, four lakes of an eventual eight-lake system will be constructed. Rainfall will fill the lakes and approximately 4 mg/d of reclaimed water will be used to offset evaporation and percolation.

To date, all of the necessary land for the project (555.29 acres) has been purchased, and when combined with existing local and state parks along the canyon, creates a 1,350-acre continuous greenbelt through the city. In 1973, the City Parks Department acquired a bulldozer, front-end loader, maintainer, and three dump trucks with general revenue-sharing funds and initiated a concentrated cleanup of the canyon. Clark Equipment Company, a local manufacturing firm, has donated large earth scrapers to be tested in excavation of lake areas. The transformation in the canyon has been remarkable. Four dams have been built and approximately nineteen acres of park development have been completed. Future plans include over twelve miles of bicycle trails, picnicking areas, and various forms of water recreation. Initially all water sports in the four lakes will be limited to secondary contact; however, future monitoring and testing of the water may allow primary contact.

FUTURE WATER REUSE APPLICATIONS

Future application are uncertain. In all probability they will consist of variations of existing agricultural, public use, industrial, or recreational applications. Because of Lubbock's limited sources of new domestic water, multiple reuse of water will continue to be a necessity, rather than a discretionary alternative.

The Lubbock experience seems to be a fulfillment of a forward-looking prediction in an early publication on water reuse of 1965: "Re-use of water through many cycles will be routine practice in fifty years."[15]

NOTES

1. Freese, Nichols, and Endress, Consulting Engineers, *Feasibility Report on the Canyon Lakes Project* (Lubbock, Tex., 1969).
2. R. M. Sweazy and G. A. Whetstone, "Case History of Effluent Reuse at Lubbock, Texas" (Paper presented at Spray Irrigation Seminar, Harrison Hot Springs, British Columbia, April 1975).
3. Freese, Nichols, and Endress, Consulting Engineers, *Report on Makeup Water for the Upper Canyon Lakes* (Lubbock, Tex., 1971).
4. City of Lubbock Planning Department, "Methods of Storing and Using Renovated Waste Water for Lubbock, Texas," *An Expanding Lubbock ... Reclaimed Water for a Growing City* (Lubbock, Tex.: April 1968).
5. Sweazy and Whetstone, "Lubbock, Texas."
6. R. M. Sweazy, "Multiple Reuse of Municipal Wastewater" (Paper presented to An International Symposium—Frontiers of the Semi-Arid World, International Center for Arid and Semi-Arid Land Studies, October 1974).
7. Freese, Nichols, and Endress, Consulting Engineers *Canyon Lakes Project.*
8. Sweazy and Whetstone, "Lubbock, Texas."
9. Sweazy, "Multiple Reuse of Municipal Wastewater."
10. Freese, Nichols, and Endress, Consulting Engineers, *Canyon Lakes Project.*
11. Marcia Headstream et al., "The Canyon Lakes Project," *Journal of the American Water Works Association* 67, no. 3 (March 1975): 125-27.
12. Freese, Nichols, and Endress, Consulting Engineers, *Canyon Lakes Project.*
13. Freese and Nichols, Consulting Engineers, *Recommended Plan of Action for Development of Additional Surface Water Supply for Lubbock, Texas* (Fort Worth, Tex., 1975).
14. G. B. Thompson, et al., *Variation of Urban Runoff Quality and Quantity with Duration and Intensity of Storms—Phase III,* Office of Water Resources Research, Department of the Interior, Washington, D.C., August 1974.
15. G. A. Whetstone, *Re-use of Effluent in the Future with an Annotated Bibliography,* Texas Water Development Board Report 8, Austin, Tex., 1965.

CHAPTER 8

The Experience/Evaluation   Neil M. Cline
of Water Reuse
in Orange County,
California

Orange County, California, is a growing metropolitan area of about 1.7 million persons, situated in the near-desert area along the Southern California coastline. Twenty-five years ago the county was devoted to citrus and row-crop farming; however, since the end of World War II there has been a steady displacement of agriculture by urban development. This transformation has taken place at a rapid rate, with population increases averaging 8 percent per year.

The county receives about thirteen inches of rainfall annually. Natural flows of the Santa Ana River and its tributary creeks combine with local precipitation to provide about 25 percent of current water demand.

Orange County's greatest natural resource, the underground water supply, was used by early settlers to supplement surface flows of the Santa Ana River. As the area gradually became an important agricultural center, the increased demand upon subsurface water by the county's many wells resulted in gradual lowering of the watertable. To supplement local supplies, in 1928 the cities of Santa Ana, Anaheim, and Fullerton joined ten other communities from neighboring counties to form the MWD to import Colorado River water. The Colorado River aqueduct, built by MWD in the 1930s, is 242 miles long and sized to provide over a million acre-feet annually to the arid coastal region of Southern California. In the late 1940s it was apparent to water planners in Southern California that additional water supplies would be required, resulting in a cooperative program with the State of California Department of Water Resources to develop the most ambitious water system devised in the West to transport high-quality surplus Northern California water to the south, a distance of over 450 miles. The system, sized to supply over 2 million acre-feet, was completed in the early 1970s, and initial water deliveries from Northern California arrived in Orange County in 1973.

As the economic boom of the late 1940s got under way, it became necessary to use groundwater reserves to meet the rapidly growing water requirements in quantities that exceeded the natural recharge. The over-

Neil M. Cline is the secretary-manager for the Orange County Water District, Fountain Valley, California.

draft condition occurred during a period of relatively light precipitation, which led to serious drawdown of water levels in the local basin. By November 1956 the watertable was at or below sea level in about 85 percent of the area, resulting in seawater intrusion of the coastal aquifer. In 1949, the Orange County Water District, or OCWD, formed by an act of the California legislature in 1933 to protect and manage Orange County's massive groundwater basin, began importing vast quantities of Colorado River water for groundwater recharge. Since then the district has purchased more than 2.2 million acre-feet of Colorado River water for groundwater replenishment. High-quality Northern California State Project water deliveries for groundwater replenishment began in 1973.

There are indications that the rapid growth of the past two decades will not continue; however, the best estimates of local urban planners are that by 1980 there will be 1.8 million persons in the county and over 2 million from 1985 to 1990. The ultimate density of the county is subject to debate, but it is considered prudent practice for utility suppliers to prepare for increased demands in Southern California, particularly in Orange County. There are a number of factors that contribute to present growth pressures, including the lure of a pleasant climate, employment opportunities, and migration from older urban areas in Los Angeles County and elsewhere to newer, less uncertain communities in Orange County. (Figure 8-1 shows the location of the OCWD.)

WATER SUPPLY AND DEMAND

Current water requirements in the district exceed 400,000 ac-ft/yr. Traditionally this demand has been met by a combination of local and imported water systems. It has become apparent, however, that to prepare for future water supply requirements, another solution to Orange County's water deficiencies is necessary. Imported water supply has never been politically popular, and the difficulty is compounded as fuel costs for energy necessary to pump water from distant watersheds escalate. Southern California's allotment from the Colorado River system will be reduced 50 percent in 1985, when the Central Arizona Project is anticipated to begin deliveries from the river to the Phoenix area. Surplus water available from Northern California is a function of future demands and development of the northern part of the state and, as has been emphasized by the recent drought, there are questions concerning the amount of water in the north available to Southern California. It is increasingly apparent that the water requirements of Southern California will be extended through increased water conservation and wastewater reclamation programs. Within the

Figure 8-1. Orange County Water District

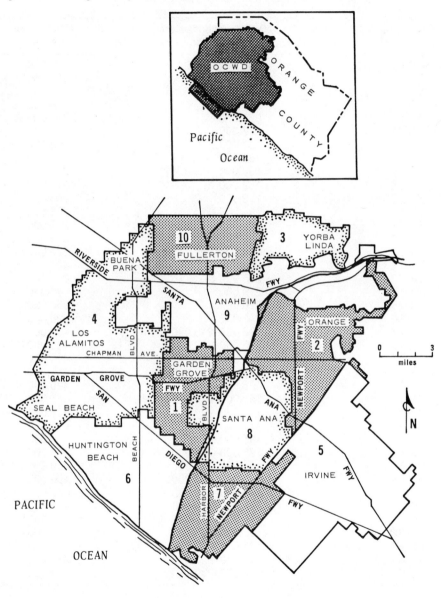

boundaries of the OCWD, anticipated ultimate requirement of 500,000 ac-ft/yr will be composed both of desalted water and of local, imported, and reclaimed sources. (See table 8-1 for a summary of the anticipated water requirements.)

Table 8-1. Summary, Anticipated Water Requirements (ac-ft)

Fiscal Year (July–June)	OCWD Groundwater Extraction	OCWD Total Water Use*
1956–57	186,000	232,000
57–58	160,000	197,000
58–59	209,000	264,000
59–60	207,000	266,000
60–61	226,000	308,000
61–62	177,000	249,000
62–63	186,000	275,000
63–64	189,000	290,000
64–65	180,000	282,000
65–66	182,000	271,000
66–67	169,000	263,000
67–68	194,000	278,000
68–69	179,000	273,000
69–70	195,000	316,000
70–71	204,000	325,000
71–72	229,000	367,000
72–73	215,000	329,000
73–74	219,000	346,000
74–75	226,000	350,000
75–76	245,000	396,000
76–77	195,000–245,000	400,000
77–78	195,000–240,000	405,000
78–79	195,000–235,000	410,000
79–80	195,000–230,000	415,000
80–81	195,000–225,000	420,000
81–82	195,000–220,000	425,000
82–83	195,000–220,000	430,000
83–84	195,000–220,000	435,000
84–85	195,000–220,000	440,000
85–86	195,000–220,000	445,000
86–87	195,000–220,000	450,000
87–88	195,000–220,000	455,000
88–89	195,000–220,000	460,000
89–90	195,000–220,000	465,000
90–91	195,000–220,000	470,000
91–92	195,000–220,000	475,000
92–93	195,000–220,000	480,000
93–94	195,000–220,000	485,000
94–95	195,000–220,000	490,000

*Does not include water purchased for groundwater replenishment.

LOCAL WATER SUPPLY: GROUNDWATER BASIN

The Orange County groundwater basin, which underlies the area of the OCWD, is the depositional plain of the Santa Ana River. The major features of the region are surrounding hills and mountains and a broad, gradually sloping alluvial plain with alternating gaps and small hill systems along the coast. A major fault zone that effectively seals the basin from the sea at deeper levels generally parallels the coastline; however, in several gaps along the ocean front there is free access between seawater and groundwater in the top 150–200 feet of recent alluvial fill. Figure 8-2 is a general cross-section of the groundwater basin. At the center of the basin it is over 4,000 feet to the base of the fresh water complex. The fresh water base rises to an elevation of 200 feet along the coast and in the Santa Ana River canyon area.

Figure 8-2.   Cross-section of Orange County Groundwater Basin

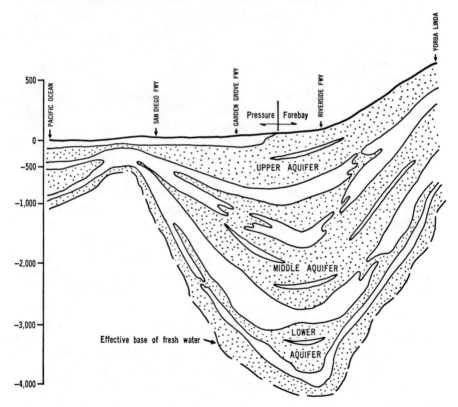

In general, there are three principal aquifer systems in the basin. The upper aquifer system extends to a depth of 1,300 feet; the middle system ranges from 1,300 to 2,600 feet deep; and the lower system, from 2,600 to 4,000 feet. The lower aquifer contains water of 1,000 parts per million (ppm) TDS, probably due to ocean water incursions during deposition.

The middle zone averages 100 to 200 ppm TDS, characterized by light organic stain. Less than 15 percent of basin water is produced from this aquifer. Water quality of the upper zone ranges from 1,000 to 200 ppm TDS. The variation is a result of access to surface percolation and subsequent reflection of the activities of man. It is presumed that water generally has free access to all aquifer systems in the forebay portion of the basin, while downstream the basin is capped by a clay zone forming a pressure area. Eighty-five percent of production in the district is from wells drilled into the upper aquifer system. There are 1,500 wells currently in operation in the district, with installed pumping capacity of about 400,000 ac-ft/yr.

Recharge of groundwater is accomplished through percolation in the forebay and, in more recent times, from injection wells in the pressure area along the coast. The OCWD has acquired over 850 acres of the Santa Ana River bed, and an additional 285 acres of off-channel property in the forebay area to percolate the natural flows of the river and the surplus replenishment water available from the Colorado River or Northern California. (Table 8-2 is a summary of imported water purchases for groundwater replenishment.)

In 1969, following thirty-six years of court action, the over 100 public agencies involved agreed to a stipulated judgment of equitable distribution of Santa Ana River water, guaranteeing Orange County 42,000 acre-feet of water in addition to all storm flows of the river. The combined waters on a long-term average will provide 100,000 acre-feet.

Within the boundaries of the OCWD, anyone has the right to drill a well and pump an amount of water necessary to furnish an adequate supply consistent with the doctrine of "beneficial use." A new industry or resident has this privilege on the same basis as a long-established firm or resident. Those that produce groundwater are required to report the amount of water extracted and to pay an assessment tax on each acre-foot produced. Moneys collected are used to purchase supplemental replenishment water to assure a continuing supply of groundwater.

To manage effectively the groundwater reserves, the OCWD has the authority generally to regulate the amount of water pumped from the subsurface. The district annually considers the amount of water in groundwater storage, the availability of both replenishment and direct service water through the import systems, and the many problems of distribution and water supply availability. The district then establishes a groundwater production percentage that permits maximum utilization of groundwater storage without the danger of overdrafting the basin. In its present procedure, the district has been able to set the percentage at 60 percent groundwater and 40 percent to be taken from direct service sources. Many purveyors cannot or do not choose to meet the 60:40 ratio. In these cases an assessment is levied against the overpumping, and the money collected

Table 8-2. Imported Water Purchased from MWD for Groundwater Recharge

Fiscal Year July 1– June 30	Imported Water Purchased		MWD Replenishment Rate		
	Colorado River Water (ac-ft)	N. Calif. State Project Water (ac-ft)	Colorado River Water ($/ac-ft)	N. Calif. State Project Water ($/ac-ft)	Total Annual Cost
1949–50	22,725.6		$ 8.00		$ 181,805
50–51	22,183.1		10.00		221,831
51–52	39,177.4		10.00		391,774
52–53	27,956.1		10.00		279,561
53–54	50,000.0		10.00		500.000
54–55	67,789.1		9.17		621,626
55–56	20,915.9		10.00		209,159
56–57	82,954.8		10.00		829,548
57–58	77,144.8		12.00		925,738
58–59	81,710.0		12.00		980,520
59–60	144,471.4		12.00		1,733,657
60–61	165,117.8		12.38		2,044,158
61–62	174,915.8		13.12		2,294,895
62–63	234,789.3		13.83		3,247,136
63–64	185,438.9		14.63		2,712,971
64–65	132,366.7		15.25		2,018,592
65–66	116,819.7		16.00		1,869,115
66–67	114,421.7		17.00		1,945,169
67–68	92,451.5		18.00		1,664,127
68–69	53,373.2		19.00		1,014,091
69–70	85,664.1		20.00		1,713,282
70–71	56,385.6		22.00		1,240,483
71–72	35,325.2		24.00		847,805
72–73	53,763.9	4,142.0	27.00	$32.00	1,584,169
73–74	49,405.3	42,795.2	30.00	40.00	3,161,047
74–75	52,632.6	46,159.9	30.00	36.45*	3,261,417
75–76	14,906.1	73,218.6	32.00	42.00	3,548,920
76–77**	15,000.0	16,000.0	36.00	42.00	1,212,000
Total	2,269,805.6	182,315.7			$42,254,596

*The cost for state project water was $40/ac-ft through September 30, 1974, reduced to $30/ac-ft for the remainder of the fiscal year. The rates for 1966–77 are $41/ac-ft for both Colorado River water and state project water.
**Approximate.

is distributed to agencies that, at the request of the district, take more than 40 percent of their requirement. Because of the generally fixed supply of Santa Ana River water and the limited power supply to move surplus water in the import systems, the long-range operations of the district anticipate that the basin production percentage will ultimately be established at 50 percent.

IMPORTED WATER SUPPLY

The MWD of Southern California, formed in 1932 to import water to the south coastal plain, has constructed the Colorado River aqueduct and an extensive distribution system within Southern California. The MWD is comprised of twenty-six municipalities or municipal water districts. There are five member agencies of MWD within the boundaries of the OCWD. Local water purveyors within the district take water either from the underground basin or from the MWD service distribution facilities. In 1959 MWD contracted with the state of California for additional water to be imported from Northern California. MWD's entitlement Colorado River water is approximately 500,000 ac-ft/yr, and the state contract with MWD calls for 2 million ac-ft. In the event of a water shortage, Orange County is entitled to approximately 20 percent of the MWD supply. (Table 8-3 is a summary of historic imported water deliveries in the OCWD for direct delivery.)

RECLAIMED WASTEWATER

Over 200,000 acre-feet of wastewater is discharged into the Pacific Ocean through the outfall sewer systems of Orange County. This municipal and industrial runoff for the most part has relatively low TDS and is available with the proper treatment for reapplication in the municipal water supply system. Wastewater properly reclaimed, monitored, and percolated in recharge areas of water basins is not a threat to public health, and with proper dilution or demineralization, wastewater is a reasonable supplemental supply.

In Orange County the wastewater salvage systems are divided into distinct categories between forebay and pressure area. Wastewater that can be intercepted and treated in the forebay has the advantage of being spread in aerobic environs, providing some treatment and, therefore, slightly lowering the cost to handle. The waters intercepted in the pressure zone are all downstream from industry and municipal users and are placed in an anaerobic condition. The water, therefore, requires additional treatment with attendant increases in cost.

Reclamation of wastewater to be applied in the forebay of the OCWD will involve processing 10,000 to 15,000 acre-feet of domestic wastewater, using conventional primary and activated sludge secondary treatment units. Tertiary treatment by chemical clarification, recarbonation, filtration, and carbon adsorption will produce water that is extremely low in suspended solids, free from virus and pathogenic bacteria and from traces

Table 8-3. Summary, Historic Imported Water Deliveries for Direct Delivery

Water Year (Oct.-Sept.)	Imported Delivery (ac-ft)
1976–77	160,000*
75–76	153,000
74–75	125,000
73–74	103,000
72–73	110,000
71–72	151,000
70–71	139,000
69–70	135,000
68–69	110,000
67–68	102,000
66–67	95,000
65–66	91,000
64–65	103,000
63–64	101,000
62–63	86,000
61–62	72,000
60–61	82,000
59–60	59,000
58–59	55,000
57–58	36,000
56–57	46,000
55–56	23,000
54–55	27,000
53–54	22,000
52–53	19,000
51–52	18,000
50–51	15,000
49–50	13,000
48–49	13,000

NOTE: The summary is applicable to agricultural, municipal, and industrial use.
*Estimated.

of heavy metals. Discharge requirements will be established to conform to drinking water standards. Depending upon the base quality of the municipal supply in the forebay area, it may be necessary to add demineralization processes to the forebay reclamation project. These facilities are scheduled for the early 1980s.

In the pressure zone of Orange County, historic overdraft has resulted in seawater encroachment in the coastal aquifers. Large-scale aquifer deterioration has been forestalled by the district's recharge activities; however, the threat of seawater contamination limits the flexibility of the groundwater reservoir. To prevent any further intrusion, the district operates a hydraulic barrier system consisting of injection and extraction wells. Seven extraction wells intercept brackish water and return it to the sea. A series of twenty-three injection wells capable of handling 30 mg/d, or 30,000 ac-ft/yr, are located about four miles inland, where water is placed in the top aquifers to prevent seawater movement. About 5 percent of the injected water is estimated to flow seaward, with the balance of the flow recharging the coastal groundwater supplies of local cities.

Water for the injection scheme is produced from Water Factory 21, the district's unique water treatment facility: an advanced wastewater reclamation plant that treats 15 mg/d of trickling filter effluent from the county sanitation districts of Orange County. The process includes lime clarification, ammonia stripping, recarbonation, filtration, carbon adsorption, and chlorination. Thirty percent of the treated wastewater is then processed through a reverse osmosis demineralization plant that removes 90 percent of the dissolved mineral load. The demineralized water is subsequently blended with the remaining AWT product water and mixed with varying amounts of deep-zone groundwater to attain an average quality of 550 ppm TDS for injection and indirect reuse. Water Factory 21 is capable of producing 15,000 ac-ft/yr of reusable water. Table 8-4 is a summary of the quality of water produced by Water Factory 21. It is anticipated that when increased amounts of Northern California water are utilized in the county, the TDS concentration will be significantly reduced, permitting expanded reuse of reconstituted waste flows.

Within a five-mile radius of Water Factory 21, over thirty potential users of reclaimed water for irrigation of parks, golf courses, cemeteries, and greenbelts have been identified. Present plans call for the construction of an additional treatment facility and a distribution system to provide reclaimed water for ornamental purposes by 1979. The activated sludge effluent from the county's sanitation district will be filtered and chlorinated prior to distribution. The reclaimed irrigation supply will be limited to the district's pressure zone to prevent excessive salt concentration in the groundwater supply. It is estimated that 5,000 acre-feet of water will be reclaimed for these purposes.

In addition to the OCWD reclamation projects, one of the member agencies within the district's boundaries, in the Irvine Ranch area, is developing extensive reuse systems to offset its anticipated increased demands.

WATER COSTS

Water costs in Southern California continue to escalate, reflecting the total vulnerability of the costs of supply on the increasing expenses of energy.

Table 8-4. Water Quality Comparisons, Water Factory 21

Constituent	Units	OCWD Effluent	WF-21 Product Water	Regulatory Limits
Minerals				
Ammonia-nitrogen	mg/l	43.0	0.6000	1.000
Total nitrogen	mg/l	50.0	1.5000	10.000
Boron	mg/l	1.0	0.4000	0.500
Calcium	mg/l	104.0	42.0000	
Chloride	mg/l	229.0	120.0000	120.000
COD[a]	mg/l	107.0	10.0000	30.000
Electrical conductivity	umho	1,843.0	787.0000	900.000
Fluoride	mg/l		0.7000	0.800
Magnesium	mg/l	25.0		
pH	mg/l	7.7	7.8000	6.5–8.0
Phosphate	mg/l	5.2		
Sodium	mg/l	207.0	110.0000	110.000
Sulphate	mg/l	291.0	79.0000	125.000
Total hardness	mg/l		126.0000	220.000
MBAS	mg/l		0.0460	0.500
Phenol	mg/l		<0.0002	1.000
Cyanide	mg/l		0.0030	0.200
Physical characteristics				
Color	units		19.0	
Turbidity[b]	JTU	24	0.4	1.0
Coliform	MPN/100ml		0.0	
Heavy metals				
Arsenic	mg/l	0.0020	0.0010	0.050
Barium	mg/l	.0820	.0100	1.000
Cadmium	mg/l	.0090	.0004	0.010
Chromium	mg/l	.2040	.0080	0.050
Copper	mg/l	.2910	.0020	1.000
Iron	mg/l	.1900	.0050	0.300
Lead	mg/l	.0360	.0060	0.050
Manganese	mg/l	.0380	.0070	0.050
Mercury	mg/l	.0004	.0030	0.005
Selenium	mg/l	.0070	.0010	0.010
Silver	mg/l	0.0040	0.0010	0.050

[a]Limit applied only to carbon column effluent.
[b]Limit applied only to filter effluent.

All water distributed in Orange County is pumped either from the ground or from great distances east or north. There are estimates that Southern California water will cost $300/ac-ft by 1990. Because of the uncertainty involved in attempting to predict local, national, and global economy, the OCWD currently bases its long-range cost figures for advanced planning purposes on the energy necessary to furnish water supply. (Comparisons of energy requirements are shown on table 8-5.)

Table 8-5. Energy Requirements for Orange County Water Supply

Source	Quality ppm TDS	Energy Cost kwh/ac-ft
Colorado River	750	2,100
Groundwater*	500	2,900
Water factory 21	680	3,000
State water project	300	3,320

*Adjusted to account for artificial recharge energy costs.

CONCLUSION

The future availability of imported supply from the north or from the Colorado River is always subject to curtailment in periods of drought. Considering the vagaries of politics and weather and the international energy supply crisis, wastewater reuse appears to hold the most promise for assuring an adequate quantity of water to satisfy future increased demands in Orange County.

Table 8-6. OCWD Anticipated Water Supply

Source	ac-ft/yr
MWD replenishment	120,000
Santa Ana River	100,000
Wastewater injection	10,000
Wastewater irrigation	10,000
Wastewater recharge (forebay)	10,000
Total	250,000

By utilizing the groundwater conjunctively with imported direct delivery systems and by providing wastewater reclamation and reuse systems along with conservation measures, it is anticipated that Orange County will continue to be able to meet the water requirements of its citizens. Assuming a total ultimate demand 500,000 ac-ft/yr for the OCWD, it is anticipated that the groundwater basin will supply 250,000 acre-feet. (Table 8-6 is a summary of anticipated supply.)

CHAPTER 9

Opportunities and Constraints in the Reuse of Wastewater

Donald E. Matschke

This report will cover reuse in all its broad spectrums via perspectives developed in the Chicago-South End Lake Michigan (C-SELM) Wastewater Management Study conducted by the Chicago District, U.S. Army Corps of Engineers, with the assistance of Bauer Engineering, Inc. Reuse will be discussed in context of the resulting C-SELM work products along the outline of table 9-1, highlighting opportunities for reuse and also the possible reuse constraints in the following areas: potable supplies, recreation, aquaculture-maraculture, navigation, irrigation, energy dissipation, industrial and industrial-municipal reuse.

The C-SELM study addresses regional solutions of wastewater-related problems in northeastern Illinois and northwestern Indiana. The region encompasses over 2,600 square miles of area and includes watersheds of four major river systems (figure 9-1.) Politically, the C-SELM study has impact on seven counties located within the two states and also affects a host of other agencies with political powers. Demographically, it has impact on a currently projected population of 11 million by 2020. It envisions this population living in densely populated urban centers, suburban areas with lesser density, and loosely populated rural areas. Technically, it involves the study and possible implementation of a number of types of water reuse.

POTABLE SUPPLIES

The necessity of an adequate potable water supply for satisfying all the needs of a community is self-evident. Potable water should be of reasonable temperature and free from turbidity, color, odor, and any objectionable taste. There is also a more exacting set of quality specifications that quantitatively define potable water quality in terms of chemical and biological constituents. Such water is termed *potable* or *drinkable*, meaning

Dr. Donald E. Matschke is president of the D. E. Matschke Company, Hinsdale, Illinois. The company is an engineering consulting firm.

Table 9-1. Reuse of Wastewater

Possible Reuse Opportunities	Possible Reuse Constraints
Potable Supplement existing supplies	TDS, pathogens, carcinogens Cost of redistribution User Apprehension
Recreation Maintain required flow for fishery and partial or full body contact recreation	Control nutrients to minimize eutrophic potential Observe channel erosion limits Cost of redistribution
Aquaculture-maraculture Supply growth medium for food for aquaculture or maraculture to produce a fish, shellfish, or crayfish crop	Pathogens, Carcinogens, and accumulation of potentially toxic materials such as heavy metals
Navigation Maintain adequate depths for boat passage Provide lockage flows	Cost of redistribution
Irrigation Supply optimum amount of water for crop growth Supply vehicle and source for crop fertilizer	Land ownership Cost of conveyance distribution and possible drainage systems Likely restrictions to nondirect food chain crops
Energy dissipation Provide cooling for power generation facilities Provide commercial or industrial cooling water Provide warming for agricultural soils	Increased evaporative loss Storage lagoon size related to cooling load Increased TDS concentration
Industrial Utilize partially treated internal wastewater to ful- fill fresh water require- ments, thus conserving avail- able supplies Minimize treatment costs	Increased concentrations of refractory and TDS constituents
Industrial-municipal Utilize municipal sewage treatment plant effluent for supply of industrial process and cooling water	Observe industrial process water quality requirements Increased TDS concentration

Figure 9-1.   C-SELM Wastewater Management Study Area

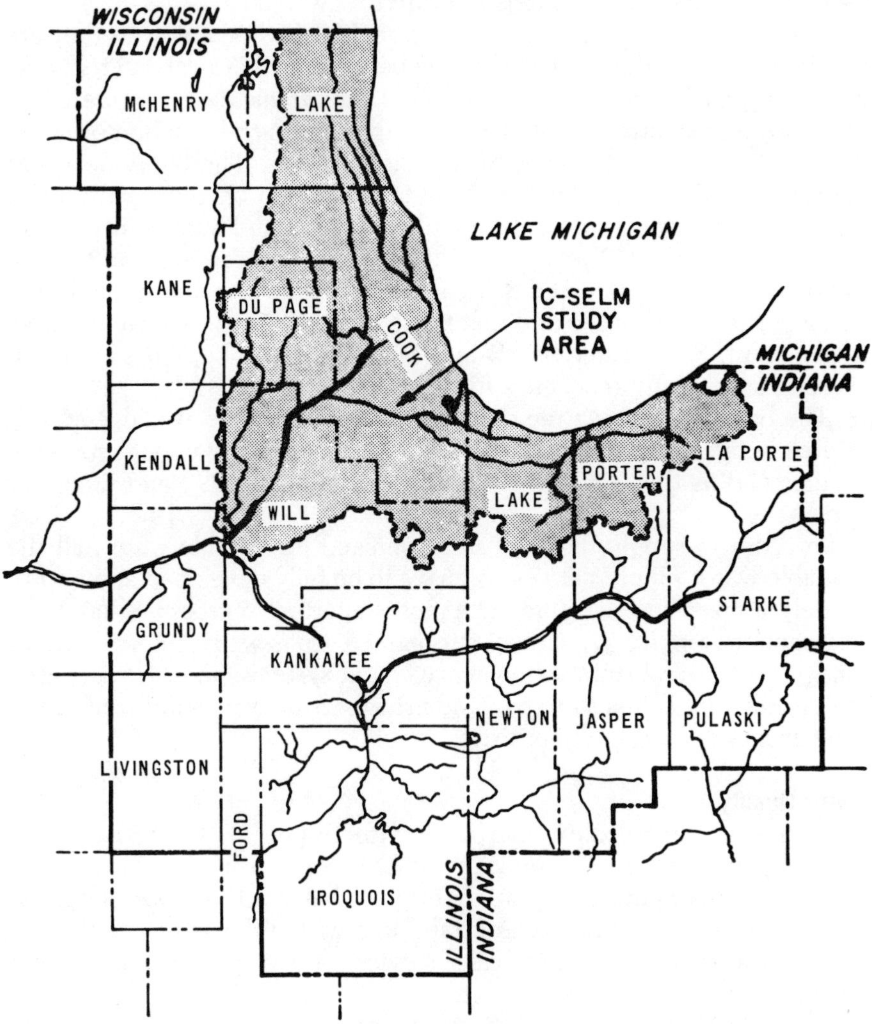

that it may be consumed in any desired amount without concern for adverse effect on health. Long-range plans for any community must by necessity include planning for the supply of this high-quality potable water resource at a reasonable price.

Supplementing Existing Supplies

Long-range plans of communities within the C-SELM study area recognize this need and outline possible future sources of supply. The sources are: groundwater, Lake Michigan water, renovated stormwater runoff, and renovated municipal and industrial (M&I) flows.

Groundwater supplies are not being replenished as rapidly as they are being drawn down, and the difference between withdrawal and recharge is growing each year. Probably the most important reuse consideration, however, is the current United States Supreme Court limitation on withdrawals from Lake Michigan by Illinois residents. The Supreme Court limitation of 3200 cfs places a definite restriction on the quantities of water available to the densely populated urban and suburban areas of northeastern Illinois. The state of Illinois, however, can petition to have the diversion limit increased if it can show that all available supplies are being prudently managed and that the inadequacy of the available supply is imminent. Stormwater runoff and M&I flows can be, but are not, at present, sufficiently renovated for potable reuse.

The balance between the demand for water and the available supply is already upset in some parts of C-SELM region and will become more pronounced as the C-SELM design target dates of 1990 and 2020 are approached.

In order to supply the increasing demand for potable water, all the available water supply sources will have to be fully developed and appropriately utilized in the future. The most important sources are: (a) Lake Michigan water, (b) groundwater obtained from wells, (c) stormwater renovated via rural stormwater management systems, and (d) renovated M & I flows, including suburban and urban stormwater runoff from treatment plants or land treatment sites.

Water Quality

TDS. A water quality constraint with respect to the reuse of reclaimed flows for potable supplies is the TDS concentration, which differs in each source of potable supply. In order to balance the TDS concentration, a mix of flow supplies was established within the service area. The purpose was to balance the C-SELM service areas with respect to potable reuse TDS concentrations.

The present TDS concentration in Lake Michigan is approximately 160 mg/l. Regional C-SELM AWT reclaimed water projected TDS concentrations are in a range between 500 and 535 mg/l, depending on the treatment technology in question. Rural C-SELM stormwater and groundwater concentrations are projected to be 130 mg/l.

Standards for drinking water quality, as established by the 1961 revision of the Public Health Service Drinking Water Standards, list a recommended maximum limit for TDS at 500 mg/l. WHO sets the potable limit for TDS at 750 mg/l. Many areas in the western parts of the United States have 1,000 to 3,000 mg/l of TDS in their potable supplies. A threshold concentration (a value that might normally not be deleterious to fish and other aquatic life) of 2,000 mg/l TDS has been established as an upper bound for healthy aquatic life in fresh water.

It is evident that a great deal of difference exists between the present TDS in Lake Michigan and the higher levels of TDS considered acceptable. Nevertheless, if the total quantity of dissolved solids discharged into Lake Michigan per year remains as at present, and the management of flows into and out of the lake also remains unchanged, a steady rise in the TDS concentration in the water in the lake can be projected, so that a concentration of 500 mg/l could be reached in several hundred years.

There are ways in which such an inevitable rise in TDS could be mitigated. Lakes Michigan and Huron, for example, are near all-time-high elevations, making substantial lowerings desirable. If *all* discharges into, for example, lower Lake Michigan could be avoided during these wet periods, some reduction in maximum lake level could be achieved, and the average rate of increase in TDS could be substantially reduced.

During periods of low lake level, on the other hand, it would be desirable to return treated flows to the lake to mitigate the unwanted effects of low lake level. A return of 3,000 mg/d to the lake for ten years could add a volume equivalent to one foot of depth over the approximately 50,000 square miles of Lakes Michigan and Huron. This foot of depth could be useful and beneficial during such dry periods.

Toxic Materials.   Phenol is an example of a potentially toxic ingredient in drinking water. The safe level of phenol concentration in potable water supplies is typical of the water quality questions that arise from time to time. The best knowledge that is available in the literature pertains to a 0.001 mg/l phenol concentration that is based on nuisance, taste, and odor, not on human health criteria. If one asked a public health official for a safe level for human consumption, he might answer 0.1 mg/l. The present writer has made an intensive search for the basis upon which 0.1 mg/l phenol concentration in water is held to be safe. The only studies uncovered to date demonstrate the adequacy of this limit for fish life.

The answer to the question, What is the safe concentration for human consumption of phenol or many other potentially toxic materials? is just not available because investigators have not yet, or are only beginning to, ask and attempt to answer the vital questions.

Distribution

Another important constraint is distribution. The trend today is to regionalize, to abandon smaller treatment plants and go to fewer and larger plants with more advanced technologies further removed from the tributary population. If reuse of this reclaimed water is desired for potable or other uses, regionalization poses an awkward situation because, after regionalization, it becomes necessary to build a conveyance system that will return the water to the population centers. As a net result, regionalization causes a longer pipe to be built both ways. This problem did occur during the C-SELM study.

Regardless of the technology being used to treat the water, the feasibility of operation will relate back to the cost of conveyance and redistribution system for the reused water. When setting down plans for management of the water resources, water reuse and distribution should be incorporated in the future vision.

User Apprehension

User apprehension can be a most important factor in potable reuse. Often the technical merits are not the decisive factor in whether potable reuse of water can become an immediate reality. Personal preferences in some instances can be afforded if other, albeit more costly, water resources are available. Since the C-SELM is not at present a water short area, this remained largely a social-political issue to be grappled with sometime in the future.

RECREATION

Recreation is another type of reuse that may be developed. One opportunity is maintaining the required flow for fisheries; another is water for partial or full-body contact recreation. Fishery experts limited recommendations to minimum necessary water depths for fishery maintenance.

Recreational flow needs were determined from observations of existing flow regimes in selected streams within the C-SELM area. Supplementary flows were then designed to be supplied to designated streams through pipes to headwater and downstream supply points to provide a year-round base flow.

Flows were supplied to area streams at injection point locations. Points were selected on the basis of recreational needs within the C-SELM area. Actual flows supplied to injection points were between minimum and maximum desirables and were based on total flow available for reuse. Recreational flows were supplied from reclaimed municipal and industrial flows from either treatment plant or land treatment systems.

The maximum flow criteria were set by susceptibility of local soils to erosion. Minimum flow criteria were determined from minimum stream depth consistent with a viable fishery. The flow quantities of water for one purpose may cause problems for another purpose. In the C-SELM area, for example, there is naturally slow stream flow. Optimum flow desired by the fishery managers is a good deal greater. This raises the question of restructuring nature and perhaps not doing a good job.

Water Quality

Recreational water quality restraints center mainly around the establishment of a viable aquatic community and the creation of an esthetic visual resource. The aquatic considerations are greatly enhanced through the establishment of permanent flows of high-quality reclaimed water in the area streams. Preventing unregulated and untreated stormwater flows from reaching the stream system helps to insure the quality of the streams established through the injection of recreational reuse flows.

In addition to established flow regimes, it is equally important to consider the quality of the water that is being reused to establish the aquatic community. Any action that might interrupt or overstimulate the natural food chain in the aquatic community at any level is serious to all organisms higher up on the chain. The nutrient, or "fertilizer," concentration in the various no-discharge-of-critical-pollutants (NDCP) reclaimed waters associated with the treatment technologies presented in the C-SELM study are not so low or so high as to cause this type of reaction in the stream system.

Another concern in any aquatic system is the suffocation of aquatic organisms by lowered or completely removed oxygen concentrations. For this reason the BOD and oxygen relationships of the reclaimed water are very important. This is not a concern in the systems envisioned for C-SELM reuse since, in addition to the extremely high quality of the reclaimed water with respect to these particular parameters, the very action of delivering the waters to the streams enhances their dissolved oxygen content. Additional aeration, for example, could be accomplished by an injection point mechanism that induces further aeration by passing water over a series of steps or small rapids as it leaves the injection pipe.

AQUACULTURE-MARACULTURE

Partially reclaimed wastewater such as a typical secondary effluent from a municipal treatment system contains the essential nutrients for raising valuable waterborne crops. Typically, the effluent would be added to the basin where algae and other flora would be produced. In the case of maraculture, the effluent would be mixed with seawater to produce saltwater forms of plant life. The resulting plant life then becomes food for higher forms of life, such as catfish, oysters, lobster, trout, etc.

At Woods Hole Oceanographic Institute (WHOI) the process has been carried one step further. The waste products from the higher forms of life are scrubbed, in a third stage, with Irish moss, a free-floating higher plant form that is capable of directly assimilating the soluble nutrients contained in the waste products. The resultant water exiting the third stage is reported to be of relatively high quality. The fishery by-products are potentially valuable as food, while the Irish moss is marketable as raw material for the manufacture of certain chemical additives.

At last report the program at WHOI was investigating a potential constraint, the occurrence of any accumulation or other abnormal effects involving pathogens, carcinogens, or heavy metals in the fishery products.

NAVIGATION

With navigation reuse, there is an obvious opportunity for maintaining sufficient or augmented depths for vessel passage. A second incentive is conservation of fresh water supplies by substituting renovated water for lockage flows. In the Chicago area, a great deal of water is passed through lockages because of the procedures by which locks are manipulated with a resulting loss of availability to the area. By introducing reuse flows and by using air curtains to prevent the reused water from diffusing back into the fresh water supply, very significant conservation of fresh water can be accomplished. In the case of the C-SELM study, some 60 mg/d of fresh water were conserved.

Navigational flows are based upon individual lockage requirements. This is a reflection of the actual number of lockages in any specific period. In addition to the pump-back, closed-lockage system designed for the C-SELM study, an air-bubbler system is provided to prevent any mixing between reuse flows in the streams and Lake Michigan at the lock interface. This system is provided at each end, or gate area, of the locks. A diffusion system is envisioned in which compressors deliver air to a bubbler manifold located on the bottom of the lock at a rate sufficient to establish a barrier to intermixing. Pump-back facilities are designed to empty or fill the standard lock chamber within a period of four to five minutes.

Navigational flows are supplied through a complex distribution system, which may be very costly in some areas. This could be an important constraint in this type of water reuse development.

IRRIGATION

An irrigation or land treatment system presents an interesting opportunity for beneficial reuse. The land treatment system can be described in terms of the operational functions of its physical parts (figure 9-2). Aside from the pipeline network transporting the raw wastewater from the metropoli-

Figure 9-2. Land Treatment Components

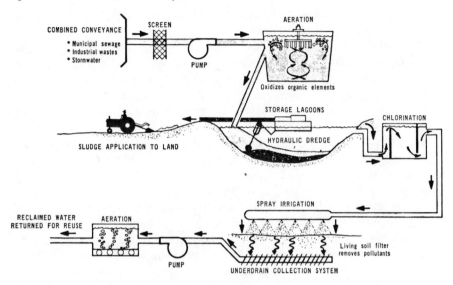

tan area to the land treatment site, the first part consists of two types of lagoons connected in series. In the first, or aerated, lagoon, oxygen is added by mechanical aerators and mixers that constantly aerate, mix, and churn the raw wastewater. The added oxygen provides the environment necessary for microbial organisms living in the water to decompose municipal and industrial wastes, thereby transforming the organic and soluble wastes into suspended solids. The treated wastewater is then transferred to a much larger storage lagoon, where the suspended solids settle on the bottom. There the solids or sludge continue to be broken down by further bacterial action until the solids residue is relatively stabilized. The stabilized sludge, which is high in nutrient and organic value, is then removed for subsequent reuse. This sludge can be used either on the adjacent farmlands as a source of fertilizer for agricultural production or transported outside the land site area where it may be used as a source of organic material for improving soils and disturbed areas (e.g., strip-mined areas) having low existing productivity.

At this point in the process the wastewater has received the equivalent of primary and secondary treatment. This is the same level of water quality currently being achieved by most of the major sewage treatment plants in the study area. At present the treated wastewater from study area treatment plants is discharged into nearby streams. The wastewater, however, is still rich in the plant nutrients carbon, nitrogen, phosphorus, and potassium. If discharged directly into a stream, the carbon, nitrogen, and phosphorus would stimulate growth of aquatic plants in the stream and cause a eutrophic condition. During the cycle of growth and decomposition of these aquatic plants, dissolved oxygen in the water sometimes would be periodically depleted to the point of causing a fish kill.

The land system design seeks to take advantage of the nutrient value in the treated wastewater by spraying it on the soil and letting the crop cover take up the soluble nutrients. Before being applied to the land, the treated effluent is chlorinated to kill disease-level organisms. The chlorine residual concentration is at a level not harmful to the crops.

The treated wastewater is transported from the storage lagoon to the croplands, where the water is applied by the use of a centerpivot or other available types of irrigation systems. Applying the treated wastewater to the land is the final, or polishing, stage in the treatment process. The water is renovated by the entire biosystem of both the soil and cover crop. Involved are the complex physical and chemical reactions, the biological processes of the soil's bacteria and fungi, and the natural crop uptake—all of which form the basis for determining the farmers' present fertility program and cropping practices. By the time the wastewater percolates through the soil column and reaches the underdrain system, the wastewater has been renovated (figure 9-3). The renovated water, which is of potable quality, is then collected by a system of drain tiles and/or drainage wells and projected to be returned to the C-SELM area for reuse.

Wastewater irrigation, thus, supplies the vehicle as well as the fertilizer itself for a farming operation. And that is very profitable to the farmer. How much is it worth? Fertilizer prices have risen markedly in the past few years; phosphorus prices have increased four or five times; and nitrogen prices have increased over three times. Per pound, nitrogen costs 10 to 15 cents; phosphorus, about 50 cents; and potassium, about 10 cents.

Because the manufacture of inorganic nitrogen fertilizers is very energy dependent, we are not apt to have stability in nitrogen production or pricing for some time. Phosphorus is a material that can be mined and developed only as a finite resource and with great pollution costs at the phosphorus processing point. As phosphorus is utilized it becomes widely distributed and eventually finds its way to the oceans. Thus, although it is not consumed, its availability is very significantly decreased. Thirdly, we have potassium. Potassium prices have been more stable as contrasted with the prices of nitrogen and phosphorus. At present, there are new nitrogen sources being developed in the Middle East, where cheap energy is available. New phosphorus deposits are also being developed so that eventually the prices may come down as new sources of supply are brought into the market.

Using the above prices and estimating the cost to fertilize a 150 bu/ac corn crop, there would be needed 200 lb of nitrogen for a cost of $20 to $30/ac. For the likely phosphorus need, there would be an additional cost of $15/ac. That is a total of $35 to $45, plus 30 to 60 lb of potassium,

Figure 9-3. Land Treatment Process

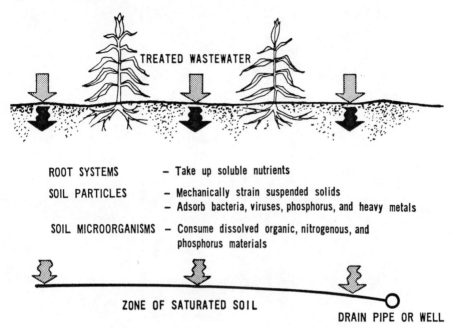

ROOT SYSTEMS   — Take up soluble nutrients

SOIL PARTICLES   — Mechanically strain suspended solids
                      — Adsorb bacteria, viruses, phosphorus, and heavy metals

SOIL MICROORGANISMS — Consume dissolved organic, nitrogenous, and
                      phosphorus materials

ZONE OF SATURATED SOIL

DRAIN PIPE OR WELL

depending on the kind of crop. Approximately $40 to $50/ac of fertilizer value could be supplied with this wastewater. Wastewater applied by such an irrigation system will supply the nitrogen crop needs and will additionally take care of the phosphorus needs and most, if not all, of the potassium needs.

The agricultural utilization of sludge employs it as a fertilizer or soil conditioner and is applied to the agricultural land at a controlled rate on a yearly basis. Both biological, organic sludges and physical-chemical, inorganic sludges can be applied to the land for agricultural utilization. Inorganic sludges are used for their acidity control and soil-conditioning values.

An optimum sludge application rate for the agricultural utilization of conventional and land treatment sludges over a fifty-year period is 13.5 dry tons/ac/yr (table 9-2). For advanced biological sludges, the corresponding rate is 28.8 dry tons/ac/yr. The sludge application rate is adjusted so that the total nitrogen applied to the land is equal to the nitrogen uptake of crops, plus the nitrogen lost through volatilization and soil denitrification. Increasing the organic nitrogen content of the topsoil is ignored as a means of consuming additional nitrogen, as a limit could be reached in this process before the end of the design fifty-year period. Thus

Table 9-2. Characteristics of Waste Sludge and Land Application Rates

Types of sludge	Yield Dry Tons/ MG	% Solids for Pipeline Transmission	Agricultural Application Rate (dry tons/ac-ft)	Accumulation in 50 Years (dry tons/ac*)	Land Reclamation Application Rate (dry tons/ac)	Accumulation in 50 Years (dry tons/ac)
Advanced biological	1.64	6	28.80	1,440.0	213	213
Chemical-Physical	1.13	10	1.73	86.5		
Conventional biological	0.77	6	13.50	675.0	100	100
Land treatment	0.77	6	13.50	675.0	100	100

NOTE: These sludges are all amenable to greater dewatering. This would be appropriate for alternative transportation systems, such as unit train or barge transport.

*The amounts are believed to be acceptable from the point of view of accumulations of heavy metals that accompany all sewage sludges. These metals are kept largely insoluble by maintaining a pH of about 7.

a maximum crop yield can be expected without a simultaneous groundwater pollution problem. The fifty-year accumulation of these sludges is not expected to produce excessive accumulations of the associated heavy metals, based upon existing test experience over periods of years.

The optimum sludge application rate for the agricultural utilization of physical-chemical sludge is a 1.7 dry tons/ac/yr. This application rate is determined by the alkalinity of the sludge and, at this level of application, does not contribute very significantly to the crop nutrient requirements.

Land Ownership

What are the constraints on land treatment? In many areas the price of land is currently high. The ideal situation for cities is to provide supplemental wastewater to a farmer who needs more water to grow his crop and who is willing to pay for both the water and the nutrients. The city would not buy the land in this case, but there would be the cost of conveyance of the water to the farmer. This type of system is possible in arid parts of the United States. If, on the other hand, the irrigation system is part of a city wastewater treatment system in a humid part of the country, the first purpose is to treat the wastewater. In this situation, it is desirable for the city to acquire the right to use the land for irrigation of the treated wastewater by paying the owner a lease or rental price that is agreeable to both parties and that encourages and allows the farmer to remain a farmer and to continue his association with the land. A system can be designed that is relatively compatible with prevailing farming practice and that would encourage participation by a farmer.

Distribution

The cost of conveyance to and from an irrigation site can be great. It is advantageous to have the irrigation and treatment site as close as possible to the sources of the raw wastewater. The closer it is, the less costly. To be right on the periphery of a town area is ideal because there is a short conveyance and a short return distance.

Restricted Use

There may exist institutional restrictions for the use of wastewater irrigation on some varieties of crops. Likely, the restrictions will apply only to direct food chain crops. Illinois, Michigan, and other midwestern states will not allow the application of chlorinated or nonchlorinated secondary wastewater to any food crops other than those, such as grass or feed grains, used for animal feed. Consideration will be given to sugar beets or other crops that undergo a processing step prior to human ingestion. Other states have different restrictions. In California, for example, wastewater is being used to irrigate nut trees and tomato crops.

ENERGY DISSIPATION

Some of the facilities of the land treatment and irrigation system can be used jointly for water resource management and electric power generation. Predictions of future energy requirements have been given in a number of studies, and in most cases these energy forecasts have been based on the assumption that the large increases in energy needed in the next fifty years would be substantially provided by the generation of electric power.

One such forecast is the Federal Power Commission's (FPC) National Power Study compiled from 1966 to 1968. This study forecasts that the minimum energy demands would require a doubling of installed capacity every ten years for the next thirty years. This prediction was based on a projection of the energy demands experienced over the past twenty years, including an allowance for decreasing population growth rates. Using this projection the minimum commitment for generating facilities in 2000 would be approximately seven times the 1973 levels.

In another study, Earl Cook, professor of geography and geology at Texas A & M University, pointed out the possible need to conserve resources to minimize the associated pollution problems and to maintain adequate reserves for future generations. This reasoning leads to a leveling-off of power consumption by approximately 2010 and 2020 at a level of about four times that of 1973. To achieve the result envisaged by Cook would require unprecedented public policy changes, as it would call for an arbitrary limitation of consumption of resources.

The C-SELM estimate for this study area assumes it would be wise to make a minimum commitment for generating facilities at about seven times 1970 levels for 2020, or 65,000 MW, as compared to twelve times present levels as predicted by local power companies. This estimate falls between the two projections listed above, although it does seem to fit more nearly with the conservative projection of Professor Cook.

Cooling for Power Facilities

The utilization of land treatment storage lagoons for the dissipation of the waste heat generated during the production of electric energy has been investigated for the C-SELM study. In making this investigation, certain basic assumptions and design criteria were established.

The first and primary assumption made is that a nuclear power generating station located near the land treatment sites would provide the additional power needed to meet the energy requirements of the C-SELM study area through 2020. According to the energy forecast of the previous section, an additional 55,000 MW of electric-generating capacity would be required to supplement the existing, or 1970-installed, capacity of

10,000 MW in order to meet the 65,000 MW projected requirement in 2020. The waste heat to be dissipated from the generation of this much power amounts to 8,780 billion Btu/d. The cooling pond surface area required for dissipating this heat is approximately 70,000 ac, provided that the temperature of the cooling pond is allowed to exceed 80°F during the summer. This surface area requirement for heat dissipation is on the same order as the surface area provided by the land treatment storage lagoons in 2020. The storage lagoons provided by the land treatment alternative thus could be fully utilized as part of the waste-heat dissipation system for the generation of power at the projected 2020 levels.

Figure 9-4.   Conceptual View of Land Treatment System Associated with Power Station

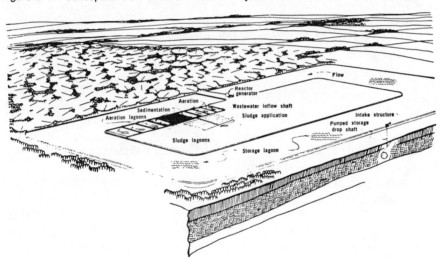

Figure 9-4 shows the general arrangement of a modular land treatment system in combination with a nuclear power generating system. The wastewater being pumped into the treatment system through the inflow shaft would be distributed to the aerated lagoons for biological treatment. The effluent from the aerated lagoons would be directed to the sedimentation lagoons, where most of the suspended solids would be removed. The effluent would then be directed into the storage lagoon, and the sludge would be stored and thickened in the sludge lagoon. The thickened sludge would be applied to the land allocated for sludge application. The power station cooling system would pump cool wastewater from one end of the lagoon and discharge heated wastewater into the other.

There is a constraint associated with energy dissipation: increased evaporation loss. The premise is, however, that it is preferable from an economic and resource allocation standpoint to evaporate secondary effluent as contrasted to fresh water. The total make-up water required to replace the water lost by evaporation during the heat dissipation process is estimated to be 43 mg/d, or approximately 16 percent of the 265 mg/d average flow coming into a land treatment modular system in the C-SELM study.

Warming for Agricultural Soils

Another use of effluent discharge is to provide warming for agricultural soils. Secondary effluent temperature rarely falls below 55°F, even in the winter in the Midwest, and rarely exceeds 70°F in the summer. Because it stays within that range, the water could be applied to agricultural soils and hold these soils warm for longer periods, thus establishing a longer cropping time. Experiments along these lines have been reasonably successful in the state of Washington. It was concluded that periods of agricultural activity could be extended by application of effluent.

INDUSTRIAL

Many industries generate wastewater with quality characteristics perfectly adequate for recycling for further industrial use. Sometimes minimal pretreatment is required for recycling. Recycling accomplishes two goals: (1) it minimizes demands on an often overtaxed water resource and (2) it minimizes the quantity of wastewater that will ultimately be rejected or blown down for treatment prior to discharge to a receiving water. As treatment requirements and, thus, treatment costs become more demanding with increasing water and effluent quality goals, it is advantageous to minimize the final flows requiring ultimate treatment.

The power industry is an example of an industry that commonly employs recycling of cooling water. In the relatively water-abundant C-SELM area, power industry recycling is motivated by a desire to minimize discharge of waste heat to natural waters in order to control the effects of thermal pollution. Existing federal and state standards specify the conditions under which cooling water discharges are acceptable to receiving waters. Those standards apply not only to the power industry, but also to any other potential discharger of waste heat.

The C-SELM evaluation of impact of existing and NDCP future standards considers the impact of recycling on critical industries. For the purpose of the study, recycled, blowdown flows from industrial recycle systems are considered acceptable to the C-SELM regional treatment plants. No deleterious effects are ascribed to the increased TDS concentrations associated with these blowdown flows.

The steel industry, because of the extent of its water use, is an industry critical in the C-SELM area. At present, the water requirements of advanced-technology, integrated steel mills would be approximately 40,000 gal./ton of steel, of which 19,000 gal./ton, or 47 percent, is required for indirect cooling; 7,000 gal./ton, or 18 percent, is required for direct cooling; and 14,000 gal./ton, or 35 percent, is required for process use.

A generalized maximum recycle strategy for the integrated steel industry is:

1. All cooling flows and the sinter plant, steel-making processes, and hot and cold rolling mill process flows are reclaimed and recycled repeatedly until TDS concentration approaches inhibitory levels.
2. Blowdown from the recycling flow, described above, is successively used for the by-product coke plant cooling and process requirement, followed by the blast furnace process requirement.
3. Pickling wastes are regenerated with a hydrochloric acid thermal recovery system; tin-plating and galvanizing wastes are essentially stripped of their heavy metal contents by adsorption recovery systems and discharged to local or remote and, as required, advanced waste treatment.
4. Reclaimed iron solids are recycled to either blast furnaces or steel-making processes via sintering, as required; reclaimed oil is classified and reused or sold for further reclaiming; recovered zinc, tin, and chromium are selectively reclaimed, when economically feasible, and reused.
5. Sanitary flows are transmitted to local or remote primary, secondary, and, as required, advanced waste treatment.

Utilizing this strategy, the make-up water required per ton of steel can be reduced by approximately 92.5 percent. The remaining 7.5 percent of recycled water ultimately is blown down to final and advanced treatment. The increased unit cost for advanced treatment is offset by the reduced flows requiring treatment. The net result is NDCP, or advanced treatment with little, if any, increased cost to the steel industry.

The other critical water-using industry in the C-SELM area is the petroleum industry. In recent years, the potential make-up water requirement for crude oil for both processing and cooling has decreased from 440 to 60 gal./bbl. This has been possible largely through recycling of cooling water. Further reduction in wastewater production per barrel of crude is still possible. An ultimate make-up water requirement of approximately 40 gal./bbl was projected in the C-SELM study.

The wastewater parameters of the various petroleum production sub-processes are compatible with conventional primary, secondary, and advanced waste treatment, as required. Pretreatment for oils and sulfides is frequently required.

A review of large (greater than 5 mg/d effluent discharges) petroleum refineries in the C-SELM study area revealed that recycling of cooling water was not intensively practiced and that most potential reductions have not been achieved. With an ultimate recycle strategy in the petroleum industry within the C-SELM area, it is possible to hypothesize a major reduction in petroleum industry wastewater requiring treatment.

Table 9-3. Industrial Reuse Potential of Municipal Effluent

Industry	Reuse Potential
Steel	For coke and slag quenching, gas cleaning, and hot rolling operations, secondary effluent quality would be acceptable.
	For cold rolling and reduction mill waters, secondary effluent would have to be pretreated (coagulation, sedimentation, filtration), mainly to reduce suspended solid content. Pickling and cleansing rinse waters require a softened or demineralized water.
Petroleum	Pretreatment of effluent for suspended solids and turbidity removal is necessary to enable use as process water for desalting, washing, and product transportation operations. Utilization of wastewater for brine removal from crude oil produces synergistic effects through wastewater renovation of certain pollutants, such as phenols.
Food processing and pharmaceutical	The reuse of secondary effluent for process water is not acceptable, since all water for washing, transport, and blanching operations must be of potable quality.
Explosives and soap	The reuse of secondary effluent for process water would require pretreatment, including coagulation, sedimentation, and filtration. Further treatment may include softening and demineralization for the particular desired water quality.
Power and boiler feed and cooling operations	The reuse of secondary effluent for cooling and boiler feed operations may have limited use. Cooling water use in the steel and petroleum industries far exceeds the process water use in these industries. Pretreatment will be dependent on specific installations. Generally, pretreatment for boiler feed will be necessary for solids and hardness control.

Again, as in the steel industry, this is not estimated to result in significant additional costs to industry over costs currently being met to treat to present standards.

INDUSTRIAL-MUNICIPAL

The opportunity for the reuse of secondary effluent from municipal treatment plants for industrial process waters is great. The quality of intake waters for a number of C-SELM industries is not significantly different from that of secondary municipal effluent. At present a number of industries operate raw water pretreatment facilities to condition properly their process water. The incremental cost of pretreating municipal effluent versus present pretreatment operations may prove to be feasible when viewed as a water-conserving technique. Table 9-3 presents selected industrial reuse opportunities. The municipal treatment plant should be in close proximity to the particular industry. Industrial reuse of such water may not be economically feasible in areas where there exists an abundant water supply or where industrial water consumption is much larger than nearby municipal wastewater flows.

PART 3

PROSPECTS

CHAPTER 10

Planning
for Water Reuse
in Denver, Colorado

Richard D. Heaton

HISTORICAL ASPECTS

To appreciate the wastewater reclamation and reuse necessity in Denver, one must understand some of Colorado's history, as almost every event is in one way or another related to water development.

In the late 1800s, eleven small water companies competed for business with the six-gun and force as the primary sales gimmicks. The quantity and quality of water were of a secondary nature in that highly competitive atmosphere. Horse-drawn wagons went into the mountains, where the numerous barrels were filled with clear stream water. Returning to town, the water sold for 5 cents a bucket to those on the first floor and 10 cents a bucket to those on the second.

This system lasted until the early 1900s, when waterborne typhoid eliminated 600 customers. The small water purveyors were consolidated into one water utility that used filtration and chlorination to eliminate the disease threat. This utility was later purchased by the city and county of Denver. For the Water Department to remain politically and financially independent of the city, a separate Board of Water Commissioners was formed. Thus, all the revenues from water sales go into the Water Department treasury and not the city's. No tax monies are used for support.

The water utility today serves close to 1 million persons with a service area of 300 square miles. In 1976, 68 bg of water was served to customers. This equates to a yearly average consumption of 207 gal./capita/d, one of the highest in the country. Figure 10-1 provides more details of the actual water use.

In Colorado itself, close to 95 percent of the water goes to agricultural pursuits, with only 3 percent representing municipal supply. Of the 220 gal. stated previously, 52 percent, or 115 gal./capita/d, is for residential use. The majority of that is for home landscaping, as shown in the bottom bar graph of figure 10-1.

Denver today is experiencing the common pains of urban sprawl. Be-

Richard D. Heaton is the director of the Water Reuse Project for the American Water Works Association, Denver, Colorado.

Figure 10-1. Typical Water Use

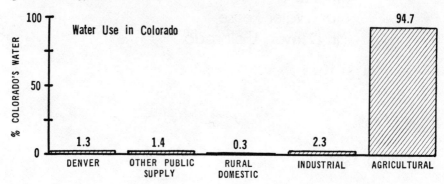

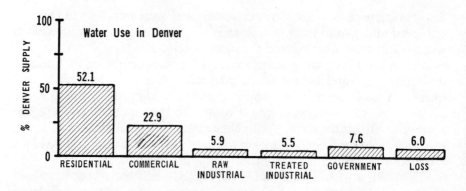

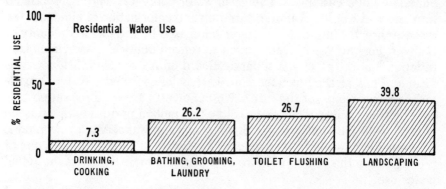

cause of the lack of water, geographically it is situated where a major city should not be. The city itself lies on the semi-arid eastern slopes of the Rocky Mountains, which receive on the average only twelve inches of precipitation per year. Most of the Pacific storms dump their snow loads on the western slopes of the continental divide; these become tributary to the Colorado River system.

Figure 10-2.   Denver's Water Supply System

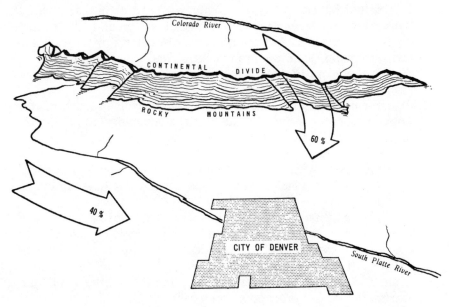

It was apparent early in Denver's history that the indigenous eastern slope streams became insufficient to meet the growing demands. Through far-sighted planning, Denver purchased water rights on western slope sources; and, through a system of dams and tunnels underneath the Divide, the city now brings this water to the drier eastern plains. As shown in figure 10-2, this transmountain water presently accounts for 60 percent of Denver's supply, and this amount will increase in the future.

WATER SUPPLY ALTERNATIVES

To meet the expected overwhelming demands in the future, the Water Department is committed to a logical and multifaceted approach to develop additional water supplies. But *develop* means many things in the West. It can take the form of any one of the following:

1. *Weather modification.* Bureau of Reclamation studies indicate that proper cloud-seeding can increase runoff and yield up to 15 percent. But the actual use of this extra water is limited by the "appropriations doctrine" in western water law. Rivers are consid-

ered *over-appropriated* when more than one entity's demands could be satisfied, but one entity receives an amount greater than needed.

2. *Watershed management.* This form of development includes optimizing runoff and yield from proper forest cutting, vegetation patterns, snow fences, evaporation control, and canal lining.

3. *Raw water acquisition.* This alternative can range from purchasing agricultural rights or capturing spring runoffs.

4. *Water conservation.* This fourth method involves teaching the public proper watering methods and changing vegetation patterns to inverse rate structures, total metering, or rationing and restrictions, if necessary.

5. *Miscellaneous.* Other areas of investigation include transcontinental pipelines, glacier melting, desalination, and groundwater studies.

6. *Exchange and reuse.* These last two areas are closely related and will receive considerable attention in the future. Exchange may be a new principle to eastern water ideology. In essence, discharged sewage effluent is used to satisfy agricultural demands downstream, while a like amount of water is diverted at the utility's intake upstream. Before this procedure was legally resolved, large quantities of water had to bypass the water intake to satisfy the use downstream. Sewage or other return flows were just an unmeasured bonus.

All of the above methods serve to increase water availability, many without physical construction or environmental damage.

WASTEWATER REUSE

But Denver views reuse as one of the more viable means of supplementing future supply. The words *reuse, recycle,* and *reclaim* are interesting. They all sound good, and recycling of resources appears at first to be a logical and efficient conservation process. But reclaiming wastewater poses a unique set of problems.

For the last ten years, Denver has been evaluating all of the reuse potential in the area. In every reuse scheme, save direct potable reuse, a dual distribution system is required: one line to convey potable water and the other, a lesser quality product.

Industrial Reuse

Industrial reuse was the first of several alternatives evaluated. If a city is fortunate enough to have its heavy water-using industries near the sewage source, the most logical approach would be to offer those industries reclaimed water and thus conserve the potable supply. Industry, however, is not centralized in Denver, nor is it always located adjacent to a sewage treatment plant. This form of reuse, then, requires an expensive additional pipeline and pumping facility that may or may not be justified by economics or water shortages.

Other factors require consideration, as well. Industrial reuse may be the most logical, but not necessarily the most efficient, method. There does exist in Denver a large coal-burning power plant within 2,000 feet of the municipal wastewater treatment plant, an ideal situation geographically. The plant uses in excess of 10 mg/d of water for cooling and stack scrubber purposes. Existing sources of water include shallow wells and diverted ditch water purchased from the Water Department. The cost approaches 6 cents/1,000 gal. To provide the plant with an equal amount and equal quality of reclaimed effluent would cost 30 to 40 cents/1,000 gal., which is five to six times the present rate.

The industry cannot realistically be expected to convert to a more expensive source, even for public relations benefits. Secondary effluent, available at no charge, is of insufficient quality to serve the plant needs. Tertiary treatment would be required to remove scale-forming phosphates and corrosive ammonia. Faced with an EPA discharge permit that limits TDS, the power plant must exert careful control over concentration cycles. Using reclaimed water with an initially higher TDS content would limit tower concentrations, thus requiring purchase of even more of the expensive product.

The Water Department also receives considerable revenue from sale of the ditch water. Substituting another source automatically eliminates that revenue, as no other market is available. Exchanging the water right to another diversion point practically eliminates the quantities involved. Forcing use of the more expensive reclaimed water in a drought situation is impractical, as the plant's wells could suffice. It is difficult to compete economically with a mere pumping charge, especially when the power is inherently owned.

Industrial reuse is an acceptable plan and is being successfully implemented countrywide, but it is not the panacea for all communities. When properly planned, sewage effluent can readily serve new industries or those that can adapt to a different quality of water. Some thought has been given to establishing a new industrial park where the businesses are amenable to secondary effluent. As to the creation of a new water market, questions such as growth encouragement arose that did not comply with the initial conservation theory in Denver.

Municipal Reuse

A second alternative for reuse involves municipal application. This plan calls for an extensive dual distribution system to serve parks, golf courses, recreational lakes, or perhaps individual home needs (lawn watering and toilet flushing).

A major year-long study was undertaken in Denver to evaluate a dual pipe system in a new and completely planned community of 10,000 persons. A secondary pipeline of highly treated wastewater would have served the needs of a recreational lake, a golf course, and the needs of many private homes. Several combinations of reuse were evaluated. All costs being considered, the resultant price of the reclaimed source was more than the potable water in neighboring communities. But who would subsidize the cost differential?

1. The water utility for demonstration purposes? A losing economic venture was not needed, as the future did not look that promising.
2. The developers themselves? Adding the increased price onto the home would jeopardize an already sensitive market.
3. The recreation association? Its mandatory monthly fees were already prohibitive.
4. The homeowners, through higher rates? Why should they pay extra just for the privilege of living in an experimental, conservation-minded community? They expected a rate reduction.

The high system costs were due strictly to:

1. Intensive treatment requirements, since the recycled water was expected to be at least biologically safe in case of short-term accidental ingestion.
2. The dual piping system, dual meters, home plumbing modification, and resultant increased O&M costs.
3. The lack of a winter market for the product in Denver's climate.
4. The storage, holding, and flow equalization necessity. Large summer irrigation demands would have caused undesirable water level fluctuations in the recreation reservoir. Control measures and costly sizing were necessary for a successful operation.

In addition, proper training in the use of the dual system would have required a definite change in individual lifestyle. For these reasons the project was deemed infeasible. In other situations, a dual system may be practical and advantageous, due to its inherent water conservation. Utilities have been trying for years to instruct the populace in wise water use, with very little success among adults. The real results have been among children, who are more ecologically minded. The impact of their water savings will not be felt for fifteen to twenty years. Recycling, in essence, performs the water conservation and moves the responsibility from the customer to the utility.

Agricultural Reuse

The use of sewage effluents directly or indirectly in agriculture is widely practiced. It is often the only source of water and relieves some demand on rivers or well systems.

Unfortunately, knowledge is insufficient regarding any deleterious health effects in the food chain from uptake of toxic substances. In addition, highly polluted agricultural return flows are even more concentrated if sewage effluents are the feed source.

In the Denver region, major agricultural reuse is simply prohibited by certain water rights decrees. This particular legal condition will become more apparent as municipal demands increase along the eastern slopes of the Rockies.

Groundwater Recharge

Where extensive underground aquifers exist or saltwater intrusion is evident, groundwater recharge with highly treated sewage effluents is a viable means of increasing supply or detering a problem.

With respect to the Denver situation again, the underlying geology is simply not amenable to recharge. And with complicated western water law, it is not clear whether injection of x gallons of water at one point in an aquifer justifies the same x withdrawal at another. Ownership is highly questionable once control through injection is lost.

Potable Reuse

Each city considering the reuse alternative should evaluate each mode before making a decision. Denver has looked in depth at all of the potentials and has concluded that the most efficient and logical reuse of wastewater is in the potable system, or the reclaiming of sewage effluent to a product suitable for human use and consumption.

As legally determined in the state supreme court, the only water available for reuse is the 60 percent transmountain flows. In terms of volume, however, it represents close to 100 mg/d available for reuse by 1985. The total of all the industries' and parks' water use in the area does not approach this tremendous, usable resource. Using only a part means wasting, wasting something that was purchased once and that represents millions of dollars in potential revenue if sold again.

Potable reuse eliminates the dual distribution concept, but the same arguments against the other alternatives can be used against potable reuse. It too is expensive, from the sophisticated treatment—for guaranteeing reliability—to the years of health-effects research for insuring safety.

PUBLIC ATTITUDES

When the decision has been reached to approach potable reuse, several attitudes become prevalent. The first of these can be properly entitled the "yuk syndrome." This is the "no, never, not at any cost" attitude: "I'll move first, truck in bottled water, steal it, whatever, but not me, brother!" The second is toned down a bit and says, "Yes, go to potable reuse, but only as a last alternative. Exhaust every means first. Wait until the farms are dry and my grass is dead. Even if it's cheaper, hold off as long as possible."

The third attitude is a positive one that views potable reuse as a viable means of supplementing future water supply. "When it becomes economical and safe to apply, do it." This last attitude is, of course, the one Denver is pursuing and encouraging. The decision is sound and no shame need be implied by its admittance.

The public relations studies conducted thus far are, in fact, very positive in terms of acceptance. An original premise was that no program could succeed without the approval of an informed public. Thus every effort has been made to publicize the program.

Table 10-1.   Initial Reuse Attitude Survey

Question: How would you feel about using treated and purified sewage water for drinking . . . to take care of future water supply problems?

	(%)
Strongly approve	17
Slightly approve	23
Total	40
Slightly disapprove	19
Strongly disapprove	41
Total	60

A first survey in 1971 covered 500 persons. When first confronted with a reuse question, the response was definitely negative, as shown in table 10-1. A short reuse information paragraph was read to the participants and the question, rephrased. A slightly more positive response is noted in table 10-2. With even more discussion and the question given as indicated in table 10-3, 85 percent of those surveyed were willing to drink reclaimed water if the quality were as good as or better than existing supplies.

The initial survey revealed two important facts: (1) Education is important: The more one knows about potable reuse, the more positive is his

Table 10-2. Second Reuse Attitude Survey

Question (after reading short reuse information statement): If Denver announced that it was considering the use of renovated wastewater as a part of its drinking water system, what would be your personal reaction?

	(%)
Strongly approve	23
Slightly approve	29
Total	52
Slightly disapprove	19
Strongly disapprove	29
Total	48

Table 10-3. Final Reuse Attitude Survey

Question: Would you drink renovated wastewater if its quality were the same as that of your present house water?

	(%)
Yes, definitely.	53
Probably so.	24
Not sure, tend to think so.	8
Total	85
Not sure, tend to think not.	5
Probably not.	4
Definitely not.	6
Total	15

response; (2) A rather formidable task is to produce a snow-melt equivalent water from secondary effluent.

A second survey was conducted by a professional organization in March 1975. A random group of 452 persons was selected by age, sex, income, ethnic background, and geographic location. In conjunction with other statements on growth and water supply, the question shown in figure 10-3 was asked. The graph indicates that 63 percent of the respondents were in favor, with about 25 percent against and 12 percent having no idea.

Variations in response pattern were found to be statistically significant. By age, persons in the two youngest groups (18–24 and 25–44 years) were considerably more in favor than those in older groups (up to 75 percent). This age-response difference appears significant in terms of ecological awareness. The popularity of a recycling scheme is a great selling point at this time. It was the surveyor's opinion that more public education is all

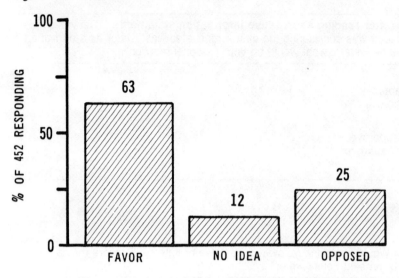

Figure 10-3.   Public Reactions to Potable Reuse

QUESTION 16:   Water reuse is the treatment of sewage water,
                     purified to the same quality as our present supply, so
                     that it can be introduced into the drinking water supply.

WOULD YOU FAVOR OR OPPOSE A WATER REUSE SYSTEM FOR DENVER?

that is necessary for an even higher favorable response. A third survey in 1975 indicated a favorable response, as well.

All of these results may differ somewhat from studies conducted elsewhere, and this occurrence may be attributable to the attitude of the interviewers or to Denver's extensive public information program. The important point is that, while a national public information program would be helpful, it is the response of Denver citizens that is important to Denver. Acceptance must remain a local function.

INDIRECT VS DIRECT REUSE

Once the potable reuse decision has been made, two modes of operation become available: the direct or indirect system. The possibility exists in Denver to let secondary effluent flow downstream a few miles before being picked up at the reclamation plant. This procedure, according to many, allows nature's "magic mile" of stream to dilute or purify the sewage. Perhaps it is more esthetically pleasing to see water being withdrawn from a river than from an outfall.

Many problems exist, however, with the indirect mode of operation. For some months with low stream flow, sewage effluent is the basis of the South Platte River. There is practically zero dilution. When there is flow, the quality is highly questionable with storm runoff, industrial discharges, upstream sewage plants, and the more-consistent-than-not accidental spills. As the discharge standards become more stringent and the quality of sewage effluent improves, it is a shame to put it in a dirty receiving stream.

Some European rivers used for water supply purposes are close to 100 percent returned sewage flow. This concentration has essentially been ignored, and conventional water treatment cannot safely handle the source. The percentage of sewage in U.S. streams is increasing as well, with some figures as high as 50 percent noted.

Direct reuse, where the sewage outfall is connected to the reclamation plant intake and this plant's product is taken directly to the distribution system, is safer than indirect methods. The main reason is that the source is acknowledged. The treatment, monitoring, and control of product will be much more sophisticated than conventional water treatment because of the inherent dangers.

Quality Aspects

Product quality and standards are going to be very important in potable reuse because it is a whole new ball game. In all probability, more stringent standards will have to be developed for recycled water.

The 1962 U.S. Public Health Service Drinking Water Standards listed twenty chemical parameters, only nine of which serve as absolute grounds for rejecting a supply as unsafe. The new EPA and WHO standards contain only a few more. None of these standards lists more than a few synthetic organic and inorganic compounds, despite the fact that hundreds of these chemicals find their way into wastewater.

Conventional drinking water standards were originally based on the premise that water for human consumption would generally be drawn from groundwater sources or from protected, uncontaminated surface water supplies. Although the assumption is rarely true for most surface supplies today, it definitely does not apply to sewage effluent.

Two alternatives are then open to an agency considering potable reuse. One is to wait a number of years until the research work is done, until the in-depth toxicological and epidemiological studies are complete. The other method is adequately to monitor, with available equipment, the reclaimed water and attempt what is called "use-increment removal," or the renovation of secondary effluent to its original pristine state. With monitoring sophistication, this method would alleviate many problems with possible deleterious effects.

The latter approach has been chosen by the Denver Water Department and offers side benefits of considerable merit. First, use-increment removal offers a hedge against future standards. It is the more severe standard, with guessing at the future not required. Second, the idea of "as-good-as-or-better-than the original source" has a tremendous public relations benefit and satisfies the attitude surveys mentioned earlier.

Table 10-4. Use-Increment Removals

Parameters	Denver Water Composite	Secondary Effluent	Removal Increment
Coliform/100ml	0.000	160,000.000	160,000.000
COD*	<5.000	62.000	57.000
TOC*	<2.000	25.000	23.000
Phosphate*	0.040	8.700	8.600
TKN*	0.100	28.200	28.100
Lead*	0.030	0.082	0.052
Iron*	0.273	3.000	2.700
TDS*	124.000	480.000	356.000
Suspended solids*	0.000	98.000	98.000

*mg/l.

With current technology, monitoring pollutants below certain concentrations is not possible, and the health danger of every sewage constituent is now known. For this reason, the only logical approach for this highest order of reuse is a combination of use-increment removal and medical health effects studies. Both are needed. The latter then assumes a secondary, or fail-safe, role. (Table 10-4 indicates what is required to achieve use-increment removal for Denver's water.)

Treatment Requirements
How does one arrive at the concept of producing a snow-melt equivalent water? This question has been the subject of one year's work conceptually to design a potable reuse plant. In the fall of 1974, the first attempt was to collect, from a number of experts in the AWT field, their opinions on what treatment scheme would accomplish the goal. This information, plus subsequent technical input, has resulted in a predesign report published in August 1975, by CH$_2$M-Hill Engineers.

Figure 10-4 is the selected treatment sequence to produce a drinkable product. Many design objectives are incorporated into the proposal. First and foremost, the plant had to represent the best currently available technology and must incorporate within its design unit processes capable of

Figure 10-4. Process Flow Diagram

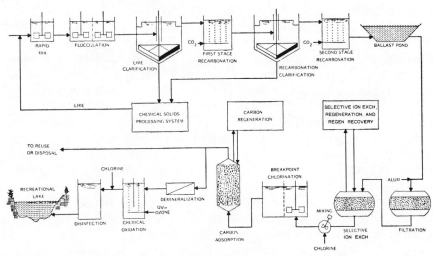

reducing to acceptable levels all harmful or undesirable substances. Additionally, the facility must be of a size sufficient to utilize equipment similar in nature to that which would be used in a full-scale facility. It must further contain sufficient flexibility to allow uninterrupted operation and new technology input. It must be as self-sufficient as prudent use of funds will allow. This requirement dictates that all known problems be faced today, not left for later solution. It must finally be visible and accessible to the public.

Because the plant must essentially be a fail-safe operation, two types of redundancy have been stressed: *In-kind redundancy,* with backup duplicate tanks, dual pipes, and standby equipment; and *process redundancy,* where one or more unit operations may perform the same function as another.

Taking all of these factors into consideration has resulted in the figure 10-4 flow sequence. The selected size is 1 mg/d, which takes the plant out of the pilot plant category and into the demonstration plant terminology.

Flow Stream Description

Secondary effluent from the metropolitan sewage treatment plant is pumped to the headworks of the reclamation facility for flow measurement. Chemicals such as lime, alum, iron, and polymers are added and violently mixed. Gentle stirring follows to allow flocculation. Subsequent clarification of the high pH lime sludge will effectively remove phosphorus, suspended solids, many trace metals, bacteria, and viruses. Two-stage recarbonation allows more softening to occur, with further removal of undesirables.

A ballast or flow equalization pond follows that allows the downstream processes to operate at variable flow rates. Several of these processes involve backwashing and regeneration steps that dictate start-stop operation and highly variable recycled flow streams. The pond isolates the continual flow processes from those that must be operated cyclicly.

Water is then pumped to pressure trimedia filters to remove all remaining suspended matter. The clear, solids-free filter effluent then flows to a selective ion-exchange system. Clinoptilolite resin therein removes the major nitrogen compound ammonia. Residual amounts are converted to nitrogen gas via breakpoint chlorination. The water is essentially bacteria- and virus-free at that point.

Activated carbon columns that follow, effectively remove trace amounts of organic material, as well as taste-, odor-, and color-producing substances. Demineralization will be accomplished by reverse osmosis. Salt removal is necessary to accomplish the use-increment removal goal, but the membranes offer additional protection against organics, bacteria, and viruses. At this point in the treatment sequence, flow is reduced to .1 mg/d for economic purposes.

The now highly purified water emerging from the reverse osmosis step is still not considered adequate for long-term human ingestion. Organics may still be a problem, and ozonation, perhaps coupled with ultra-violet light as a catalyst, will follow. A synergistic effect occurs with almost complete destruction of organics. Product water leaving the chemical oxidation system will receive a small chlorine dose for residual disinfection before entering a small recreational lake on-site; here the public will have full access to the reclaimed water.

Table 10-5.   Quality Goals, 1 mg/d Potable Demonstration Plant

Parameter	Expected Product Quality
Turbidity	0.50
Suspended solids*	0.00
TDS*	150.00
Total nitrogen*	0.05
Total phosphate*	0.07
Hardness*	88.00
Alkalinity*	60.00
Bacteria	0.00
Virus	0.00
Toxic metals*	0.01
Gross organics*	<1.00

*mg/l.

Although the treatment scheme has been chosen, many side streams will be researched in light of new discoveries. Some of these may include polymeric adsorption, ion-exchange, or different sequencing. Expected plant quality is shown in table 10-5. It is comparable to those values shown in the use-increment table (table 10-4).

Solids Handling and Regeneration

With respect to solids handling, figure 10-5 indicates some of the steps involved. No biological solids will be generated, but there will be 7,000 lb/d of lime sludge.

Figure 10-5.   Chemical Solids Handling

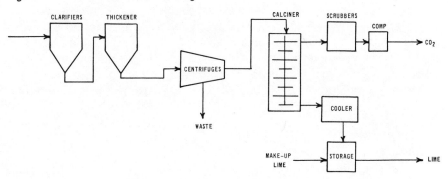

Clarifier underflows at 1 percent solids will first go to gravity thickeners and reach a 4-percent consistency. Classification and dewatering centrifuges will separate the phosphorus-rich stream from the reclaimable lime solids. Dewatered lime sludge will be fed to a calcining furnace for recovery of the product. The CO_2 generated is used in the recarbonation process. Approximately 20 percent make-up lime is required.

Lime recovery at the 1 mg/d scale is very uneconomical, but for demonstration purposes it is necessary. Carbon will be regenerated in furnaces as well, then recycled. Again, the process is not justified at 1 mg/d, but any recycled chemical or stream that can affect quality will have to be tested.

The brine solution from the demineralization process will be disposed of at the sewage plant. Ultimate disposal will be by solar evaporation.

Nitrogen removal and recovery is perhaps the only new or undemonstrated process in the plant (figure 10-6). When the clinoptilolite resin is exhausted, a brine solution of NaCl that re-exchanges sodium ions for ammonium ions is run through the beds. They are then ready to use again. The ammonia-laden stream reaches a clarifier where NaOH is added to raise the pH. $Mg(OH)_2$ is precipitated out because of its interference with the selective resins. From the clarifier, the liquid enters the ammonia

Figure 10-6. Nitrogen Removal and Recovery System

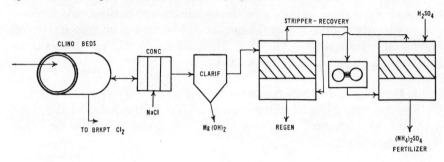

removal and recovery process (ARRP) for closed-loop stripping. As the water trickles down over open media, ammonia gas is stripped out with blowers. As the gas enters a second tower, H_2SO_4 acid is added and the product is fully recovered as a fertilizer, $(NH_4)_2SO_4$. This method eliminates the previous stripping problems of scaling and temperature sensitivity. The recovered product is near a 50-percent concentration and is highly marketable.

Economics

In terms of capital cost, the 1 mg/d plant will run as shown in table 10-6. The figures are based on July 1975 dollars. O&M costs, as indicated in table 10-7, will approach $460,000. At the 1 mg/d scale, the final product will cost $3/1,000 gal. But in the future, economies of scale will apply and the projected cost will range from 70 to 80 cents/1,000 gal. in the 100 mg/d range. Although this cost appears high, it is highly competitive to some of the other raw water projects now being contemplated.

RESEARCH NEEDS

What is needed for the success of a potable reuse endeavor? The first need, of course, is a plant to produce the reclaimed water. The second is many years of health effects research.

It is encouraging to see the increased federal interest in the potable reuse field. Indicative of this interest are the provisions in the new Safe Drinking Water Act that authorize reuse funds. For a number of years, the EPA Office of Research and Development (OR&D) has devoted effort to the demonstration of wastewater treatment processes capable of produc-

Table 10-6. Capital Cost Estimate, 1 mg/d Potable Demonstration Plant

	Cost (millions of dollars)
Influent pump station and pipelines	0.31
Lime treatment with two-stage recarbonation	0.50
Lime sludge recovery	1.40
Filtration	0.40
Selective ion exchange	0.40
ARRP recovery	0.30
Breakpoint chlorination	0.12
Activated carbon adsorption	0.37
Regeneration facilities	0.68
Demineralization at 0.1 mg/d	0.15
Chemical oxidation at 0.1 mg/d	0.06
Disinfection at 0.1 mg/d	0.02
Laboratory equipment	0.10
Administrative and process operations building	0.68
Public relations items	0.15
Special monitoring	0.25
Land and utilities	0.17
Yardwork	0.30
Engineering, legal, administrative, and contingencies	1.79
Total	8.15

Table 10-7. Annual O&M Costs, 1 mg/d Demonstration Plant

	Annual Cost
Labor	$297,400
Power	21,300
Fuel	6,700
Chemicals	76,700
Parts	57,800
Total	459,900

NOTE: Capitalized O&M = $1.20/1,000 gal.

ing high-quality effluents. The goal, however, was primarily pollution abatement, not reuse. A reassessment of EPA priorities, therefore, is necessary to place potable reuse in the proper perspective.

A unified health effects program nationwide is needed because the problems are not unique to Denver. In fact, many areas where the reuse alternative is attractive are faced with water shortages. The public health aspects of questionable potable water derived from approved sources like

New Orleans should be reviewed in the same light as potable reuse. In many instances, the public health aspects are the same.

Answering the health effects questions in potable reuse essentially answers those in all other reuse alternatives. The socio-economic aspects of potable reuse have not paralleled treatment technology.

PROGRAM SCHEDULE

In terms of planning, the Denver program is graphically shown in figure 10-7. It is designed to incorporate at each step lessons learned in previous steps and to answer all questions as the program progresses. The 1 mg/d potable reuse demonstration plant is expected to be on line in the early 1980s.

Figure 10-7. Denver Reuse Program

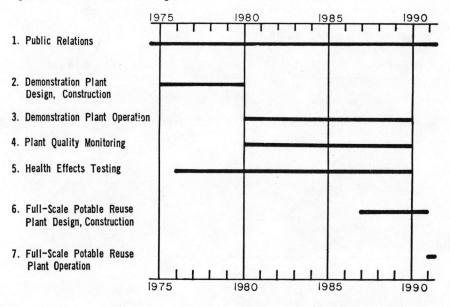

While potable reuse may not be an attractive, economically feasible resource for all cities, Denver believes it will be a valuable addition to its ongoing water development program. Fears of the unknown are not needed and should not be allowed to negate beneficial research. The potential benefits in water supply are too great.

CHAPTER 11

Present
and Future Directions
for Municipal Wastewater
Reuse Research

John N. English

Abundant supplies of clean surface and underground waters in the United States have been taken for granted until recent years. Severe contamination of many surface supplies has occurred. Increasing instances of groundwater contamination are being found. Thus, our relatively fixed volume of water may become less and less usable. Adequate pollution control measures must be taken, and conservation and reclamation of resources must become the rule.

Sound management of water resources must include consideration of the potential planned reuse of properly treated municipal wastewater as an alternative for meeting future water demands. While the need for additional water supplies is greatest in the arid Southwest, some areas in the eastern part of the country are also observing water shortages. Groundwater in many places is being mined or used faster than it is being replaced by natural means. In groundwater-using areas such as Southern California and Long Island, New York, alternate methods of obtaining water are very expensive. Where the cost of new water sources is high or where legal constraints are placed on new sources, wastewater reuse may be an attractive alternative. The potential benefits of wastewater reuse were recognized in PL 92-500, the Federal Water Pollution Control Act Amendments of 1972, and, more recently, in PL 93-523, the Safe Drinking Water Act of 1974. There is a clear national mandate to conserve our water resources by renovating and reusing wastewater.

PAST REUSE RESEARCH

The EPA OR&D, through its Municipal Environmental Research Laboratory and predecessor organizations has, since 1960, devoted effort to the development and demonstration of AWT processes capable of producing effluents of high quality suitable for a range of reuse or recycling appli-

John N. English is a sanitary engineer and staff specialist for the Wastewater Research Division, U.S. Environmental Protection Agency, Environmental Research Center in Cincinnati, Ohio.

cations. EPA health effects and socio-economic research relating to wastewater reuse, however, has not paralleled wastewater treatment technology developments. Only since 1974 has EPA, through its Health Effects Research Laboratory (HERL) in Cincinnati, initiated health effects studies directly related to the reuse of wastewater. Research to determine the socio-economic aspects of reuse has also received only minor attention. Additional studies are needed to determine whether recycled water can be efficiently and equitably integrated into the economic and social framework of existing water supply systems.

The treatment technology capability can be identified for reuse applications in areas such as agriculture, recreation, and industry, where quality requirements have been defined. The state of California has already established water quality standards for wastewater used for agricultural and recreational purposes.[1] Treatment technology capability exists for most reuse purposes, with the primary exception being potable reuse. Since there are public health questions in this country concerning the degree of treatment for potable reuse, the necessary treatment technology is less well defined for this purpose than for other reuses.

The emphasis on reuse and the need for research in this area have come about as a result of the potential availability of highly treated wastewaters that are "too good to throw away." These waters have attracted the attention in water-short areas of those agencies that are responsible for maintaining adequate sources of supply.

POTABLE REUSE AS A LONG-TERM GOAL

Until adequate health effects data are obtained on the residues in high-quality wastewater treatment effluents, any potential reuse situation that has a health question associated with it will not be sanctioned by regulating agencies. An example of such a situation is the long-term research program identified by the state of California as necessary to provide sufficient data before it will allow a proliferation of projects for the recharge of groundwater with reclaimed water.[2] Recharge is being considered as an important water resources management technique not only in California and other areas of the arid Southwest, but also in other communities in the Midwest and East, around the city of Chicago, and on Long Island—all of which rely on groundwater supplies. Due to the lack of adequate health effects research data on which to base reasonable regulations, however, the concern for safety may cause state agencies to propose regulations that may retard wastewater reuse for groundwater recharge.

The use of wastewater for domestic purposes is, of course, not the only means of establishing reuse as a viable water resource management technique. Source substitution that is not dependent on long-term health studies and allows the higher quality, conventional water supplies to be used only for potable purposes is a means of conserving these supplies. It is, however, imperative that support of health research is continued and expanded, since in areas in the United States such Denver, Long Island, areas in Southern California, and other localities where source substitution will not provide sufficient water resources to meet the domestic water supply needs of a growing population, the feasibility of potable reuse must be determined. Without health effects research this cannot be done. It is the highest priority research in the wastewater reuse program, since it requires a long-term program that must be implemented now if it is to have an impact on future national water needs.

The Water Pollution Control Federation (WPCF) and the AWWA issued a joint resolution that urged the federal government to support a massive research effort to develop needed technology and evaluate potential health problems related to recycling of wastewater to domestic supplies. These organizations underscored the lack of adequate scientific information about possible acute and long-term effects upon man's health from such reuse, and also noted that the essential fail-safe technology to permit such direct reuse has not yet been demonstrated. The resolution recognizes the need for an immediate and sustained multidisciplinary, national effort to provide the scientific knowledge and technology relative to the reuse of water for drinking purposes in order to assure full protection of the public health. (For the AWWA proposed policy statement (1977), see appendix C of this volume.)

In Cincinnati a relatively new program dealing with the health effects associated with the potable reuse of municipal wastewater has been by HERL. The projects implemented in this program are based on the results of a workshop held in March 1975, to identify "Research Needs for the Potable Reuse of Municipal Wastewater."[3] The objectives of the program are: (1) to determine the nature and concentrations of organic, inorganic, and microbiological contaminants present in AWT plant effluents that actually or potentially may be used as a source of potable water supply; (2) to conduct long-term toxicological and epidemiological studies to determine the health effects of consuming such waters; and (3) to provide health effects criteria for the reuse of renovated wastewater to assure the safety of the product. Active projects in this program include:

1. analysis of organics in AWT effluents;
2. mutagenic testing of AWT organic concentrates;
3. biological (mice) evaluation of toxic effects of organics present in AWT effluents;
4. health effects of consumption of renovated water-chemistry and cytotoxicity studies;

5. pyrogenic activity of carbon-filtered wastewaters;
6. the effects of ozone on organics in wastewater.

The above-described health effects research needed to establish confidence in overt potable reuse parallels that planned and under way for presently used water supplies. Since we are living in a world where covert potable reuse is a reality and millions of persons are already using wastewater indirectly for potable purposes, the same questions must be answered, regardless of whether reuse is direct or indirect. What are the health effects of reusing wastewater either directly or indirectly? What technology is needed to remove potential health-hazardous constituents? Comparative health effects data for present domestic water supplies and properly treated wastewater used for potable purposes can be established by applying the contaminant measurements and toxicity testing techniques, already developed or being developed, to both of these waters.

NEAR-TERM REUSE EXPANSION CONCEPTS

The volume of wastewater available for potential planned reuse is significant; however, the quantity presently reused is small. The U.S. Water Resources Council estimated that in 1970 municipalities used 9,850 bg of water of which 7,670 bg, or about 78 percent, was returned as wastewater.[4] In 1971, only 135 bg of municipal wastewater treatment plant effluents were being reused for planned purposes.[5] This represents less than 2 percent of the available waste flow. Unplanned reuse, or the return to receiving waters for subsequent reuse, accounts for the remainder of the available waste flow.

A 1971 survey of reuse identified 358 reuse sites within the United States and 55 within foreign countries.[6] Of the types of reuse noted, by far the greatest number of plants practice reuse for irrigation. Of the 358 U.S. sites, 209 were judged to be very small irrigation disposal operations. In terms of volume, however, irrigation reuse accounts for 77 bg, or slightly more than half the reuse reported, with industrial reuse a close second. It should be mentioned that one large industrial reuser, the Bethlehem Steel Corporation in Baltimore, Maryland, uses 44 bg of the 54 bg reported.

In spite of the meager amount of planned reuse, a study by Stone in California has shown that the public is ready for large-scale wastewater reuse for nonbody contact purposes and, to a lesser extent, for body contact purposes.[7] The study involved a survey of the general public, industrial plant managers, public water resources officials, and water resources management experts. The results indicated favorable attitudes toward reuse. The true driving force that will eventually bring about reuse, however, is economics. When the cost of the renovation of wastewater becomes measurably less than the cost of alternate sources, interest will increase rapidly.

Because of the health effects questions and associated high costs to treat wastewater to provide a safe potable quality water, it is anticipated that the priorities for reuse will pattern themselves in a way such that water of high quality is not used for a purpose that can tolerate a lesser degree of purity. Source substitution is a means of conserving approved sources of potable water in water-short areas by using poorer quality water for purposes that can readily adapt to it. The lack of cost-effective multiple distribution systems has generally inhibited source substitution as a means of expanding reuse. In the vicinity of the wastewater treatment, plant distribution to large users of renovated water can be simple and cost effective. An example is the 30 mg/d wastewater treatment facility presently under construction at Contra Costa, California, a facility that will provide effluent to nearby petro-chemical industries primarily for cooling purposes. If the users are widely dispersed and redesigning of existing distribution systems to accommodate a dual system is necessary, however, high costs may be involved. Dual water supplies can be planned for new communities or for the industrialized areas of these cities. Since only about 25 percent of water used in the home is for potable purposes—i.e., drinking, cooking, laundry, and bathing—the potential for source substitution for uses such as toilet flushing and lawn watering is significant. Studies are needed, however, that determine the design problems, adequate public health protection, and the cost effectiveness of having separate distribution systems for delivering renovated water to homes, industries, and to other nonpotable water users. One method that will expand the dual distribution system concept is to make such systems eligible for federal construction grants.

Source substitution as a viable reuse expansion concept also depends on the ability of the industry—if an industrial use is involved—to adapt its technology to enable use of a lower quality water. Many industries use the municipal potable water supply in their processes, and they often do not know if they can maintain product quality with a less pure water.

As the cost of the municipal supplies increases due to expanding the water treatment requirements to remove recently identified health-hazardous materials associated with many conventional surface supplies, industries will be looking around for cheaper sources of water. Until studies are undertaken to determine quality requirements, however, expansion of industrial reuse will be hampered. A case in point concerns a large, highly specialized flower grower in California who operates a nursery and grows poinsettias and Easter lilies. The irrigation volumes required amount to about 20 percent of the local water district municipal water demand. Since the district has to import water, it is concerned with reducing costs, and it is considering source substitution of treated wastewater for the potable supplies for flower irrigation as a means of reducing the potable water demand. The grower is concerned, however, about the effect of the reused water on the quality of his poinsettias and resists using a lesser quality water until he is assured it will not affect his product. Similarly, other industrial users require data to demonstrate that they can adapt their processes to lower quality municipal treatment plant effluents.

Reuse has potential as an effective water quality management tool. Where receiving waters have stringent water quality criteria in order to protect them from pollutants, the cost of wastewater treatment to meet the stream standards may be greater than the cost of a lesser degree of treatment to meet an industrial or other use combined with the cost of transporting the effluent out of the basin for needed reuse elsewhere. The treatment facility at Lake Tahoe, California, is a classic example of interbasin transfer of a high-quality wastewater effluent out of the lake basin to insure protection of the high-quality lake waters and provide for subsequent reuse of the effluent in a recreational reservoir and for irrigation purposes. Federal support of the pumping costs for interbasin transfer for reuse purposes where the cost of discharge in the originating basin is prohibitive may be a viable method of expanding reuse.

Section 208 of PL 92–500 deals with the development and implementation of areawide waste management plans. Although wastewater reuse is built into the law, it is not receiving sufficient attention. It should be addressed in the 208 planning process and special consideration should be given to reuse as a water quality management tool in each 208 planning area.

DIRECTIONS OF REUSE RESEARCH

The EPA OR&D reuse program should follow two avenues of research: The first is the more near-term, less controversial nonpotable use of wastewater. The goal of this program is the establishment of feasible methods to extend valuable water supplies by source substitution. This goal should be achieved by 1982. Potential near-term nonpotable research projects to accomplish this goal are:

1. identification of applications for the reuse of wastewater and development of institutional arrangements for bringing reclaimed water into our systems;
2. determination of potential users' (e.g., industry's) ability to adapt to various water qualities;
3. evaluation of dual distribution systems and economic incentives to promote their use;

4. compilation of water utility experiences with conservation programs, such as installation of water meters, public education, and the use of water-saving devices.

The second avenue of research is the implementation of research and experimental demonstrations that prove the feasibility and practicability of reusing wastewaters for potable purposes. This goal should be achieved by 1987. It will correspond to the timing of the legislative mandate for "nonpolluting discharge," as well as currently identified local needs, such as groundwater requirements in California and Long Island, and Denver's potable reuse requirements. Potential research projects to accomplish this goal are:

1. characterization of biological, organic, and inorganic residues in wastewater effluents;
2. study of large-scale treatment systems for the reliable removal of potentially harmful residues;
3. studies of the behavior of pollutants in soils and sediments in the underground environment;
4. assessment of toxicological risks of ingesting wastewater residues;
5. research and application of monitoring techniques and strategy for regulation programs;
6. epidemiology studies of exposed populations;
7. socio-economic aspects of potable reuse.

Industries, municipalities, and the general public will make the decision for reuse when the time is right for their particular situation. EPA is attempting to provide the necessary research information to allow each concerned water user to determine the proper place for reused wastewater in its water resource management program.

SUMMARY

The development of AWT technology capable of treating wastewater to a reusable commodity that is "too good to throw away" has attracted the attention of agencies in water-short areas that are responsible for maintaining adequate water supplies. The amount of reuse, however, is presently rather meager; less than 2 percent of the available municipal wastewater is being reused on a planned basis. The lack of adequate health effects data on the residues in high-quality effluents will delay implementation of any potential reuse situation that has health questions associated with it. The sparsity of information on the feasibility of source substitution as a means of increasing planned reuse and the deficiency of water resource management concepts that address reuse are hampering its development for less-controversial purposes.

Near-term research efforts should be initiated in EPA as part of a program to identify applications for reusable wastewater other than for potable purposes and to develop the institutional arrangements for bringing this water into our systems. A long-term demonstration and health effects research program should be implemented that addresses potable reuse and will impact the needs of communities where source substitution cannot provide water resources sufficient to meet their future domestic water supply needs. It is anticipated that this program will require a ten-year period to complete.

NOTES

1. State of California Department of Public Health, "Statewide Standards for the Direct Use of Reclaimed Wastewater for Irrigation and Recreational Impoundments" (Sacramento, Calif., May 1968).
2. State of California Water Resources Control Board, "Report on the Consulting Panel on Health Aspects of Wastewater Reclamation for Groundwater Recharge" (Sacramento, Calif., June 1976).
3. Environmental Protection Agency, "Research Needs for the Potable Reuse of Municipal Wastewater," EPA Technical Series, EPA-600/9–75–007, December 1975.
4. National Water Commission, "Water Policies for the Future" (Washington, D.C.: Government Printing Office, 1973).
5. Ibid.
6. C. J. Schmidt et al., "Municipal Wastewater Reuse in the U.S.," *Journal of the Water Pollution Control Federation* 47 (1975): 2229.
7. Ralph Stone, "Water Reclamation: Technology and Public Acceptance," *Journal of the Environmental Engineering Division, ASCE* 102, no. EE3, Proc. Paper 12193 (June 1976): 581–94.

APPENDIXES

U.S. Environmental Protection Agency
Policy Statement on Water Reuse

The demand for water is increasing both through population growth and changing life styles, while the supply of water from nature remains basically constant from year to year. This is not to imply that we are or will shortly be out of water, although water shortages are of great concern in some regions, and indirect reuse has been common for generations. We must recognize the need to use and reuse wastewater. Therefore,

1. EPA supports and encourages the continued development and practice of successive wastewater reclamation, reuse, recycling, and recharge as a major element in water resource management, providing the reclamation systems are designed and operated so as to avoid health hazards to the people or damage to the environment.
2. In particular, EPA recognizes and supports the potential for wastewater reuse in agriculture, industrial, municipal, recreational, and groundwater recharge applications.
3. EPA does not currently support the direct interconnection of wastewater reclamation plants with municipal water treatment plants. The potable use of renovated wastewaters blended with other acceptable supplies in reservoirs may be employed once research and demonstration have shown that it can be done without hazard to health. EPA believes that other factors must also receive consideration, such as the ecological impact of various alternatives, quality of available sources, and economics.
4. EPA will continue to support reuse research and demonstration projects, including procedures for the rapid identification and removal of viruses and organics, epidemiological and toxicological analyses of effects, advanced waste and drinking water treatment process design and operation, development of water quality requirements for various reuse opportunities, and cost-effectiveness studies.

American Water Works Association Policy Statement (1971)

1. Identify the full range of contaminants possibly present in treated wastewaters, which might affect the safety of public health, the palatability of the water, and the range of concentrations.
2. Determine the degree to which these contaminants are removed by the various types and levels of treatment.
3. Determine the long-range physiological effect of continued use of reclaimed wastewaters, with various levels of treatment, as the partial or sole source of drinking water.
4. Define the parameters, testing procedures, analytical methodology, allowable limits, and monitoring systems that should be employed with respect to the use of reclaimed wastewaters for public water-supply purposes.
5. Develop greater capability and reliability of treatment processes and equipment to produce reclaimed water of reasonably uniform quality, in view of the extreme variability in the characteristics of untreated wastewaters.
6. Improve the capabilities of operational personnel.

The Commission also recommends that research focus on advanced treatment processes that incorporate or replace secondary treatment, on other methods of reducing the amount of advanced treatment, and on the practicability of installing and operating dual water supply systems—one for human consumption and the other for manufacturing purposes.

The net cost of treatment of water for reuse should be compared with the costs of such alternative sources of water as desalting and interbasin transfers before any such alternative is adopted.

American Water Works Association Proposed Policy Statement (1977): Use of Reclaimed Wastewaters as a Public Water Supply Source

The American Water Works Association recognizes that properly treated wastewaters constitute an increasingly important element of the total available water resources. In relation to this situation several factors are important. These are as follows:

1. Ever increasing amounts of treated wastewaters are being discharged to the waters of the Nation and constitute an increasing proportion of many existing drinking water supplies;
2. More and more proposals are being made to introduce reclaimed wastewaters directly into various elements of domestic water supply systems in certain water short areas;
3. The sound management of our total available water resources may include consideration of the potential use of properly treated wastewaters as part of drinking water supplies in certain instances;
4. Insufficient information exists concerning acute and long-term effects on human health resulting from such uses of wastewater; and
5. Fail-safe technology to assure the removal of all potentially harmful substances from wastewater is not available.

Based on these factors the policy of the American Water Works Association is [1] to urge the Federal Government to support an immediate and sustained multidisciplinary national research effort to provide the scientific knowledge and technology relative to the future use of reclaimed wastewaters as a public water supply source in order to assure the full protection of the public's health, and, . . . [2] that any advocacy of such direct use of reclaimed wastewaters as a public water supply source await[s] the development of the needed scientific knowledge and treatment technology.

Reprinted from the *Municipal Wastewater Reuse News*, no. 1 (October 1977), p. 11, by permission of the publisher.

The Model

The model TINKLE simulates a municipal water supply, demand, and waste treatment operation (See figure 3-4.) These three major systems on the model are combined in a simulation consisting of a main routine and thirteen subroutines. The design and testing of the model was carried out over an eight-month period. An experienced programmer, Roy A. Wyscarver, worked full time writing and debugging the model in close collaboration with Daniel Dworkin. The model requires a synthetic record of stream flows and rainfall. The record is simulated by the use of the U.S. Army Hydrologic Engineering Center's HEC-4 program (1971) and stored on tape or disc for use during the simulation. The main program, which serves as the executive routine, is designated TINKLE. In running a simulation, TINKLE first obtains data on the system from INPUT and then reads rainfall and stream flows generated by HEC-4 (figure *App D*-1).

MAIN ROUTINE

1. *Limiting stream flows.* The monthly flow of each stream used in the system is decreased under the following circumstances: (1) if the diversion works or pipeline is unable to pass the required flow; (2) if restrictions require a base flow before diversion; and (3) if senior rights and intervening rights must be satisfied. The limitations can be set for seasonal variations in restrictions. In addition to limiting flows, the water may be designated as local or imported for those areas in which reuse is limited to water originating outside the basin. The editing parameters of the program can be set to print net stream flows for each year; or, if only a sampling of flows is desired, the frequency of the net stream flow print-out can be reduced to as little as once during a fifty-year simulation.

2. *Historical data.* The past history of monthly flows is supplied to the program as part of the input data. As each monthly flow is read into the program, it is used to update the historical data file. At the end of each year, the total flows for the year are added. This sum of yearly flows and that of the previous flows are ranked from 0 for the lowest flow to 1 for the highest. This ranking is used as part of the decision process at the end of each year to determine whether to increase conventional capacity.

3. *Modifying the recycling status.* If the simulation is using recycling intermittently, a monthly check of whether the recycling status should be changed is

---

Reprinted from Hydrolic Engineering Center, *HEC-4 Monthly Streamflow Simulation* (Davis, Calif.: U.S. Army Corps of Engineers, 1971).

Figure app. D-*1.*   Main Routine Tinkle: Stream Flows and Rainfall

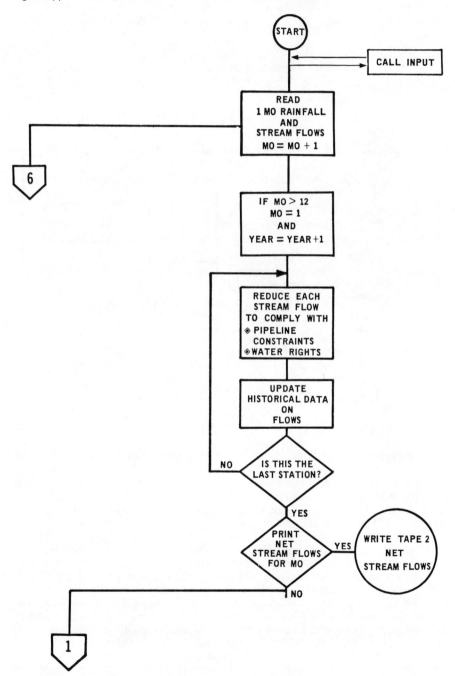

initiated. The decision to recycle is based on reservoir levels. There are two specified: a lower one that starts recycling and a higher one that ends the recycling process. This is done in a series of comparisons of present and past levels, and in present levels with the "on" and "off" levels for recycling (figure *App D*-2).

Figure app. D-2.   Main Routine Tinkle: The Decision to Change the Recycling Status

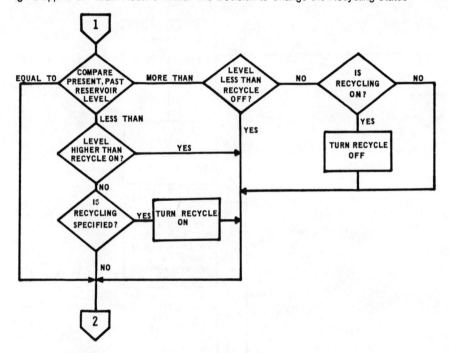

4. *Reservoir levels.* This section is designed to manage the reservoir by increasing or decreasing the supply in storage, based on the net of stream flow, reservoir losses, and demands for water from storage (figure *App D*-3). When water is spilled or the level of water drops below the conservation pool, the information is collected and reported in the final output. If the reservoir is empty, the subroutine OUTPUT is called and the program ends.

5. *Adding new capacity.* There are two methods of adding capacity: either from conventional supply from streams, reservoirs, wells, or projects or from an increase in the amount of reused water continually processed and distributed. The first is by scheduling the increase for a specific time during the simulation. The second is a decision that at the end of each year is based on monitoring reservoir-level use for the past, with the rank of the past year's stream flow compared to the historical record of flows. A check on these variables is made: (1) Is the current reservoir level above an expansion level EXPR? (2) Is the ratio of minimum level to annual use larger than EXPL? (3) Is the last year's stream flow rank less than or equal to PROB, the rank of flows? (figure *App D*-4).

If all these conditions are negative—that is, not fulfilled—then the conditions

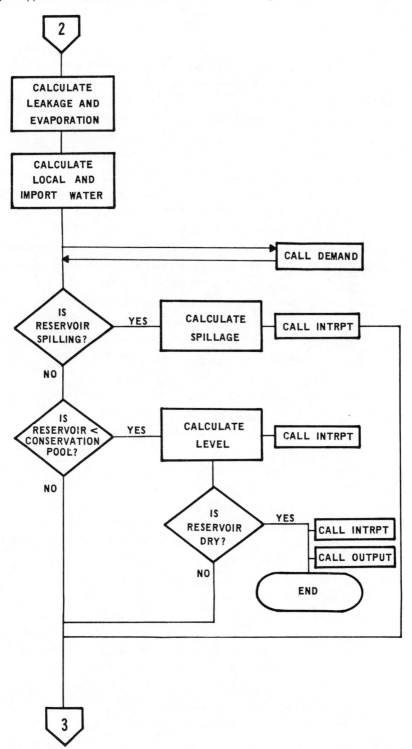

Figure app. D-4.   Main Routine Tinkle Adding New Capacity: Time and an Alternate Decision Process

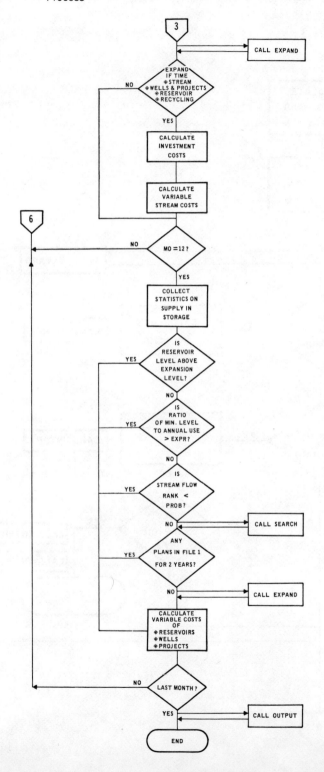

Figure app. D-5.   Subroutine Demand: Reducing the Reservoir Drain by Reuse or Rationing

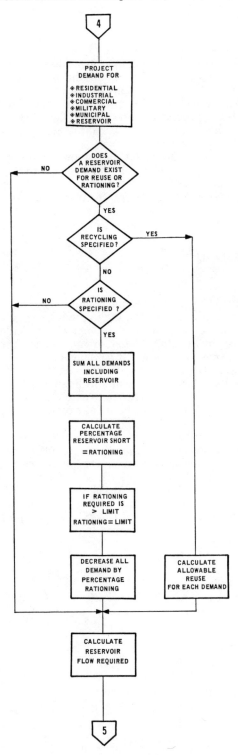

for expansion have been satisfied. Before expansion is undertaken, a subroutine SEARCH is called to examine the current plans for time-dependent expansion. SEARCH calls planning file 1, which contains the data on new projects scheduled for expansion at a fixed time. If no plans are scheduled for the next two years, a subroutine EXPAND is called, which transfers the next plan in file 5, containing the details and plans not dependent on time to file 1. The lag time to allow for implementation of the plan is instituted, and the expansion will be completed at the end of the delay period.

In this section of the program, statistics on the variable cost of streams, reservoirs, wells, and projects are collected. Before beginning a new month, the cumulative total of months is checked against the total number of months to be simulated. If the monthly run completes the series, the output subroutine is called and the simulation ends.

SUBROUTINE DEMAND

The subroutine DEMAND calculates the monthly values for the variables that are used to determine monthly water use. It also produces reused water when specified either as a continual supply or when the appropriate conditions are met during the simulation. If specified, DEMAND also rations water use during shortages.

1. *Reducing the reservoir drain.*   If rationing or reuse is specified in the program input parameter, the subroutine, on the basis of reservoir levels, determines whether to reduce the use of potable water by limiting use or supplying appropriately treated effluent. Both rationing and reuse are limited to percentages of demand. The subroutine calculates all the flows required for each demand sector (figure *App D*-5).

2. *The waste treatment operation.*   Wastewater is treated by any combination of activated sludge, granulated carbon absorption, filtrations, and ion exchange. Other processes can be included by changing the treatment equations. Only the amount of water needed to satisfy the demands for reused water is processed, unless an option is specified that requires all water to be treated to a secondary level before discharge. The subroutine finally calculates and collects all statistics and costs using subroutines COST and CCOST (figure *App D*-6).

Figure app. D-6.   Subroutine Demand: The Waste Treatment Operation

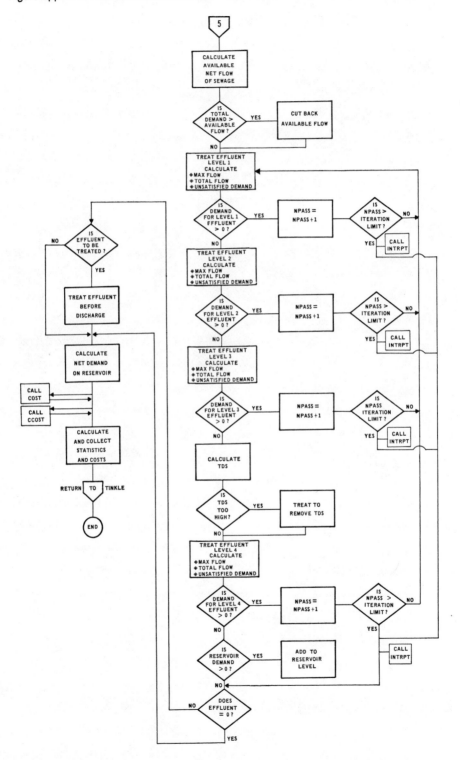